MARITAL ACTS

MARITAL ACTS

Gender, Sexuality, and Identity

among the Chinese Thai Diaspora

JIEMIN BAO

University of Hawai'i Press
Honolulu

Library of Congress Cataloging-in-Publication Data

Bao, Jiemin.
   Marital acts : gender, sexuality, and identity among the Chinese Thai diaspora / Jiemin Bao.
      p.   cm.
   Includes bibliographical references and index.
   ISBN 0-8248-2740-6 (hardcover : alk. paper) — ISBN 0-8248-2879-8 (pbk. : alk. paper)
   1. Chinese—Thailand—Bangkok—Kinship.   2. Chinese—Thailand—Bangkok—Ethnic identity.   3. Chinese—Thailand—Bangkok—Sexual behavior.   4. Chinese Americans—California—San Francisco—Kinship.   5. Chinese Americans—California—San Francisco—Ethnic identity.   6. Chinese Americans—California—San Francisco—Sexual behavior.   7. Thai Americans—California—San Francisco—Kinship.   8. Thai Americans—California—San Francisco—Ethnic identity.   9. Thai Americans—California—San Francisco—Sexual behavior.   I. Title.

DS570.C5B36 2005
305.895˙10593—dc22

                                                     2004016097

Earlier versions of portions of chapter 3 appeared in the *Journal of Southeast Asian Studies* 34:1, 2003.

University of Hawai'i Press books are printed on acid-free paper and meet the guidelines for permanence and durability of the Council on Library Resources.

To my beloved parents

I occasionally experience myself as cluster of flowing currents. I prefer this to the idea of a solid self, the identity to which so many attach so much significance. These currents, like the themes of one's life, flow along during the waking hours, and at their best, they require no reconciling, no harmonizing. They are "off" and may be out of place, but at least they are always in motion, in time, in place, in the form of all kinds of strange combinations moving about, not necessarily forward, sometimes against each other, contrapuntally, yet without one central theme. . . . With so many dissonances in my life I have learned actually to prefer being not quite right and out of place.

—EDWARD SAID, *Out of Place*

Contents

Language Conventions

CHINESE AND THAI terms are sprinkled throughout the text. I use the symbol [M] to distinguish Mandarin from Thai; for Mandarin I use phonetic transcriptions of Chinese characters. For Thai, I follow the system in *Romanization Guide for Thai Script*, except for terms that are in common usage such as "Teochiu." When a word or term is expressed in both Thai and Mandarin, I translate the Thai first, followed by the Mandarin; for example, "blood" (*luat/xuetong* [M]).

Thai sources are cited in the text and listed in the bibliography by the author's first name.

Preface

I OFTEN FIND myself living in one place and longing for something in another. For example, I seldom enjoy Thanksgiving or Christmas in the United States because it makes me homesick for my family in China. In 1999, after twelve years of living abroad, I came back to Shanghai to visit my family for Chinese New Year. On New Year's Eve—and at midnight on the fourth day of the New Year (when people welcome the Money God)—the constant din of fireworks was so loud that even inside the house I had to shout to make myself heard, and the air outside was so full of smoke that we dared not open the windows.

In the morning our street was a vast red carpet of spent firecrackers. The New Year's celebration was more commercialized and far noisier than what I remembered. I found my mind drifting back to a Thai New Year's celebration (the *Songkran* water festival) with my old friend Ming Mama and her family in Chiang Mai in 1992. Ming Mama's children, grandchildren, and I all piled into the bed of an old pickup truck with a big barrel of water. We crept through the streets flinging water on everyone we met and getting thoroughly drenched ourselves. The water symbolized purification, "washing away bad things." I had great fun. With the temperature over 100 degrees, it felt good to get soaked. It made me feel like a kid again, in a way that the New Year in Shanghai somehow had not. Maybe nostalgia has distorted my memory, or maybe China is simply changing too fast. Or maybe both. I know I've changed, and am changing still.

In the summer of 1988—just nine months after I left Beijing to come to the United States to do graduate work at UC-Berkeley—I joined a Study Abroad Program and traveled to Bangkok and Chiang Mai, Thailand. When introduced to people of Chinese ancestry in Thailand, I was astonished to discover that some did not consider me a "real Chinese" because I had grown up in "communist China." They reasoned that since Mao's regime had attempted to destroy all "Chinese traditions," anyone who had grown up during that time would be ignorant of "real" Chinese culture. Along with two of her friends, Ming Mama, who had immigrated from

Shantou, China, more than fifty years earlier, tested me: I was asked to read a classical Chinese poem and explain its meaning to them. Until I passed that test, I had been treated courteously but kept at a distance. Before coming to Thailand, it had never occurred to me that I would not be perceived as Chinese. I was also surprised to find that, contrary to what I had read, the Chinese Thai whom I encountered had not been "assimilated." I began to ask myself: what does it mean to be Chinese outside of China?

At that time, studying identity formation among ethnic Chinese in Thailand was politically sensitive. In Berkeley I once met Thailand's former minister of foreign affairs and asked him a question about Thailand's ethnic Chinese. Without bothering to sound diplomatic, he responded bluntly, "There are no Chinese in Thailand." Researching the formation of Chinese identity was even more delicate in my case because I held a Chinese passport and could be accused of working for "communist China."

While my interest in Chinese Thai identity was just awakening, I had long been interested in issues of gender inequality. Growing up under Mao, my training had been to think about all relationships in terms of class. I remember reciting Chairman Mao's teaching: "class struggle must be talked every year, every month, and every day." As I grew older, I came to realize that gender inequality could not be explained by class alone, for inequality exists between and among men and women who share the same class status. So I decided that marriage, where so many aspects of identity actually intersect and which was also considered a "safe" anthropological issue, would be my official topic. Using this strategy, I eventually became the first Chinese scholar granted permission to conduct research on the ethnic Chinese in Thailand.

The stories that the Chinese Thai told me are deeply informed by hybridity, gender inequality, and ambiguity. Ming Mama, for example, considered herself "very Chinese," but she loved to wear a Thai sarong after her bath, and her food was often a combination of Thai and Chinese cuisine. She urged her children to marry someone Chinese, but she got along well with her Thai daughter-in-law. She complained about her womanizing husband—she cried so much that she had ruined her eyes—but she never wanted to divorce him. Her Chinese-ness and her everyday activities were filled with contradictions.

Since living and working outside of China, I have personally experienced the ambiguity of being Chinese. In the summer of 1991, after living in Berkeley for four years, I went back to Shanghai for the first time to visit my family. My five-year-old nephew, Sunsun, called me "American Auntie," because all he could remember about me was that I lived in the United States. "No, I am not your American Auntie," I corrected him. "Call me Auntie." This reminded me that a white American friend in Berkeley had advised me to change my name to Jasmine, because Jasmine corresponds to a feminine image and Jiemin is too difficult to pronounce. But for me Jasmine is an alien social marker, whereas Jiemin is part of my cultural identity. I have taught those few who have asked how to pronounce Jiemin correctly to say it with an English inflection, because the Chinese tone is just too hard for most English speakers to hear and replicate. But occasionally I miss the sense of affection and intimacy I feel when my family and Chinese friends say my name. Thus when I hear the word Jiemin, I enter a diasporic space in which I become aware of the speaker's own cultural background.

Now whenever I visit Shanghai my younger sister, Sansan, always teases me about my out-of-fashion clothing, calling me "the American farmer's daughter." In the winter of 1999 my mom got very upset with me when I wore my old handmade Laotian scarf instead of her new one. "In all of Shanghai," she said, "no one but you would wear such an ugly farmer's scarf." So "the farmer's daughter" has become my family nickname. I gradually came to realize that my cultural taste had changed, and it was colliding with a Chinese notion of modernity. Finally, to keep from distressing them, I learned to dress according to local standards—just as I did during my fieldwork. It was a small concession in the larger process of negotiation.

Writing in English is where I feel my cultural displacement most keenly. Writing in Chinese is like peeling an onion: you begin with the general, work toward the specific, and finally reveal the key argument toward the end. In English, I need to reverse the order. As I was taught in graduate school, "You have to sell yourself immediately in the first paragraph"—a phrase that comes from the heart of capitalism.

As a scholar living in the United States, I have the freedom to choose my topic and to conduct my own research. But my choices are still disciplined by grant money, by the sensitivity of the research topic, by university politics, and so on. Moreover, "you need to write a book to get tenure." In a capitalist society, productivity is greatly emphasized, whether you are a farmer or a professor, and I cannot escape being disciplined by capitalist institutions. I am conforming to these politics, and I am writing this in English instead of Chinese or Thai, which would be more relevant for the people who shared their stories with me. All of these experiences have led me to agree with Ien Ang's contention that Chinese-ness "is a category whose meanings are not fixed and pregiven, but constantly renegotiated and rearticulated, both inside and outside China" (1993:5). Writing about diasporic Chinese Thai cultural identities and gender inequality, at least for me, is a political act.

While conducting research in Thailand, my personal background and ambiguous identity elicited great curiosity and many questions. Some people treated me as being similar to them: a Chinese person living outside of China. Some thought themselves "more Chinese" than I when I confessed that I never practiced ancestor worship. Some thought I was trustworthy partly because I was from China; others were suspicious of my motives because I was from "Red China" (*chindaeng*). Many were curious about my personal life, especially with regard to what country I would choose to settle in, and what sort of person I would marry. The questions they asked and the assumptions they made gave me insight into what they meant by Chinese and Thai in various contexts and revealed how our different views were informed by our own particular experiences.

My research activities were also shaped by gender expectations in Bangkok. Although I did interview a few women in coffee shops and restaurants, most were so busy that they preferred being interviewed in their homes or their shops, where they could keep doing their work and avoid dealing with Bangkok's notorious traffic. Men preferred being interviewed away from home—in restaurants, coffee shops, or their offices. Except in cases where I knew both wife and husband, I rarely telephoned a man at home, where his wife could imagine that he was involved with "another woman." Thus I contacted the men at work, unless they worked at home in family businesses. I never had this kind of concern when I called the women. My own uneasiness about where and how to contact the men illustrates how, in a very short period of time, my thinking was influenced by local gender-specific concerns.

During conversations with me about the commercial sex industry or polygyny, some Chinese Thai men emphasized their masculine prowess, assuming an appreciative female audience. In contrast, women appreciated me as a sympathetic listener when they talked about their husband's or father's extramarital sexual activities. In general, I found that women talked more easily about men's extramarital sexual activities than their own.

My fieldwork in Thailand was conducted during the summer of 1988, between July 1991 and June 1992, for a month in 1996, and four weeks in December 2002 and January 2003. In all, I interviewed over one hundred people, including *chinkao*, the first generation (lit., "old Chinese," now used to refer to Chinese who immigrated to Thailand before 1949); *lukchin*, the second generation (lit., "Chinese children"); *lukkhrung* ("half-Chinese"); and undocumented immigrant Chinese women newly arrived in Bangkok. In this book, I use material from forty extensive life histories compiled from in-depth interviews with seventeen chinkao and twenty-three lukchin, and I also draw upon interviews, gossip, and other stories elicited from family members, domestic workers, neighbors, and friends.

Most chinkao speak Teochiu, a southern Chinese dialect that I do not understand. All of them can speak some Thai, but often not enough to express themselves with the clarity and subtlety they wanted, so we conversed in Mandarin. In the emigrant regions before 1949, Mandarin was regarded as the intellectuals' language. In Thailand, chinkao who speak Mandarin usually have had more formal education or were motivated enough to learn the language on their own. Therefore, the ability to speak Mandarin became an indicator of class status among chinkao.

When I interviewed lukchin, we spoke Thai, Mandarin, English, or Lao. Sometimes we used three or four different languages in a single interview. For example, Phi Pasuk spoke Mandarin when recalling her childhood, but switched to English, her professional language, when we talked about sexuality. When referring to Thai Buddhist practices or ethnic stereotypes, she mixed in Thai and Teochiu expressions. The ease with which she switched languages highlighted the deep sense of hybrid identity felt by many lukchin.

In addition to conducting interviews, I lived with three different families between 1991 and 1992, altogether for a total of more than six months. I observed and participated in their daily activities, such as birthday parties, ancestor worship, weddings, funerals, and evening gatherings. This firsthand experience enabled me to see how individuals play with dominant ideologies and negotiate cultural rules in a rich variety of contexts.

To better understand the chinkao, I twice traveled to emigrant areas in southern China to trace chinkao roots and to get a sense of the effects of southern peasant culture on the Chinese Thai. I also surveyed 102 chinkao and lukchin households (with a total population of 921). While conducting the survey I discovered that some chinkao counted only sons when asked how many children they had. Subsequently I asked for the exact number of daughters and sons. The survey information—on marital choices and practice, ethnic identities, residence patterns, the division of labor, occupations, education, religious beliefs, and notions of a "good" wife and husband—

provided abundant information about the diversity and complexity of the Chinese communities in Bangkok, which I have used mainly as a background reference for this book.

My research on Chinese Thai Americans began with my connections to Thai and Chinese Thai American communities in the San Francisco Bay Area. The more I wrote about the chinkao and lukchin, the more I wanted to understand Chinese Thai Americans. I gradually came to realize that the process of identity formation among Chinese Thai Americans is a continuation of a cultural struggle that began in Thailand.

Between 1994 and 1998 I conducted thirty-seven life history interviews and dozens of nonsystematic interviews with Thai and Chinese Thai Americans in the Bay Area. My knowledge of Thailand and China and my ability to speak Thai and Lao were appreciated and taken to mean that I was serious about the project. A Thai Buddhist abbot sometimes introduced me by saying, "Khun Latsami [my Thai name] is Chinese, but in a previous life she was Thai." On other occasions he introduced me as "Dr. Jiemin Bao." His introductions gave me an insight into how he used his religious authority or my social capital to initiate my contact with people of different socioeconomic backgrounds.

People I interviewed in the Bay Area included transnational capitalists, restaurant owners, professionals, monks, Americans who married or dated Thai, college students, and primary school students. Almost all of the people I interviewed have had remarkable transnational experiences. The abbot, for example, grew up in rural northeastern Thailand, studied Buddhism first in Bangkok and then in India, and later served as a monk in several temples in Thailand and the United States before finally being elected abbot at a Thai temple in the Bay Area. At the end of this book, I include only a small fraction of the stories told by the Chinese Thai Americans in this project. But that will be enough, I hope, to enable us to reconsider the ethnic Chinese experience in Thailand in a different light, from a new angle of vision.

Acknowledgments

LIKE MILLIONS OF other students, during the Cultural Revolution I was sent to the countryside—in my case to Heilongjiang Province, China's Siberia—to be "reeducated by peasants." Before I left, my grandmother gave me a good-luck charm: a small brown bottle filled with Shanghai soil. She believed that by carrying some native soil with me, I would more easily adapt to rural life and stay healthy. Grandma, I miss you and often think about how you opened my eyes to the meanings inscribed in people, migration, and homes.

Since this book is one product of a long journey that began in China, moved on to Thailand, and continues to this day in the United States, I owe many debts of appreciation for the guidance and assistance I have been given along the way. First, I would like to thank Robert Reed and Herbert Phillips for their support and encouragement. I am especially grateful to Aihwa Ong, my mentor, for her remarkable intellectual energy and for her guidance and care. Without her as an inspiration and a steadfast source of new ideas, this book would never have been written.

Much of my research in Thailand, China, and the United States has been financially supported by various fellowships and grants, including two UC-Berkeley Regents Fellowships; two Luce Foundation Grants (through the Center for Southeast Asia Studies at UC-Berkeley); an Alice Galloway Memorial Fellowship; a Social Science Research Council Dissertation Fellowship; two UC-Berkeley Graduate Research Grants; three International Peace Scholarships; a Mabelle McLeod Lewis Memorial Fellowship; a Social Science Research Council International Migration Fellowship; and three University of Nevada, Las Vegas Stimulation, Implementation, Transition and Enhancement Awards.

I greatly appreciated the support of two postdoctoral fellowships: one at the East-West Center in Hawai'i, and the other a Rockefeller Foundation Postdoctoral Fellowship for the Study of Sexuality, Gender, Health, and Human Rights at Columbia University. The weekly seminars and monthly lectures organized by Carole Vance, the program's director at Columbia, provided a congenial and stimulating environment in which to read, think, and write; I greatly enjoyed Carole's intellectual rigor, quick wit, and activist spirit. Many thanks also to the other fellows and seminar participants for their inspiring discussions—which made me understand how marriage and heterosexuality stand in much need of rethinking and deeper analysis.

I wish to thank the National Research Council of Thailand for granting me permission to conduct research in Thailand. I am grateful for the institutional sponsorship, assistance, and consideration that I received from Dr. Khien Theeravit at the Institute of Asian Studies at Chulalongkorn University and from Dr. Juree Vichit-Vadakan at the National Institute of Development Administration. My thanks also go to Dr. Vatana Vonggiad of the Social Research Institute of Chulalongkorn University, who provided technical assistance for the survey, and to Hua and Lu for their work as Teochiu interpreters and consultants during the months that the survey was conducted. My gratitude also extends to many other faculty members for their generous help and valuable assistance, in particular: Drs. Bhassorn Limanonda, Chai Podhisita, Phonchai, Suriya Veeravong, Suwanna Satha-Anand, and Yupha Klangsuwan. I owe special thanks to M. L. Walwipha Burusratanaphand for sharing with me her insights into ethnic Chinese communities and for her unfailing support during different stages of this project.

The following colleagues, friends, and students have given valuable suggestions and criticism in regard to various parts and versions of the chapters in this book: Wurlig Bao, Rick Camp, Nancy Chen, Lenore Manderson, Sucheta Mazumdar, Ali Miller, Chantal Nadeau, Aihwa Ong, Oliver Philips, Svati Shah, Kanokwan Tharawan, Carole Vance, and Rebecca Young. Lindsay French's astute feedback, sense of humor, and warm friendship throughout the project made the writing especially rewarding. Bruce Lockhart's professionalism and his insightful suggestions significantly enhanced the first three chapters of the book.

Mary Beth Mills provided a careful reading of this manuscript for the University of Hawai'i Press, and she has been very supportive since the beginning of this project. I want to thank her and the second, anonymous reader, not only for their suggestions and criticisms but also for their special insight into the manuscript. I also deeply appreciated the enthusiastic support of Pamela Kelley at the University of Hawai'i Press. The manuscript greatly benefited from Gene Tanke's graceful editing. His resistance to jargon and his sensitivity to language have made the book much more readable. My thanks also go to Kanokwan for checking my Thai translations, to Victoria Fisher for making the bibliography consistent, and to Dave Melton for creating two maps for the book. My colleagues in the Department of Anthropology and Ethnic Studies, University of Nevada, Las Vegas have been very considerate, for which I am very grateful.

I owe special thanks to Leo van Munching for his friendship, generosity, and wise counsel for over a decade, and to Carrie May and Jim Bailey for their unflagging hospitality and encouragement. My warm thanks also goes to Sandra Cate, Emily Chao, Donna Goldstein, Lynn Kwiatkowski, and Sydney White for the friendship, support, and companionship they have provided since I was in graduate school at Berkeley.

The debt I feel most personally goes to the women and men I interviewed in Thailand, China, and the San Francisco Bay Area, for allowing me into their families and their lives. Without their stories, their tears, and their laughter—and many delicious meals—this book would not have been possible. To preserve the ethics of this research, they must go unnamed; but I am sure that those who can read English will recognize themselves when they see their own words and their stories told in the following pages. I write of their experiences with great sincerity and deep respect for the openness with which they addressed the issues discussed in this book, and I hope they will forgive my mistakes and any misrepresentations.

Finally, I want to thank my family. Without my parents' unconditional love and great trust, this journey would never have been undertaken. I owe my deepest gratitude to my husband, Jerry Robinson, who has nurtured me with a loving spirit. This book has become the "third party" in our relationship and a memorable part of our life together.

Part I

Positions

1

Introduction

TWO WAVES OF transnational migration, first from China to Thailand and then from Thailand to the United States, have played an important role in the formation of identity in three generations of diasporic Chinese Thai. In this book I focus on how cultural identities, seen through the lens of marriage, are constructed and acted out in Thailand and in the United States. I argue that there is no sex that is not already gendered, classed, or ethnicized, and that cultural identities are informed by regulations of sexuality. Sex, as much as gender or class, is central to understanding the formation of boundaries and cultural membership. Whether the individuals travel to or dwell in China, Thailand, or the United States, sexuality and gender remain salient for identity formation.

Diasporic Chinese are recognized as "people always in transit" (Ong 1999:2). I would add that among diasporic Chinese, men and women are transformed *differently* because they never stop negotiating with the ever-changing cultural constructions of masculinity and femininity. Flexible citizenship is accompanied by flexible sexual conduct, especially since sexuality serves as a key marker of diasporic masculinity and femininity.

What's in a Name?

In Siam (as Thailand was called before 1939) only royal family members and appointed nobles used surnames. Five of Siam's kings—Rama I (1782–1809), Rama II (1809–1824), Rama III (1824–1851), Rama IV (1851–1868), and Rama V (1868–1910)—used Chinese names to show their respect when making tribute payments to China (Kasian 1992:107). A Chinese name embodied a source of social capital that could be used to gain entrance into certain networks and access to valuable resources. However, the increasing presence of European colonialists in the mid-nineteenth

3

During the time of Rama V, hair worn in a braided queue was an important symbol of being Chinese. (By permission of the National Library, Bangkok.)

century destabilized the hierarchical relationship between China and Siam, and the value of having a Chinese name declined.

Ordinary Siamese began using family surnames in 1913 when King Rama VI (1910–1925) decided that the practice would help establish Siam as a "modern" state (Vella 1978:129). In 1939 Siam's name was changed to Thailand, thereby emphasizing the Thai, one of the country's particular ethnic groups. This marked the end of an era in which the monarchy had expressed its pride in ruling over a diverse ethnic population. While the old Siam had embraced all ethnic groups, the new name masked cultural, ethnic, and religious heterogeneity in the name of national uniformity.

In the 1940s Thailand's regime requested that men and women assume first names "appropriate" to their gender. A man's first name was to indicate masculine attributes such as strength and bravery; a woman's, feminine characteristics such as beauty, fragrance, and gentleness. For example, General Somchit Chamanan changed his name from "Somchit," meaning "fulfilled wish," considered feminine, to "Kriengsak," meaning "full of dignity" (Sumalee 1995:132). The creation of family surnames, the change in the country's name, and the requirement for "gender appropriate" first names were all motivated by the dream of establishing a modern Thai identity.

The politics of names continues to play a key role in regulating Thai citizenship. According to the elderly Chinese I interviewed, early Chinese immigrants were required to add the prefix *sae* to their surname as an indicator of Chinese-ness.[1] Sae—the Teochiu word for "family name"—has been absorbed into the Thai language; it is used to emphatically single out those who are ethnic Chinese. Thai law states that Chinese immigrants who retain their Chinese nationality are "Chinese" (*khonchin*) or "Chinese with citizenship" (*sanchat chin*). From 1956 to 1972 the Household Registration Office classified Chinese immigrants who had changed their nationality and their Thailand-born children as "Thai with Thai nationality of Chinese ethnicity" (*khonthai sanchat thai, chuachat chin*); by the third generation, they were legally classified as Thai. But in practice these categories were full of ambiguity, the result of interethnic marriages, the constant manipulation of immigration laws, and the changing rules for citizenship.

Based upon official Thai government statistics, in 1989 there were only 254,777 Chinese in Thailand (Office of the Prime Minister 1990:85). But by 2002, according to the CIA's World Factbook, ethnic Chinese made up about 14 percent (8.7 million) of Thailand's total population (62.3 million) (World Factbook 2002). The size of the ethnic Chinese population in Thailand continues to be a much-debated demographic and political issue.[2]

Throughout most of the twentieth century in Thailand, the category "Chinese" has been inscribed with negative meanings. One might avoid blatant discrimination in certain circumstances by becoming a Thai citizen, but adopting a Thai family name is a condition for acquiring citizenship. So the Chinese are caught between their need to change their citizenship and their desire to keep their Chinese surnames, which is, after all, a link between themselves and their ancestors. Changing surnames means abandoning one's ancestors, who are thought to be watching over and protecting their descendants. Thai surnames do not carry the same kind of cultural meaning.

To overcome this dilemma, Chinese Thai invented Thai surnames that contained their Chinese surnames. First, they transcribed their Chinese surnames into the Chinese dialect they spoke rather than into Mandarin. For example, "Chen" in Mandarin became "Dang" in Teochiu, so that dialect-group identity was articulated. But since the Thai regime allows *only* those who share kinship relationships to share the same surname, thousands and thousands of Teochiu Chinese who had the same surname had to create a new family name. For example, one might add the term *charoen* (prosperity) to Dang. So what began as the Chinese surname Chen ended up being transformed into the Thai surname Dangcharoentham. By doing this, individuals preserved their Chinese surnames within the Thai configuration. But so many Chinese Thai have done so that the long, hybrid names have themselves become indicators of Chinese-ness in Thailand.

When Chinese Thai Americans settled on the west coast of the United States, they confronted a landscape of identities very different from that they had experienced in Thailand. The Thai index of ethnic hierarchies had no significance in an American context. Many Americans knew nothing about Thailand, often confusing Thailand with Taiwan or mistaking Thai immigrants for "Indochinese refugees." It was very rare for an American to read the hidden meanings of a hybrid Chinese Thai name, and as a practical matter Americans found these family names too hard to pronounce or too long to remember. Therefore many immigrants restored their Chinese family names—for example, using Dang in the United States, but Dangcharoen in the Thai American community and in Thailand. Thus, the name itself bears a transnational print: Dang originated from Chen but also departs from it.

Names are more than social markers. They can indicate power relationships between nation-states and subjects, and give a glimpse of how various social categories—such as Thai, Chinese, or American—are formed. Diasporic Chinese Thai often have both Thai and Chinese names, and some have English names as well. Some use a Chinese name at home and a Thai or an English name at school or work. Using names situationally expresses a flexible cultural identity and multiple belongings. It may also reflect the name-holder's educational background and class status. To respect this practice, I have given the individuals whom I write about Thai, Chinese, or English pseudonyms based upon the name they used when first introduced to me.

In Thai society one important way to show respect is by addressing someone with the proper kinship term or professional title. I address people in the book just as I did in the field. I often address Chinese Thai men formally with Chinese appellations such as *laoban* (head of the business), *jizhe* (journalist), or *xiansheng* (Mr.). Some I addressed with Thai designations such as *achan* (professor or teacher) or *thaokae* (head of the business), a Teochiu Chinese term that has been integrated into the Thai language. I addressed only a few men with Chinese kinship terms such as *bobo* (elder uncle). In contrast, I commonly addressed many of the women as *nainai* (grandma), *mama* (mother), *ayi* (younger aunt), or *jie* (older sister), and occasionally I used a Thai kinship term such as *pa* (aunt). I also addressed one woman as *xiaozhang* (principal) and another as *laoshi* (teacher), their occupational titles in Chinese. The Thai kin term *phi* refers to men and women who are older than the speaker; and the designation *khun* is a respectful term corresponding to "Mr." or "Mrs." used before someone's name. It can be replaced by less neutral and more informal kinship terms; such fictive kinship relationships emphasize seniority and social status and help organize the flow of everyday life. Indeed, seemingly straightforward relationships often take place within a complex web of hierarchical systems.

Unlike those who speak Western languages, Thai speakers have multiple ways to say 'I,' each with particular resonances and connotations of deference, social status, intimacy, and formality, and similar interrelated factors (Voravudhi and Diller 1999:114). Self-reference in Thai is called *kan wang tua*, literally "the placing of self" or "speaking position" (ibid., 117). In addition, a junior man is required to use the term *khrap* at the end of a sentence to show his respect. A junior woman uses the term *kha* to show her respect. These terms, and most of the others used for self-reference, are gender-specific. Thus, names and linguistic conventions set the tone for the most basic components of Thai social life and Thai cultural identities.

Names can also move people closer to or further away from resources and privilege. One of Thailand's top news stories in 1991 involved a very public confrontation between Supreme Commander General Sunthorn Kongsompong, his wife, and his mistress. The mistress, Ampapan, a former nurse, told journalists that she claimed the right to use the general's family name, Kongsompong. It was unprecedented for a mistress to use the media to confront a lawful wife. Ampapan said, "I felt as if I had had a previous relationship with this man, that we used to live together. . . . I knew that very second that I would eventually be this man's wife" (Sanitsuda 1991). She portrayed her relationship with General Kongsompong as natural and inevitable, a result of the karma she and the general had accumulated from a past life together.[3]

The public and the press referred to Ampapan as the general's *mianoi* (minor wife). This term has negative social connotations, for in Thai society a woman who lives with a married man other than her husband is often referred to as his minor wife regardless of her marital status. To complicate matters, in some cases the "major wife," *mialuang*, may never have legally registered her marriage, having had a ceremonial marriage instead. Therefore, I often use the term polygyny in this study as it is defined by local discourse and practice rather than by the law.

To counter the negative category "minor wife," Ampapan described herself as the genuine "mother of the house" (*maeban*), who took care of every aspect of the general's well-being, from selecting his toothpaste to choosing his clothes; she said she wanted nothing more than the chance to "serve" the general legally (ibid.). In crafting this public image of herself, she minimized the significance of any economic advantages that she gained from her relationship with the general. According to the media, however, this former nurse was now a land developer "embarking on a golf-course project covering more than 4,500 *rai*" (180 acres) (ibid.).

The general's legal wife, Khunying Orachorn, an elite-class woman whose honorific title "*khunying*" had been conferred by the Thai royal family, had no choice but to respond to this public challenge. She filed a lawsuit to prohibit Ampapan from using her husband's family name. Like Ampapan, Khunying Orachorn portrayed herself as a "good" woman: she responded to her husband's affair with wifely virtue, by "tolerating," "keeping silent," and "letting things pass by" (ibid.). This stance gained her considerable public support. Newspapers quoted readers who applauded her with such comments as "Good, this will teach the *mianoi* her place" (ibid.).

However, Ampapan had asked the general's mother to adopt her so that she could use the general's prominent family name. In the end the court ruled that Khunying Orachorn did not have the right to monopolize the general's family name, thereby supporting the general and implicitly validating polygyny. Khunying Orachorn, who had conceived of herself as a defender of legality, found herself defeated by the judicial system.

The general himself was noticeably absent from the heated media discourse. His power conferred on him the privilege of remaining silent throughout the controversy. However, the actions of his two wives did influence the public's perception of him. A local Chinese newspaper titled one report: "It is easy for the general to play politics, but it is difficult for him to play with his women" (*zhengzhi yigao, nüren nanwan* [M]) (*World News Daily*, 24 June 1991).

This episode took place while I was conducting fieldwork on how marriage shapes the ongoing construction of ethnic Chinese cultural identities in contemporary Bangkok. I was particularly interested in how various constructions of gender, sexuality, ethnicity, and class—the stuff of identity—conflated at the site of marriage, and this event allowed me to observe firsthand how local gender ideologies influenced the ways in which many upper- and middle-class Chinese Thai identified themselves. Because this confrontation took place over a period of months in such a public forum—indeed, it became a sort of soap opera—people from every walk of life avidly followed its twists and turns and readily expressed their opinions on it; diverse attitudes towards marriage, sexuality, and ethnic differences all bubbled to the surface.

What struck me was how class status and gender politics affected the process of defining and rejecting others, and how men's collective sexual privilege was taken for granted. Like most Thai men, many middle-class Chinese Thai men regarded the general's sexual privilege simply as a demonstration of a "man's nature" (*pen thamachat khong phuchai/nanren de tainxing* [M]), the result of essentialized biological differences between men and women. At the same time, the Chinese Thai men usually described themselves as "responsible" (*khuam rapphitchop/fuze* [M]) family men, in contrast to "irresponsible" working-class Thai men who "lay eggs" everywhere, but do not support the family. From this perspective, while both Thai and Chinese Thai men might lay eggs outside the home, being a successful breadwinner—a key symbol of middle-class respectability—delineated the boundary between Chinese and Thai. However, because of the general's elite-class status and his clear ability to support his dependents, the Chinese Thai men focused on his inability to maintain "peace" between his wives. Some commented that the Chinese kept the peace between their wives much better than the general did. Several, for example, mentioned Teko, a celebrated lukchin polygynist whose seven wives and nearly two dozen children lived "harmoniously" under one roof; furthermore, Teko and all his wives worked together at a family-owned meatball factory. Through the process of ethnicizing along class lines, middle-class Chinese Thai men articulate their class respectability by emphasizing their sexual privilege, their breadwinner role, and their ability to maintain family harmony.

The Chinese Thai women were more interested in Ampapan and Khunying Orachorn and focused their criticism on Ampapan rather than the general. Ampapan was denounced as being "worse" than a sex worker for having "stolen" another woman's husband. One elderly woman, my neighbor in Bangkok, praised Khunying Orachorn for her tolerance, saying she was "like us Chinese" (*xiang women zhongguo ren* [M]). Many women supported the elite-class major wife while condemning Ampapan for "not knowing her own social status" (*mairu thana/buzhi gaodi* [M]).

Chinese Thai men and women were interpreting the conflicts in the story of the general and his wives in gendered and class-specific ways. The men focused on the general's inability to maintain family harmony instead of on his economic responsibility; the women focused on the necessity of tolerating male sexual privilege and on hierarchies between wives. To borrow Stuart Hall's remark, they spoke "from a particular place and time, from a history and culture which is specific." What they said was "always 'in context', positioned" (1990:222). Similarly, my attempts to understand unfamiliar combinations of ethnicity, sexuality, gender, and class were shaped by the nature of my relations with the people I interviewed, by current academic discourse, and, of course, by my own culture-bound modes of thinking.

Just as individual identity comes from a specific position within a power structure, names and labels are also located within cultural systems and power structures; they are tied to an individual's gender, ethnicity, class, cultural identity, citizenship, and access to socioeconomic resources. I have named this book *Marital Acts* because it locates marriage as a site for exploring different ways that identities are constructed and acted out in the interactions between sexuality, gender, class, and ethnicity or race. The notion of acts refers not only to national and cultural forms of (self) regulation or discipline—the various guises of governmentality—but also to *practices*—negotiation, play, and disguises. I hold that it is impossible to understand identity unless the processes of discipline and self-identification are examined. I want to avoid treating transnationalism abstractly, as a collection of dematerialized cultural flows. Instead, I pay special attention to everyday practices when examining how identities work, and how and why they change in certain ways.

Three Generations: Chinkao, Lukchin, and Chinese Thai Americans

The book is organized into four parts. Part I (chapters 1–2) provides an introduction and illustrates various class, gender, ethnic, generational, individual, and theoretical positions in this book. Part II (chapters 3–5) focuses on the chinkao, the China-born first generation, while Part III (chapters 6–9) deals with the lukchin, or Thailand-born second generation. Throughout Parts II and III, I use three key themes—kinship, the division of labor, and conjugal sex—to characterize everyday practices and contextualize identity formation. Part IV, the conclusion, examines how particular aspects of the culture brought over from Thailand, as well as American culture and identity politics, inform the ongoing cultural struggle of Chinese Thai Americans.

Most chinkao in this project were born in southeastern coastal China, in Guangdong and Fujian provinces, and came to Thailand via steamship in the 1930s and 1940s. While the immigrants included speakers of five Chinese dialects—Teochiu, Cantonese, Hakka, Hainanese, and

Hokkienese—Teochiu-speakers were the most prominent. After arriving in the new land, chinkao were confronted with an emerging Thai nationalist movement, followed by an anti-communist campaign during which some chinkao and lukchin were accused of working on behalf of communist China. Diplomatic relations between Thailand and China were suspended from 1949 until 1975, during which time most chinkao were cut off from their family members in China—some for as long as twenty-six years. In addition to encountering displacement and marginalization in Thailand, chinkao also had to contend with China's antagonistic policies toward "overseas Chinese" (*haiwai huaren* [M]) at that time. The houses and land that some had purchased for retirement back in China were confiscated during the Land Reform movement in the early 1950s, and some had relatives who were persecuted as "spies" during the Cultural Revolution (1966–1976) simply for having received remittances or parcels from Thailand. Overseas Chinese were openly scorned as the bourgeoisie, and thus a threat to socialist China.

Under these conditions some chinkao began referring to themselves not as overseas Chinese but as "overseas orphans" (*haiwai guer* [M]). Eventually, as they involved themselves more deeply in Thailand's economy and ethnic politics, they became aware of growing differences between themselves and the Chinese in China. Gradually they switched from renting to buying houses in Thailand.[4] The shift from sojourner to dweller—from migrant to immigrant—was based on personal choices, but those choices were strongly influenced by the policies of the Thai and Chinese regimes toward the ethnic Chinese.[5]

Chapter 3 explains that most men came to Thailand as labor migrants, whereas women usually came because of marriage or family reunification. The dialectical relationship between immigration and marital practices reveals that immigration is both an economic endeavor and a complex process of cultural reproduction in which Thai and Chinese regimes compete. Chapter 4 demonstrates how Chinese identity is characterized by masculinized economic production and feminized reproduction. Chinkao women transformed much faster than men in the work domain. With greater access to labor markets in Bangkok, chinkao women can add an income-producing job to the unpaid work of housekeeping and childcare. Nevertheless, their economic upward mobility and choice of occupation are still heavily influenced by family gender politics. Chapter 5 analyzes how chinkao men conform to the Chinese ideal of masculinity—to be a reliable breadwinner—while embracing aspects of the Thai ideal of masculinity—

especially the notion of being a virile womanizer. Thus, these transformations among chinkao—men changing their sexual behavior and women transforming their work behavior—characterize their gender-specific ways of belonging in Thailand and China. This reworking of feminine and masculine identities constitutes a central part of the cultural struggle within transnational space.[6]

Part III—especially chapter 6—focuses on the hybrid character of lukchin identity. By examining three weddings, chapter 7 further illustrates how Thai "modernity" (*thansamai*) and lukchin hybrid identities are expressed in class taste and ethnic identities. Born, raised, educated, and dwelling in Thailand, lukchin have experienced a different set of regulations than their chinkao parents and have been exposed to many more aspects of Thai and Western culture. Most have learned about Chinese culture only from the stories told by their parents and from their own experiences living in Thai society. When they identify themselves as Chinese, *khonchin*, they often distinguish between the Chinese in Thailand and the Chinese in China. At the same time, they are keenly aware that they differ from "real Thai" (*thaithae*) in the eyes of the state. For this reason, when I refer to ethnic Chinese in Thailand, I frequently use the term "Chinese Thai" to distinguish them from the mainland Chinese and to capture their transnational experience. I do not use "Sino-Thai" because this expression has been used to refer to the descendants of Chinese immigrants who married Thai spouses and to the relationship between China and Thailand. When referring to the Chinese Thai in Thailand and in the United States, I use the term "diasporic Chinese Thai." At the same time I also use "Chinese," "ethnic Chinese," "chinkao," "lukchin," and "Chinese Thai Americans" in various contexts to convey a sense of differences, transformation, ambiguity, and fluidity. I hope this will help convey the idea that cultural identities are socially constructed and malleable, not fixed states from which a "natural" essence is expressed in a set of distinctive attributes.

In the struggle to be accepted as Thai or to resist being discriminated against as Chinese, lukchin became conscious of the need to act "Thai." They learned to mimic a perfect Central Thai accent and imitate Thai body language. Particular Thai gestures, such as lowering the body or showing respect through hand movements (*wai*), became ways of expressing their sensitivity to the Thai social hierarchy. Some also spoke English in order to dilute or disguise their Chinese-ness.

The majority of chinkao and lukchin whom I met had moved from peasant or working class to middle or upper class.[7] Their socioeconomic upward mobility is similar to that of the ethnic Chinese in other parts of Southeast Asia and has been coincident with expanding business opportunities, an early advantage in business (Mackie 1992a:163), and the development of commercial production in Thailand "as colonialism and market forces integrated indigenous economies into the world market system" (Lim 1983:6).

However, the changes engendered by socioeconomic upward mobility are not necessarily "progressive." Accumulated economic capital has enabled some lukchin men to express certain cultural beliefs that chinkao men could not afford to practice: male inheritance and patrilocality (a married couple lives with the groom's natal family) are more prevalent among lukchin than among chinkao. Some lukchin men no longer think like their fathers that Thai women are "sexier," but assert, because of sexual encounters with newly arrived undocumented Chinese immigrant women, that "Chinese women are tastier." An old Chinese metaphor that compares women with wild or domestic flowers has been replaced with a Thai metaphor that compares women with different flavors of hot sauce. It is said that "repeatedly tasting the same hot sauce causes a man to lose his appetite" (*kin namphrik thuaikao khao ko bua*). Within the contemporary construction of Thai masculinity, fidelity to one's wife is not a crucial indicator of being masculine. Indeed, the sexual discipline that a man experiences is to be a "womanizer" (*chaochu*), not a faithful husband. Unlike his wife, he is not limited to having sex only within the marriage. In other words, the particular masculine constraints that a lukchin man experiences are often obscured by his sexual privilege as a man in Thai society.

Chapter 8 explores the effects of naturalization on conjugal sexuality and middle-class respectability. A lukchin man can boast about his extramarital affairs to express his masculine identity and middle-class respectability. In contrast, to be an active sexual agent would call into question a lukchin woman's middle-class respectability and feminine identity. As a consequence, men and women who had extramarital affairs talked about them and managed them differently. Gender-specific practices also profoundly influence the operation of a family business, the theme of chapter 9. I pay special attention to female entrepreneurs, conjugal sexuality, and emotional management, topics generally neglected in the study of Chinese family businesses in Southeast Asia. I argue that a businessman's structural privileges, embedded in kinship and the sexual domain, not only serve to disguise an exploitative conjugal labor relationship but also enable him to claim his wife's accomplishments as his own.

Chapter 10 examines how Chinese Thai Americans experience different regulations than chinkao and lukchin with regard to sexuality, citizenship, and ethnicity. In an unexpected gender-specific twist, Chinese Thai American women have begun asserting their sexual freedom, and men have had to restrain their previous womanizing. For many Chinese Thai American men, patronizing the sex industry or marrying more than one woman no longer demonstrates masculinity. Instead, monogamy becomes the ideal, and masculinity now tends to be measured by success in acquiring material goods. Nonetheless, monogamy does not necessarily mean gender equality.

The previously meaningful social categories "Thai" and "Chinese" are often lumped together as "Asian American" or "people of color" in the United States. When discussing identity politics in the United States, the term "race" must be added to the mix. Chinese Thai experiences of racial discrimination in the United States often evoke memories of discrimination encountered in Thailand. A few who had rejected their Chinese identity in Thailand are now reclaiming it, but it would be a mistake to read this as a rejection of Thai cultural identity. On the contrary, most Chinese Thai Americans are proud of being Thai, an identity they have embraced since childhood. Being forced to rethink identity politics as a result of transnational migration and displacement, they are deeply engaged in three distinct yet related cultural practices: they claim Thai-ness, they claim American-ness, and they create accounts of Chinese and Thai ethnicity that use their specific cultures and histories to challenge preconceptions of what it means to be Thai, Chinese, and American.

Generational differences have to be understood in relation to different cultural and socioeconomic systems, but generational boundaries were not always clear-cut. Some lukchin were older than some chinkao, having been born long before the chinkao immigrated to Thailand. If we focus exclusively on generational distinctions, we risk overlooking the complexity within a generation, because we can easily ascribe a certain level of artificial homogeneity to a group for whom other distinctions, such as gender and class, may have much greater meaning. Therefore, I pay attention to differences and similarities within generations as well as between them, in order to understand them both horizontally and vertically. The juxtaposition of these three generations illustrates how the formation of cultural identity is an ongoing process, taking place not only between generations but also within each one as well.

2

The Ongoing Process of
Identity Formation

Identity Games

Diasporic Chinese Thai have long confronted issues regarding identity formation and the processes of belonging, exclusion, self-assertion, and adaptation. Here is what I heard from Kayai, an undergraduate I interviewed in the San Francisco Bay Area in the summer of 1997:

> My mother's father was the chief of police in Singapore. My dad's father was prime minister of Thailand for a few years. My mom is very conscious of the fact that she is a foreigner, and she wants me to be *very Thai*. If I don't act Thai, the first thing everyone says is that mom does not know the culture, and she does not know how to teach her children.
>
> She had quite a bit of trouble when she married into my dad's family. My dad's family is so Thai, not even Chinese Thai, but very Thai. So my dad not only marries a Chinese, but, my goodness, a foreigner who doesn't know Thai culture. And so, in the beginning, my dad's mother was not very happy. She didn't smile.
>
> Playing the game is knowing the culture, knowing how people want you to act and then acting that way. And, yes, that is what in Thailand they would call two-faced (*khon songna*), not sincere. Though maybe that is too strong for what I am doing.

Although Kayai's mother, born and raised in a "Chinese" family in Singapore, worked hard to act Thai, think Thai, and raise her children to be Thai, she maintained her Singaporean citizenship. Later, she and her husband got a "paper divorce" so that Kayai and his siblings could take advantage of her foreign citizenship and attend a privileged international school in Bangkok. Despite their nominal divorce, the couple's marital life continued as before, and the children continued using their father's prestigious Thai surname. By manipulating those legal regulations that are informed by ethnic and gender politics, the children benefited from both their mother's foreign citizenship and their father's prominent family name.

Coming from such a family, Kayai was conscious of the need to play identity games. His insight—"playing the game is knowing the culture, knowing how people want you to act, and then acting that way"—was shared by other diasporic Chinese Thai I interviewed in Thailand and in the United States. Although they rarely used the phrase "playing the game," they often told stories about performing to meet the expectations of others, and tailoring their behavior to take advantage of various regulations and institutions. However, this confrontation with identity—"playing the game"—is characterized by much more than the creative agency of its individual players. Sherry Ortner suggests that games, *as a model of practice*, embody the interaction of agents and structures:

> The idea of the "game" is meant to capture simultaneously the following dimensions: that social life is culturally organized and constructed, in terms of defining categories of actors, rules and goals of the games, and so forth; that social life is precisely social, consisting of webs of relationship and interaction between multiple, shiftingly interrelated subject positions, none of which can be extracted as autonomous "agents"; and yet at the same time there is "agency," that is, actors play with skill, intention, wit, knowledge, intelligence. (1996:12)

Individual agents are both enabled and regulated by political-economic structures and by cultural regimes of truth and power—the state, the family, and economic enterprises. The effects of transnational migration, cultural and geographic displacement, and the interpenetration of different ideologies have all made identity games even more complicated.

Imagination, Identity Politics, and "In-Between-Ness"

The most recent studies on transnational migration and diasporas in Asia have abandoned older class-oriented or assimilation approaches, focusing instead on how the spread of global capitalism has rearranged class, gender, race, and nationality differences into new combinations of identity (Basch, Glick Schiller, and Szanton Blanc 1994; Nonini and Ong 1997; Ong 1999). The effects of transnational migration have dramatically destabilized Chinese cultural identities.

The three social categories—Thai, Chinese, and American—that individuals in this study have struggled with were created and defined by different nation-states, which makes them seem natural or original. But Benedict Anderson has argued convincingly that a nation is not a given reality but rather an imagined community (1991), whose most "natural" and defining features have been culturally constructed. However, he also claims that "the dreams of racism actually have their origin in ideologies of *class*, rather than in those of nation" (ibid., 149). Racism does indeed intermingle with ideologies of class. Jewish racial stereotypes in the United States, for example, are often related to "being middle-class" (Ortner 1998:10), and stereotypes about "wealthy Chinese" in Southeast Asia are similarly informed by class. But the effects of racism extend far beyond class. Ethnocentrism and white supremacy are often part of national ideologies that shape identity politics. Aihwa Ong, Brackette Williams, and others have pointed out that "even Western European and American civic nationalisms depend on the invention of a unitary substance—the 'blood' of kinship and race—to cement their links to a social and political unit and to an economic system" (Ong 1999:56). Indeed, in this project, many believed that Chinese or Thai "blood" determined the authenticity of cultural membership and therefore played a significant role in the construction of identity.

The sociologist Paul Gilroy suggests that absolutist notions of nationalism and cultural difference are inadequate for understanding diasporic experience and identity (1992). For example, to understand the black diaspora as an international experience, he urges us to go beyond nation-bounded geographies of inquiry toward a much larger analytic space; he reconfigures geographies of movements of goods, economies, people, and identities as a single complex unit based on a perspective of transnationality and interculturality.

Gilroy's approach to the chronotope of movement (following Mikhail Bakhtin) as a time-related construct and cultural intermixture within diasporic populations is powerful and influential. And yet, as Aihwa Ong points out, multiple geographies were and continue to be experienced by Chinese whose historically earlier diasporas were continually evolving into a network of family ties, kinship, commerce, sentiments, and values spread throughout regions of dispersal and settlement (1999:12). It is also important to note that, before the mid-nineteenth century, Chinese merchants entered Thai socioeconomic space in the middle rather than at the bottom, and their relationship to the state regime was much different than that which characterized the diasporic space of the "Black Atlantic."

Multiple geographies are a main characteristic of all diasporas, yet they may be too easily attributed specifically to the conditions of late modernity and the ascendance of transnational neoliberal capitalism. Shelly Errington warns us that our efforts to triumph over all meta-narratives are often "far less revolutionary and innovative and deconstructive than they pretend to be" (1998:157). To a certain extent, our old meta-narrative of "progress" seems to have been repackaged as the meta-narrative of neoliberalism, naturalizing the link between free market capitalism, democracy, and individual liberation, and celebrating as part of the condition of late modernity the emergence of new and flexible forms of identity that bring more "freedom."

Perhaps we should see such flexibility, at least in part, as another form of discipline. In *Flexible Citizenship*, Ong observes that despite the acceleration of flexible concepts and practices, which are linked to the rise of global capitalism, "there has been little or no attempt to consider how different regimes of truth and power may set structural limits to such flexible productions and subjectivities" (1999:19). Such a consideration of the *limits* of flexibility, I believe, derives from Ong's expansion of the causal significance of Foucault's notion of governmentality; she suggests that governmentality—the various regimes of discipline, including the state and institutional discourses as well as the various cultural logics of family, kin, and group identification that discipline identity in everyday practice—may be just as important, just as causally constraining, as the structure of the political economy itself.

Clearly, despite the creative agency implied in the notion of flexible citizenship and hybrid cultural identity, flexibility should perhaps be understood *not* as individual autonomy, but rather as a negotiation with the multiple regulations of different nation-states and hybrid cultural practices. Diasporic Chinese Thai understand that their rights and obligations differ from country to country and that certain behaviors are more acceptable in one country than in another. To get the best out of these various systems, they develop different strategies for engaging with different regimes. Their flexible strategies arise from the in-between spaces they encounter as they deal with regimes across national borders.

Homi Bhabha calls in-between space a "Third Space" (1994:36–39). He presents it as a theoretical space, a transnational space, a space of articulation, and a location of culture beyond national borders. For me, however, in-between-ness is not just theoretical; it is *created in and by practice*, and it exists at the *intersections* of ideology, discipline, and action. It is the space in which cultural negotiation and identity formation occur, where one conforms to, transgresses, or ignores boundaries. And in-between-ness works against ideological dichotomies and boundaries such as migration/dwelling, old home/new home, Chinese/Thai/American, and so on. These disciplined in-between spaces are never black and white but full of tension and constantly in flux and being renegotiated.

Beyond Assimilation, Double Identity, and Classed Ethnicity

Before the 1990s Western academic writing articulated three main scholarly theories about Chinese communities in Southeast Asia. One viewed them as unchanging, another as assimilated, and a third as having a class-based ethnic identity. Each approach must be understood in relation to the political conditions in which it was formulated. Theories, like ideologies, are culturally bound to specific historical-political moments and need to be understood as such.

William Skinner's work on the historical transformation of Chinese communities in Thailand was the most influential research on Southeast Asia done during the Cold War period (1957; 1958; 1964; 1973a; 1973b). Skinner challenged the persistent belief that the Chinese maintained unwavering loyalty to their own culture century after century (e.g., Mallory 1956:265). Instead, he predicted that the Chinese in Thailand would be completely assimilated by the fifth generation. And indeed, the Chinese Thai have undergone dramatic social and economic transformations and adapted to many Thai cultural practices. But the assimilation model ignores the capacity of a people to develop their own meaningful identity and denies the possibility of individuals having multiple identities; it also obscures the diversity of Chinese Thai communities. By presenting these changes as a natural progressive process, assimilation theory overlooks the power embedded within Thailand's ethnic politics. One of the challenges we face is to understand how a marginalized cultural identity can be *temporarily* silenced and constrained, without falling back on the assimilation assumption.

While Skinner advocates an American evolutionary-assimilation model, Richard Coughlin believes in coexisting but separate Chinese and Thai cultures and identities. He has proposed that the Chinese in Thai society carry a double identity and can act as either "Chinese" or "Thai" depending on the circumstances and their self-interest (1960:193–194). He has suggested that this dual character is associated with the different value systems, occupations, and family structures of Chinese and Thai society (ibid., 197). His assertion may reflect the influence of John Embree's argument that Thailand was a "loosely structured" society in contrast to the "tightly structured" societies of Japan and China (1950). Coughlin rarely discussed how, when, or *in what context* the Chinese shifted between these two identities or how these two identities could coexist in one person. Both Coughlin and Skinner seem trapped within a binary logic: the Chinese are either unchangeable or assimilated; they have either a single or a double identity.

From the mid-1970s through the late 1980s, a younger generation of Western scholars, many of them influenced by Marxist theory, began to treat class as an important category for understanding the Chinese in Southeast Asia (see Heidhues 1974; Hewsion 1981, 1989; Lim and Gosling 1983; Omohundro 1981; Szanton Blanc 1989). Some investigated commercial and kin networks, family businesses, and models of Chinese capitalism (see G. Hamilton 1991; Mackie 1992a, 1992b; Redding 1990; Siu-lun Wong 1980). Their work has provided valuable insights into the complexity of ethnic groups engaged in the capitalist mode of production. However, they tend to separate political economy from a range of cultural processes, conceptualizing class solely as an objective structural position. This class-oriented approach fails to answer some important questions. For example, why is it *more* culturally acceptable for a Chinese man to marry a Thai woman than for a Chinese woman to marry a Thai man? How do kinship and affinal exchange contribute to the redrawing of ethnic boundaries?

Indeed, class signifies more than economic differences. As Ortner points out: "At one level the term 'class' points to certain economic-cum-cultural locations defined within an objectivist perspective. Classes are not objects 'out there,' but there *is* something out there in the way of inequality, privilege, and social difference which the idea of 'class' is meant to capture specifically in its economic dimension. At the same time class is . . . an identity term and is, in fact, the only American identity term that is organized primarily around an economic axis" (1998:8). Class consists of more than economic capital; it also is aligned with cultural taste and ethnic identity.

While studies have focused on the political and economic aspects of the lives of Chinese Southeast Asians, the cultural aspects of their lives, as Leo Suryadinata has noted, have been very much neglected (1989:4–41). Building upon his insight, I argue that Chinese Southeast Asian women are mostly written out of the world of production and that sexuality is written out of identity formation.[1] Sexuality and gender are systems of difference that penetrate all domains, and we have a responsibility to analyze those differences in culturally specific contexts.

Naturalized Heterosexuality in a Political and Economic Context

In the spring of 1992 when Guoyi Mama, my neighbor in Bangkok, discovered that her husband was sleeping with their live-in Thai maid, she was outraged. "In his eyes I am worth less than a maid. But he is worth less than a rabbit. At least a rabbit does not eat the grass near its own nest." She felt especially humiliated that her husband's affair took place inside the home with a maid who held the position with the least status in the family hierarchy. Before her discovery, Guoyi Mama and her husband had been sleeping together in the same bed, but after uncovering her husband's affair, she moved into her own bedroom, resisting her husband's authority by detaching herself sexually but maintaining the marital bond. As women living in Bangkok, where the sex industry flourishes, she and her maid might well have shared the popular view that it was a "man's nature" to have a large appetite for sex. But when the two women clashed over one man, Guoyi Mama took out her frustration by firing her working-class maid.

This episode points toward the interlocking nature of sexuality, gender, class, and ethnic relations in everyday life among middle-class Chinese Thai in Bangkok. It reveals a wife's resistance to and complicity with her husband's sexual privilege. However, academic discourses on diasporic Chinese rarely use sexuality itself as a critical category of analysis. As Carole Vance points out, "Anthropology seems especially well suited to problematize these most naturalized categories, yet sexuality has been the last domain (trailing even gender) to have its natural, biologized status called into question. For many of us, essentialism was our first way of thinking about sexuality and still remains hegemonic" (1991: 880).

Heterosexuality, perhaps because it has been seen as the most "normal" of sexualities, often tends to obscure rather than illuminate our investigations into other cultural and historically specific sexualities. At the same time, homosexuality, long marginalized by heterosexual normality, has been much more variously investigated and theorized in academic discourse. Identity becomes crucial in the study of gay and lesbian sexuality, which is not the case in the study of heterosexuality. Does this mean that people who practice heterosexuality do not think about identity in relation to their sexual practices? Of course not. Rather, it is taken for granted. While heterosexual normality has been somewhat destabilized and problemitized by feminist and lesbian/gay scholarship, I am convinced that it remains largely naturalized.

In studying Southeast Asia, scholars tend to focus on the regulation of sexuality and gender *within* an ethnic group, or between indigenous people and outsiders such as colonialists, rather than on the interactions between different ethnic groups in the same society (Atkinson and Errington 1990; Stoler 1997; Van Esterik 1982b; Ward 1963). Transnational sexuality is mainly addressed in another body of literature, which deals with issues such as trafficking in women, mail-order brides, gay and lesbian sexuality, AIDS, and sex tourism.

The study of sexuality in Thailand has been quite explicitly affected by time-specific politics. Through the 1970s and 1980s, studies of sexuality primarily concentrated on the issues of population growth, fertility, post-nuptial residence, and female sex workers. But since the 1990s, so-called high-risk groups—sex workers and unmarried men—have become the major focus because of concern over how their practices affect the spread of AIDS. Recently an increasing number of scholars have ventured beyond the study of commercial sexual relations and high-risk groups to explore issues such as the representation of sexualities, married men's sexuality, and gay identities. These studies help us to understand a wide range of sexual practices and the complexity of sexuality and gender politics within Thai society. And yet, in contrast to the extensive sociological accounts of male premarital and extramarital sexual behavior, there has been near-total scholarly silence about conjugal sex, female extramarital sex, and the *connections* between class and sexuality.[2]

In this book, I argue that sexuality has to be understood within the context of power. Foucault states that "power relations are rooted deep in the social nexus, not reconstituted 'above' society" (1983:222); in other words, power relations are embedded in everyday activities. But Foucault appears much more concerned with desire than with ethnicity or gender. According to Foucault, because of Christianity in the West, sex is understood in terms of desire, and that in search of its deep meaning subjects confess their desires in order to find out who they are.[3] I contend that in Thailand and in the United States the notion of heterosexual desire is constructed along gender lines, and that sexuality is often used to ethnicize or racialize the Other. Although race as a category does not exist in the natural world, discrimination based on arbitrary social classifications certainly does exist. The diasporic "I," at least as I found it in my research, is never neutral in regard to sexuality, gender, or ethnicity/race.

Sexuality should also be read as an important class marker. As George Mosse points out, respectability—a term indicating "decent and correct" manners and morals, as well as the proper attitude toward sexuality—informs middle-class sexual norms in modern Europe (1985:1). According to Mosse, sexual restraint or self-control has been considered *the* symbol of bourgeois manhood in modern Europe. Such a notion of middle-class respectability *does* apply to the construction of femininity in Thai society, but it does *not* apply to the formation of masculinity. A middle-class woman gains class respectability by controlling her sexual behavior and being a chaste wife and a devoted mother. In contrast, a man's middle-class respectability is articulated by becoming a breadwinner and a womanizer. Thus, middle-class respectability is gendered.

Despite the various ways in which gender, ethnicity, and class serve to discipline sexuality, male sexual privilege is often thought of as "natural" and entirely separate from the moral order and socioeconomic forces. For example, according to a man quoted in a *Bangkok Post* article on polygyny and prostitution in Thailand: "To a Thai man, sex is just like scratching an itch or eating to satisfy hunger" (Cabrera 1996). In a study conducted in 1990, 80 percent of the males and 74 percent of the females responded that it was "natural for men to pursue sex at every oppor-tunity" (VanLandingham et al., citing a study conducted by the Deemar Corporation 1993:298–299). The Thai regime advises men to "cultivate good hobbies" and "have positive activities for their time and energy" as a substitute for visiting sex workers (Wasant 1991). In contrast, women are advised to offer their husbands "complete sexual pleasure within marriage, thereby making the latter's recourse to sex workers unnecessary" (Cook 1998:262).

Nonetheless, both the men and the women involved are aware that men's extramarital sex directly affects the family economy, the children's inheritance rights, and the wife's respectability. Such a contradiction—one I encountered repeatedly in my fieldwork—forced me to take sexuality seri-ously. By using sexuality as an analytical category, I illustrate how naturaliz-ing any social practice, such as heterosexuality, conceals fundamental ideas of prestige, class, ethnic stereotypes, and asymmetric gender relations. I hope this will enable us to see how naturalization occurs *within* political and economic forces, not outside of them.

"Naturalization," as Sylvia Yanagisako and Carol Delaney point out, "contains power already embedded in culture" (1995:1). The real effect of naturalization is to mask power relations in what is taken to be the natural order itself. It is easy to mistake longstanding socially constructed categories as god-given "truths." Sex, ethnic, and racial differences are probably the most deeply embedded, most deeply naturalized distinctions used in constructing cultural identities.

Naturalized Social Categories

Rites of passage play a key role in naturalizing a person's authority and privilege. Thai men are expected to enter a Buddhist monastic order as novices or monks; the length of service can vary, from days, weeks, or even years, depending on individual circumstances. Completing this term of monastic service is believed to transform a "raw" man into a mature man (*khonsuk*) (Keyes 1987b:36). Individual status, such as being born male rather than female, is understood to reflect the "merit" (*bun*)—that is, the positive karma—that a person inherits from previous lives. Karma is taken by many as a fundamental truth of Thai Theravada Buddhism. Being biologically male, and undergoing the spiritual transformation from ordinary man to monk, legitimizes a man's position of leadership, both in the family and in the public realm. In contrast, for a woman it is marriage that symbolizes the transformation into a "complete person" (*khonsombun*) (Anuman 1973:57–58). Becoming a nurturing mother is considered the crucial step that turns a woman into a full adult, for childbearing is regarded as a moral action which leads to improving a woman's karma and maturity (Muecke 1984:462; Whittaker 1999:47). Earth and rice are also linked with women, and all three are regarded as sharing "natural" nurturing qualities. Thus the criteria for becoming a complete person are responses to the gendered construction of cultural identity.

The exclusively male spiritual rite—service as a monk—parallels another exclusively male rite in which a sexually experienced man takes an inexperienced man on his first visit to a brothel.[4] Therefore, the boundaries between prostitution, marriage, and the monastery are fluid for Thai men; they can move in and out of these three institutions freely (Manderson 1992:471–472). Like the spiritual transformation from man to monk, the sexual encounter is also seen as transformative; this awakening of the mature man is both spiritual and sexual.

In a Chinese cultural context, the forms of naturalization are expressed quite differently. Cultural categories such as yin/yang, or *nei/wai* [M] (inside/outside), are particularly meaningful to Chinese for understanding gender relationships, their bodies, and the universe at large. Nei/wai attributions disguise a broad complex of power relations, which can be better understood in light of Tani Barlow's insight into yin/yang in relation to the reproduction of women in China (1994). In arguing that hegemonic *funü* [M] (women) take shape in "a system of purposes" that constitutes a genealogy in Chinese history, Barlow points out that:

> The forces of yin and yang are many things: logical relationships (like up and down, in and out, husband and wife), practical forces, "designations for the polar aspects of effects," and in a social sense, powers that inscribe hierarchy (i.e., yang subordinates yin because it encloses the lesser force into itself), but yin/yang is neither as totalistic nor as ontologically binary as the Western stereotype would have it. (1994:258)

Barlow's remarks suggest the complexity, multiplicity, and fluidity of yin/yang. The entire cosmos is understood as being in a state of vibrant equilibrium, constantly pulsing between paired counterforces such as yin and yang, male and female, day and night, warm and cold, up and down, inside and outside, strong and weak. A human body, or a physical entity such as a house, is understood as a mixture of yin and yang, forces out of which the entire universe is composed. Yin/yang are never viewed as fixed. Yang can turn into yin, or yin can change into yang, depending on the situation. On the one hand, yin/yang emphasizes balance and harmony. When yin and yang are in balance, a nation, or a family, is believed to be prospering; a body is healthy. On the other hand, yin/yang depicts a particular social order: yang is active and male; it subordinates yin, which is passive and female. Power relations are naturalized by and within these cultural logics. Nei/wai has a similar kind of dynamic and flexible quality. Both men and women can be nei or wai, or both, depending on the situation, but men gain greater structural privileges than women within the patrilineal system.

Elaborating upon Foucault's notion of governmental biopolitics—the regulation of the sexual and reproductive behavior of individuals to ensure the security and prosperity of the nation as a whole—Ong argues that the diasporic Chinese have been similarly shaped by a kind of family biopolitics, which she defines as "a set of rational practices that regulate healthy, productive bodies, and their deployment in flexible capitalist activities" (1993:755). In this book, I will explore how identity is formed under the influence of cultural logics, socioeconomic systems, and gender and ethnic politics, particularly in three realms: kinship networks, the division of labor, and heterosexual practices.

In the realm of kinship, nei/wai defines both gender relationships and the symbolic social order. Even before birth, each individual is assigned a position within the kin group and a rank within the patrilineal structure— such as male/insider and female/outsider. Thus in the emigrant areas of southern China before the second half of the twentieth century, a girl was considered an inside member of her natal family, but her position within the patriarchal family was inferior to her brother's, although she might be superior to a sister-in-law with no son. When she married, however, she became an outsider in her natal family. But marriage alone did not automatically make her an inside member of her husband's family; she did not achieve this status until she bore a son. Her children would be referred to as "outside grandson" (*waisun* [M]) and "outside granddaughter" (*waisunnü* [M]) by her own parents, while her brother's children would be given the privileged positions of "inside grandson" (*sunzi* [M]) and "inside granddaughter" (*sunnü* [M]). In contrast, a man would always be an insider in his natal family, clan, lineage, and ethnic group. This shows how gender derives central meaning from the kinship structure. Marital status would influence a man's inside membership only if he married into his wife's natal family and adopted her family name—which could happen when a son from a poor family married a daughter from a rich family that had no sons. Thus it is very important to understand kinship as consisting of cooperative units based on social, economic, and sexual ties rather than simply as naturalized kin-based domestic groups.

In the context of the division of labor, nei/wai indicates social space inside and outside the family, integrating both production and reproduction. Interestingly, women and men switch nei/wai positions in this setting. The wife, the outsider of patrilineal kinship, becomes an "inside person" (*neiren* [M]) to her husband, and the husband becomes an "outside person" (*waizi* [M]) to his wife.[5] Being her husband's inside person implicitly emphasizes a wife's domestic responsibilities and the socially constructed, family-oriented social space. Being an outside person to his wife emphasizes a husband's responsibility as the family's primary economic provider and his duties and prerogatives in dealing with public institutions beyond the family. The wife has to be nei to protect the integrity of the family, while the husband has to be wai and interact with the wai domain. His nei-ness is assured. The husband's shift to the wai economic domain, while enforcing his privileged position in conjugal relations, never conflicts with his "inside" membership in the kinship system. In other words, men and women may occupy either nei or wai positions, depending on the context and circumstances, but this does not necessarily equalize power relationships between them. The wife's nei position within the conjugal bond does not confer the same benefits upon her that her husband's privileged nei position within the patrilineal kinship system bestows upon him.

This gendered division of labor, one of the key components of Chinese nei/wai family gender politics—"men are in charge outside the family and women are in charge inside the family" (*nan zhuwai nü zhunei* [M])—directly contributed to the gendered character of Chinese migration before the twentieth century. Conventionally, men were encouraged to go outside/wai to earn money to support the family. A wife was expected to perform her inside/nei duties: raise children, care for in-laws, preserve her chastity, and work the fields. Although farming took place outside the home, it was regarded as an inside duty because family members and villagers worked together. However, the wife of a gentry man did not usually work in the fields; field labor shifted to the wai category for her. In other words, a woman from a wealthy family was more strictly confined to her home, both because her field labor was not needed and because, according to family gender politics, staying more strictly inside made a woman purer and more feminine. Nevertheless, regardless of class differences, it would have been unimaginable for a married woman to leave her husband and children behind in China in order to migrate abroad to make money.[6]

In the realm of conjugal sexuality, a husband has the structural privilege to cross nei/wai sexual boundaries, but a wife—regardless of her wealth and informal power—is structurally constrained from doing so. More important, this gendered naturalization serves to assign privilege to men and to treat resistance and boundary crossings by women as "unnatural."

In addition, when a Chinese immigrant man marries a Thai woman, he and his children continue to be considered "Chinese." But if a Chinese woman marries a Thai man, she and her future children forfeit their Chinese cultural membership. It is worth noting that the American Expatriation Act of 1907 stipulated that "any American woman who marries a foreigner shall take the nationality of her husband" (Zhao 2002:36); contemporary Thai law also states that a Thai wife assumes her foreign husband's nationality upon her marriage. It was not until June 2003 that the Names Act was finally amended so that a Thai woman had the option of using her husband's surname or keeping her maiden name after marriage (Mongkol 2003). Thus, names, cultural membership, citizenship, and

gender, rather than standing on their own, are combined into an inseparable nexus.

Much like Chinese nei/wai family gender politics, the Thai "front/
behind" (*na/lang*) family gender politics are expressed in Thai legal regulations, kinship, the division of labor, and the gender system. The well-
known Thai expression "men are the forelegs of an elephant; women are
the hind legs of the elephant" (*chai changthaona, ying changthaolang*) is often
used to illustrate the point that it is "natural" for men to lead women.
Naturalizing the social order effectively disguises the gender hierarchy.

According to na/lang cultural logic, a husband acts as the leader and his
wife as the follower. In Thai "*maeban*" literally means "mother of the
house." It may also be translated as "housewife," but I prefer "mother of the
house" because this translation better captures the emphasis placed on
motherhood and women's authority in the particular space of the house. A
maeban is expected to play many roles, including caretaker, educator, cook,
and financial planner. She does far more than just the housework although
housework and childcare are often considered "women's work" (*ngan khong
phuying*) and thus within the lang domain. The challenge is to recognize and
understand women's authority and power even though they are performing
less valued work. Thai women are structurally disadvantaged, but they are
rarely passive. On the contrary, they often act flexibly by manipulating
rules. As a Thai American nurse put it to me: "A smart woman is able to act
as if she is a follower treating her husband as a leader. But in fact she leads
her husband without letting him know he is being led."

Nei/wai and na/lang should not be erroneously associated with such
familiar dualities as "nature/culture" (Ortner 1974), "domestic/public"
(Rosaldo 1974), or "reproduction/production" (Harris and Young 1981).
Rather, nei/wai and na/lang—the embodiment of the plural nature of gender constructs—should be viewed as part of the Chinese and Thai patriarchal cultural logics that support the behavior and ideas of individuals. They
coexist, compete with each other, and capture complex aspects of power
relations—especially in Bangkok, where Chinese Thai comprise a majority
of the middle and upper class. Nei/wai and na/lang cultural logics are compatible to the extent that each assigns rank within a hierarchical order
according to gender differences. But as we shall see, they have also become
increasingly entangled where their boundaries become more fluid and
ambiguous.

PART II
THE CHINKAO
EXPERIENCE

3

The Gendered Politics
of Migration and Marriage

Marriage is everywhere intimately interconnected with social hierarchy.
—ABNER COHEN, *Two-dimensional Man*

MIGRATION FROM CHINA to Southeast Asia began centuries ago. Before the mid-nineteenth century, almost all migrants were male "Chinese merchants and their partners and employees who sojourned at overseas ports and cities, or miners and other workers organized as *kongsis* (ritual brotherhoods) to protect their industrial and business interests" (Wang 1996:5). During that time, local Chinese lineage councils would not allow wives to leave the village for fear of losing the entire family (Landon 1941:52; Skinner 1957:126).

To "fasten the heart" of a migrant son to his home in China, families often engineered a marriage for him before he left, relying upon such conventional configurations as "arranged marriage" (*baoban hunyin* [M]) or the "little daughter-in-law" (*tongyangxi* [M]). Such marriages provided a new household laborer, the daughter-in-law, and ensured the family a more generous remittance from the overseas son. By the beginning of the twentieth century, however, as restrictions on women's migration eased, these same marital configurations were producing unforeseen outcomes. Rather than pulling overseas husbands back to China, as the senior kin had planned, many "widows of living ones" (*huo guafu* [M]) used their conjugal connection to migrate abroad. Newly acquired social mobility increased the capacity of women to circumvent family discipline, establish their own nuclear families, and avoid being so closely monitored by in-laws. However, this did not mean that they challenged the patrilineal and patriarchal

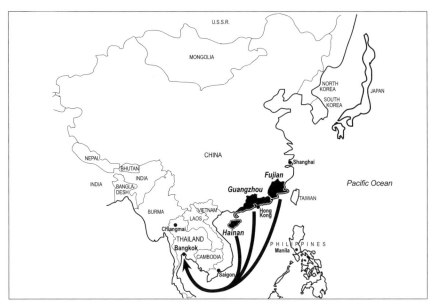

Migration from China to Thailand

family structure. On the contrary, they often used their own sons as players within the patriarchal system.

Unlike the migrant women, the men migrated because they were encouraged to fulfill their breadwinner role by accumulating economic capital for the family, even at the risk of their lives.[1] The size of a migrant man's remittance was often the measure of his moral and economic worth to his kin. Remittances also served as a symbol of masculinity and as a means of securing one's integration into the patrilineal family and kin network. As they accumulated more wealth, some migrants created new marital configurations, such as transnational polygyny or *liangtoujia* [M], which literally means "a family on both ends." Indeed, migration and marriage are best understood as interlocking parts of a dynamic process involving individuals, families, and sociopolitical structures in Thailand and China.

Male Migration and Interethnic Marriage in the Second Half of the Nineteenth Century

For centuries Siam welcomed Chinese immigrant men because laborers were in short supply (Skinner 1957:116). In particular, King Taksin (1767–1782), the son of an immigrant Chinese father and a Siamese mother and noted for leading Siam's army in defeating Burmese invaders, encour-

Chinese rice merchants in the early twentieth century. (By permission of Vitaya Vitamnuikhun.)

Young Chinese migrants in the early twentieth century. (By permission of Vitaya Vitamnuikhun.)

aged the Teochiu Chinese, who spoke the same dialect that he did, to migrate to Siam (ibid., 45–46). The Chinese of Taksin's time were known as *chinluang* or "royal Chinese" (ibid., 21 citing the *Bangkok Calendar*, 1871, p. 86). King Rama IV and King Rama V regarded the use of Chinese rather than Thai laborers as a "benevolent service to their people" (ibid., 114).

Chinese migrant men were even considered valuable enough to be employed as revenue agents and royal traders (ibid., 97).

Occupational specialization along ethnic lines was one of the most visible features of the development of Siam's economy in the nineteenth century (ibid., 91). Siamese men were subject to annual periods of compulsory (corvée) labor for the king, ancillary nobility, and patrons. Excluded from trade, they primarily engaged in agriculture (ibid., 83). In contrast, Chinese migrants participated in a cash economy; they were charged a tax, but were exempt from corvée labor service. Simply put, the Siamese paid taxes in the form of labor, the Chinese in the form of cash.

While Siamese kings welcomed Chinese laborers to Siam, China's emperors—who regarded themselves as rulers of the "Central Kingdom"—opposed overseas migration. Rulers of the Ming (1368–1644) and Qing (1644–1911) dynasties passed legislation forbidding migration abroad and declared that migrants were "low-priced people" and "unworthy subjects" (Huang 1985:7). Migration from China became a crime punishable by death (Landon 1941:198). For centuries, migration was called *guofan* [M] or "going to barbarian lands," because China was considered to be the "civilized" inside sphere, in contrast to all foreign countries, which comprised the "barbarous" (*fan* [M]) outside sphere. The notion of guofan thus succinctly captures Chinese ethnocentrism and uneasiness about migration at that time.

By the mid-nineteenth century, however, after the first Opium War (1839–1842), the Anglo-Chinese War (1856–1860), and years of intense pressure from Britain, other European nations, and the United States, Qing rulers were forced to open five ports to foreign trade and allow Western colonialists to recruit Chinese labor migrants. Shantou, located in the region where the Teochiu Chinese lived, became one of the busiest ports for exporting Chinese labor abroad. In 1893 the Qing rulers officially withdrew the migration ban, and the following year, for the first time, Chinese diplomatic and consular officers were instructed to look after the interests of subjects living abroad.

Chinese labor migrants were divided into two classes: volunteers and contract laborers or "pigs" (*zhuzai* [M]), who were virtual slaves. The majority of voluntary migrants were penniless peasants (ibid., 198; Skinner 1957:126–127). A well-known Thai phrase described Chinese migrants as arriving in Siam with nothing but "a mat and a pillow" (*suaphun monbai*). Three Chinese phrases also summarized the possible results of migration: *zuoshan*, one became wealthy; *tangshan*, one survived and made it back to

China; and *yishan*, one failed and was buried in a foreign graveyard. The migrant's dream was to make a fortune abroad and then finally return to live out a comfortable old age back in China, a "fallen leaf returning to the roots" (*luoye guigen* [M]). But as Daniel Kulp noted in his study of Phenix Village in Shantou, the majority came home empty-handed, and many never returned at all (1925:86).

In writing about pioneer Teochiu migrants in Siam, Duan Lisheng cites a poignant epitaph (year unknown) found carved on a tombstone in a Bangkok cemetery (1983:29):

> *I traveled across dark waters [the sea],*
> *Drank bitter water,*
> *Wanted to be a wealthy man* (zuoshan).
> *My wish runs away like the water.*
> *I cannot return to my hometown:*
> *This cemetery* (yishan) *is my only destination.*

With a high percentage of young men absent in emigrant regions of China, families "protected" the wives of overseas migrants, the widows of living ones. Since sexual prohibitions were more rigorously defined in these communities, the women tended to be more isolated than their counterparts in nonemigrant regions. Even within individual households, male and female members tended to be more carefully separated; for example, males were forbidden to enter the households of women after dark; and "unchastity" on the part of daughters or daughters-in-law was severely punished, sometimes even by death (Chen 1940:127, 192).

Widows of living ones were expected to remain chaste and practice filial piety even after their overseas husbands died. The following evocations of "the exemplary wife" (*lienü* [M]) were taken from Denghai County gazetteers for the year 1815:

Li was 22 years old when her husband died in Nan Yang [South Sea, i.e., Southeast Asia]. Through her strong will, she preserved her chastity after the death of her husband. Li was well known for her filial piety toward her mother-in-law. She adopted and raised a three-year-old orphan boy. When the adopted son reached adulthood he carried out his mother's wishes and retrieved his father's remains and buried him in his hometown. People praised her.

Du, the wife of Zecong Wang who was a Nan Yang migrant, was 18 years old and two months pregnant when her husband died. She had nothing but four bare walls in her house—she was utterly destitute. After the death of her husband she preserved her chastity for 50 years.

Chen, the wife of Shunzhen Li, who was a Nan Yang migrant and the son of Li Gouru, "*jiansheng*" [a student at the imperial academy], had a child after her husband died. She preserved her chastity for 37 years after the death of her husband. After her son died, she and her daughter-in-law both maintained their chastity. (Li and Cai 1815: volume 19)

These gazetteer items tell us very little about the actual lives of these exemplary women. Their full names were never mentioned; instead, they were identified by the family name of a husband, or even of a father-in-law with an official title. The motive for honoring a few wives in the emigrant regions was ideological and didactic—to strengthen control of women's behavior and sexuality generally.

While official Chinese records ignored the women's desires, folk songs of the period often revealed their suppressed emotions and their resentment of male migration:

> *Elder brother [referring to her husband] is leaving for the barbarian land,*
> *Younger sister [referring to herself] is rushing to Shantou port to stop you.*
> *You have no relatives in the barbarian land.*
> *It is easy to leave and so hard to return.*
> *Your boat will sail the ocean seven days after Shantou,*
> *You will spend seven days and nights astride measureless seas,*
> *You will not have enough food for seven days,*
> *Please take your younger sister's words for food.*
> *Muddy water becomes a clear stream if it runs far enough,*
> *Your departure leaves no trace for me to follow,*
> *Separated by mountains and rivers, I don't know where to look.*
> *I watch the sun rise at dawn and frown at the stars each night.*
> *Recruited for the pig trade,*
> *You sold yourself and left for Nan Yang to pay our debts.*
> *We said goodbye at the junction of three roads—*
> *Goodbye was a knife blow to your heart and my stomach.*
> *Elder brother, please come home, whether alive or dead,*
> *We will share the hardship together,*
> *We will drink water from the Rong river together,*
> *We will be buried together on Jieyang hill when we die.* (Bei 1988:296–297)

A common theme of these folk songs was the terrible loneliness and isolation that women endured:

I have a husband but actually I do not have one.
Every night I sleep with cold feet.
It is a pity that my pillow does not understand my words.
If my pillow knew what I was saying it would speak.

After such a long separation, a wife sometimes could not even recall the features of her husband's face:

Flowers will decorate me once again,
As my dear husband will soon return from a distant land,
Ten years I have waited for him,
I try hard to remember his face, while toiling at my spinning wheel each lonely night.[2]

By contrast, only rarely was the chastity of migrant men considered important. In the nineteenth century, prostitution was legal in Siam, and brothels were clustered in Sampeng, the heart of the Chinese community in Bangkok (Wathinee and Guest 1994:2–3). During the reign of Rama V, some rural girls were kidnapped in China and sold to brothels in Siam. A common scheme went like this: an older woman would lure a girl away by promising a visit to a Chinese opera in another village a few hours away. During the show, a fight would break out in the audience and the older woman would disappear. The girl, now alone, would be taken away or sent somewhere even further removed to work as a maid. After a few months or a year, the girl would be sold and shipped to Siam via Hong Kong (Dararat 2000:26–39). Prostitutes were first registered in Siam in 1909, and, according to the records, they were predominantly Chinese.[3] To please their Chinese customers, Siamese prostitutes also assumed Chinese names (Wathinee and Guest 1994:3). Ta Chen recorded one migrant's story:

I went to Siam as a labourer when I was a little over twenty years old. There I occasionally visited prostitutes in the company of my friends. It was quite common for the younger Chinese workmen to do so. There is a popular saying: "when the lamps are lit, forget your home"—meaning, when you can spend the night with a prostitute, forget what your relatives at home in China would say about it. (1940:191)

In China, many regarded visiting brothels as an unhealthy indulgence. For the migrant men, however, visiting brothels offered temporary escape from homesickness and the hardships of daily life (ibid., 191–192). In addition to providing easy access to brothels, Siam's regime enacted regulations that had the effect of pulling the migrant men even further away from their Chinese kin. Chinese were encouraged to smoke opium freely, which Siamese were legally prohibited from doing (Kasian 1992:110). Indeed, to acquire opium, some Siamese would pretend to be Chinese by wearing their hair in a queue, a visible marker of Chinese-ness at that time (Skinner 1957:120–121). By providing Chinese laborers access to brothels and legal opium, the monarchy increased its tax revenues and reduced the amount of money the migrants could send back to China.[4] As Skinner comments, "It is not unfair to state that while the country depended on Chinese virtues for the expansion of commerce and industry, the government relied on Chinese vices for the expansion of public revenue" (1957:120).

By the mid-nineteenth century a few Chinese women began migrating to Siam, mostly as merchants' wives and prostitutes (ibid., 196). The merchants' daughters were appreciated because of the scarcity of marriageable Chinese women in Siam, and Chinese women were "prized by the Thai for their light skin color" (Skinner 1958:8). A daughter regarded as "extra" in China could be converted into a family "treasure" in Siam; unexpectedly, migration served to increase her worth.

As other scholars have observed, men within the Siamese monarchy had been marrying women from Laos, Cambodia, and China for some time, and in the nineteenth century a ruler's ability to govern people of different ethnic groups was highly regarded (Streckfuss 1993:132). Therefore, a wife or concubine from a different ethnic background was a symbol of a man's power and privilege.

By marrying his daughter to an elite-class Siamese man, a Chinese merchant gained far more symbolic power and greater access to socioeconomic networks than by marrying her to a Chinese man. A few Chinese women even gained membership in the royal family through interethnic marriage. "Chinese of wealth," wrote the American missionary N. A. McDonald in 1884, "often become favorites with the rulers and receive titles of nobility, and these noblemen in return present their daughters to their majesties. Thus we find Chinese blood flowing in the veins of the royal family of Siam" (1884:146). For example, the "daughter of an ennobled Chinese" was taken as a wife by King Mongkut, Rama IV, and later elevated to queen. She gave birth to Princess Saowapa, later one of Rama V's queens (and also his half-sister) and the mother of Rama VI and Rama VII (1925–1935) (Skinner 1957:26). In his reminiscences, former Thai Prime Minister Khukrit Pramote described how his great-grandmother was brought to Siam from China by her father at the age of nine or ten, was presented to the royal performance group of Rama I, and finally became the concubine of Rama II (Khukrit 1983:12).

By far the most common nineteenth-century interethnic marriage was between a Chinese migrant man and a Siamese woman. Historian Sumalee Bumroongsook found that in the nineteenth and early twentieth century, rich Chinese and their offspring were considered desirable mates for Siamese women who wanted to improve their financial status, as evoked by the common saying, "marry a Chinese, eat a lot; marry a Thai, have naught" (1995:75). Other scholars have also pointed out that by marrying a local woman, a migrant (especially a businessman) could benefit from his wife's labor, her network of relationships, and her ability to deal with local customers (Landon 1941:55; Skinner 1957:127–128). It would be a mistake, however, to assume that all Chinese men who married Siamese women were richer than their wives. We have very little ethnography that describes the socioeconomic background of the interethnic couple.

The following family history, which comes from my 1992 interview with Phi Sa, a psychologist, illustrates the complex and sometimes surprising interplay of forces that can arise within an interethnic marriage.

> My grandfather came from China [in the late nineteenth century] and my grandmother was a Thai. My grandmother had about one thousand rai [1 rai = 0.4 acres or 1600 meters] of land. During the week she helped my grandfather at his shop. On weekends she went to manage the land. As a Thai, my grandmother had connections with Thai officials that my Chinese grandfather did not have. My grandfather was quite rich but did not dare to take a minor wife because he was afraid of my grandmother. My grandmother was a very strong woman.

In this case the Thai wife was at least as rich as her Chinese husband, and she was the family's decision maker too. More important, she had knowledge of local practices and knew how to deal with local officials. Phi Sa continued:

> They only had two children: my father [Fei] and my aunt. My grandfather favored my father, but my grandmother treated my father and my aunt much more equally. My grandfather wanted my father to be Chinese

so he sent him back to China to learn to speak Teochiu. My father was treated like an honorable man and was spoiled by my Chinese great-grandmother and the villagers because my grandfather sent a more generous remittance to them while my father was staying in China. In order to keep my father in China as long as possible, my Chinese great-grandmother arranged a marriage for him.

Living in China, Fei was expected to grow up Chinese, like someone born in China. Learning the language and gaining cultural knowledge in China enabled him to accumulate different forms of capital for later use in Siam, where, at the time, the Teochiu dialect was the prevailing language for doing business. In China, Fei's grandmother spoiled her first grandson; she also arranged a marriage for him to keep him there. This strategy allowed her to continue receiving larger remittances in exchange for devoting more time to turning her foreign-born grandson into a Chinese one. Fei was valued both for his position within the Chinese patrilineal kinship system and as a source of income: the longer he stayed in China, the larger his father's remittances would be. Phi Sa said:

> By the time my Thai grandmother found out about the marriage, my father already had a son. This made my grandmother very unhappy. Finally, my grandmother fell ill. People said it was because of my father. My father had no choice but to return to Thailand. Immediately my grandmother made my father join a monastery and become a monk. During the time my father was confined to the temple, my grandmother arranged for him to marry my mother, the daughter of a Thai mother and a Chinese father.
>
> Grandmother told everyone in our family that no one should ever mention to my mother that my father already had a family in China. My grandmother held a big wedding for my parents to honor the marriage.

Fei's mother used the Buddhist temple, the most influential local institution in Siam, to assist her in disciplining her son and buying enough time to arrange a new marriage, thus countering his previous marriage in China. Clearly, it was the interplay of competing forces that shaped Fei's life. Then, Fei's mother married her son to the daughter of a Siamese mother and a Chinese father—not to a Siamese woman.[5] Indeed, she apparently wanted her daughter-in-law's social status and cultural background to be comparable to her son's. Her economic and social capital enabled her to hold a big wedding to honor the marriage she wanted for her son and thereby reject her Chinese daughter-in-law and the grandson left behind in China. At the same time, the new daughter-in-law had no idea that she was marrying a man who already had a family in China. Because of his kin's maneuvering—his two arranged marriages in different countries—Fei involuntarily became a transnational polygynist. The women in Phi Sa's family were not the passive victims of discipline, nor were the men the active agents of it; rather, both were disciplined and empowered simultaneously.

Women's Migration and the Decline of Interethnic Marriage in the Twentieth Century

Mae chin, or "Mrs. Chinese," who had migrated to Siam between 1910 and 1920, "was very much embarrassed for a long time after her arrival by the sensation she created wherever she went [out] in her black Chinese trousers and neat little jacket. She was a curiosity both to the Thai and to the Chinese men of that area, many of whom had not seen a Chinese woman since their youth in China" (Landon 1941:204). But with the fall of the Qing dynasty in 1911, an improved transportation system, increasing social instability, and the occurrence of natural disasters and wars in China, the scale of immigration grew, and women's immigration, which started as a trickle, turned into a steady stream (Skinner 1957:126–127).

The political climate in Siam had, however, changed: Chinese migrant laborers were no longer valued as an important resource. In 1910, just as the British-educated King Vajiravudh (Rama VI) came to power, the Chinese in Bangkok waged a five-day strike to protest a proposed tax increase, disrupting economic activities throughout the capital city and exacerbating friction between the Chinese workers and Siam's regime. Four years later, in 1914, when King Vajiravudh had to deal with a troubled domestic economy and the reverberations of the overthrow of the Qing, he referred to the Chinese as the "Jews of the Orient," echoing the anti-Semitic movements in Europe at the time (Landon 1941:33–43).

Siam was the only Southeast Asian country never formally colonized, but nonetheless Siam's politics were strongly influenced by European, especially British, interests. Rather than complaining about Britain, which controlled 90 percent of Siam's trade, the king vented his nationalist anger on the Chinese immigrants, whom his father had deliberately imported (Anderson 1991:190). He took no significant anti-Chinese measures, however, and there was never a massacre of Chinese immigrants or their descendants, as occurred elsewhere in Southeast Asia.

Anti-Chinese sentiment did not stop Chinese immigration. Between 1919 and 1937 the number of Chinese women who immigrated to Siam increased dramatically, by 140 percent during the first decade, and then by 69 percent between 1929 and 1937.[6] From 1937 to 1947 the number of women decreased by 16.5 percent, as a result of the Japanese presence in Thailand during World War II and an increase in "anti-alien" sentiment (Coughlin 1960:24; Landon 1941:204–214; Skinner 1957:272–289).

As the sex ratio between Chinese men and women improved, the formerly extensive society of Chinese bachelors gradually disappeared, and the number of Chinese brothels in Siam decreased, from 137 in 1929 to 63 in 1936 (Skinner 1957:197). In particular, after the Second World War, as Skinner pointed out, "about half the male immigrants brought wives from China, and other China-born residents returned to China to marry or bring back to Thailand wives they already had there" (ibid., 196). This pattern held true among most of the chinkao in this project.[7] With the increase in female immigrants and a larger pool of lukchin women, the sex ratio became more balanced.

The transformed political climate in Siam and evolving demographics placed new constraints on interethnic marriages. A Chinese female immigrant's body—so prized in the nineteenth century—now lost its appeal to Siam's regime. In 1940 Thai Premier Luang Phibun Songkram publicly declared that "the average [Thai] citizen who lived in close proximity to the Chinese" should marry Thai (ibid., 269). Although interethnic marriage between Chinese and Thai continued, it declined dramatically over the rest of the twentieth century.

Among the forty households that I surveyed and the seventeen life history interviews, chinkao interethnic marriage was exclusively a male practice; not one chinkao woman had married a Thai man. Moreover, interethnic marriage occurred mainly when a chinkao man remarried or took a minor wife. When asked why only chinkao men had interethnic marriages, the chinkao thought the answer was obvious. A Thai woman who married into a chinkao home was regarded as Chinese. She was expected to worship her husband's ancestors, and the children she bore used her husband's surname and were called "lukchin." A well-known Chinese saying goes, "Marry a chicken, you run with the chickens; marry a dog, you run with the dogs" (*jiaji suiji, jiagou suigou* [M]). The "you" implied in this saying is always female, never male. In practice, a Thai woman who married a Chinese man might not act according to this cultural logic. As we saw earlier, Phi Sa's grandmother maintained her Thai identity, even though from a patriarchal Chinese perspective she was considered part of a Chinese family.

The gender-specific interpretations of interethnic marriage were informed by a patriarchal principle: the community continued to regard a Chinese man as Chinese even if he married a Thai woman. But if a Chinese woman married a Thai man, she instantly lost her membership within the Chinese community, and her children were not considered lukchin—that is, they were not considered Chinese.

In practice, interethnic marriage carried more complex meanings. Mali Bobo's interethnic marriage, for example, reflects the impact of Thai nationalism in generating negative Chinese-ness. In the 1950s the Chinese were often associated with communism, and Mali Bobo was especially suspect because he held a passport from the People's Republic of China, was an outspoken admirer of China, and unlike many others at the time, flatly refused to change his citizenship or his Chinese name. Still, he regarded Thailand as his adopted home. His ambivalence was also reflected in his choice of a spouse: although he would have preferred a Chinese woman, he married a Thai instead. He reasoned that although a Chinese wife would provide "authentic" Chinese children, she could not give him the political security that a Thai wife would supply. His interethnic marriage put to rest suspicions that he was a communist and disguised his Chinese-ness. In other words, his less worthy Chinese-ness was protected by the worthy Thai-ness he acquired through his interethnic marriage.

Although he married a Thai woman, Mali Bobo did not adopt the conventional Thai practice of living with his wife's family—not even for a token period. Even more interesting, he and his wife never registered their marriage; as he explained, the law stated that a wife assumed the nationality of her husband upon her marriage, so a female Thai citizen who married a foreigner forfeited her Thai citizenship and her right to buy land.[8] In addition his children would have been legally classified as "Thai with Thai nationality of Chinese ethnicity." By not registering the marriage, he ensured that his children would be legally classified as Thai.[9] Mali Bobo said, "I do not want my children to suffer what I have suffered."

Interethnic marriages are invested with multiple meanings and can be interpreted from different positions. The Chinese Thai community imposes its own cultural interpretations on interethnic marriage, just as the Thai state has imposed regulations on its citizens. Mali Bobo and his family lived under a set of regulations different from those that Phi Sa's grandparents had experienced.

Arranged Marriage: Transnational Matching

Mei Nainai, born in 1916, described her marriage in this way: "I was sent to my husband's home in a sedan chair. We did not know each other. [After the wedding] we were together for about three months, then he went back to Thailand again. After six years passed, I went with an agent to join him, but I was not allowed to enter Thailand because of my glaucoma. My husband and I went back to China together. I was three months pregnant when he left for Thailand again. We did not see each other after that for another seven years." Mei Nainai's experience was typical. Her husband had immigrated to Siam at age ten; at twenty he returned to China to marry seventeen-year-old Mei Nainai, the bride his natal family had selected for him on the basis of well-matched horoscopes.[10] Mei Nainai lived with her mother-in-law for twelve of the first thirteen years of her marriage.

In the first half of the twentieth century the most common marital formation in China and among migrant laborers was to have the marriage arranged by one's parents. A woman who went abroad to marry a migrant husband was called a "bride going to barbarian lands" (*guofan xinniang* [M]). A migrant man was expected to come back to China some day, not to become an outsider who lived abroad with a "barbarian wife" (*fanpo* [M]), a foreign woman. Even though all daughters-in-law were in some respects outsiders, a Chinese daughter-in-law had more value than a foreign one.

"Matching" (*pei* [M]) formed the core of an arranged marriage; it was said that "the door matches the door and the window matches the window" (*mendang hudui* [M]). The long list of desirable matches included such things as compatible social and economic status, time of birth, birthplace, dialect, region, and physical appearance.[11] Cross-dialect marriage was rare among chinkao. Within each dialect group, the preference was to marry someone from one's own county. Teochiu-speaking Chinese from Denghai County, for example, usually did not marry those from Caoyang County, which had a reputation for being overcrowded with people, hence its nickname "People County" (*renxian* [M]). However, if a wealthy Teochiu man from Denghai married a pretty Teochiu woman from Caoyang, it was considered a "good match" because the combination of masculine economic power and feminine beauty transcends county boundaries.[12]

Affection between individuals was often considered dangerous because it could conflict with familial, economic, and social interests. For those who were going to wed, the key cultural principle was to "follow parental orders and the advice of the go-between" (*fumu zhi ming, meizhuo zhi yan* [M]).

"The main purpose of marriage in the village," notes Hsiao-Tung Fei in his study of peasant life in central China, "is to secure the continuity of descent" (1939:30). Only sons could continue the family line. Villagers usually looked down on a family without a male heir. For emigrant families this was an even greater concern. Uncertain when her husband would come back again, and not knowing whether she could ever bear him a son, Mei Nainai took her mother-in-law's advice and adopted a baby boy, nursing him together with her newborn daughter.

In 1946, thirty-year-old Mei Nainai took her adopted son with her to Thailand and left her biological daughter behind with her mother-in-law. The son, the insider of patrilineal kinship, provided Mei Nainai with a status that no outsider daughter could provide. As she observed, "A Chinese [mother] has to live with her son even if he is a beggar." Although she did not refer to family gender politics, Mei Nainai understood the importance of a son in her own terms. In attaching herself to two strangers—first her husband, then her adopted son—and downplaying her relationship with her daughter, Mei Nainai sought to increase her status within the patriarchal family.

Mei Nainai did not return to China for nearly forty years. Only when she received word that the daughter whom she had left behind was dying of liver cancer did she rush back. But she arrived too late; her child had died just a few hours earlier. She had not expected her daughter's early death and anguished over not having said goodbye. Her decision to leave her daughter behind in China was a rational concession to the patrilineal kinship system, but she suffered greatly because of it.

A few Chinese women emigrated to Thailand in order to escape arranged marriages. Hui Xiaozhang, born into a gentry family in 1912, was engaged to a young boy from a wealthy family when she was only five years old:

> My parents wanted me to marry when I turned seventeen. I did not like the man they had chosen for me. I found an excuse to visit my aunt in Shanghai. Then I wrote to my father that I wanted to continue my studies. He loved me, so he really had no choice; he sent me money to support my education. After I graduated from the Female Normal Sports School and the Shanghai Obstetrics Institute, I wrote my father that I was going to marry a fellow student who came from Thailand. My father was outraged. He thought I had humiliated the family. He wrote up an announcement in the local newspaper in which he cut off any relationship with me. It was hard on my mother.

Hui Xiaozhang was one of just three girls in her county to attend middle school, and the only one to attend college. In choosing her own spouse, she was influenced by her higher education and by the ideals of China's May Fourth Movement, which rejected many conventional Chinese practices, including arranged marriage. Her father was considered open-minded because he had invested in higher education for his daughter, but he considered the fulfillment of marriage arrangements a matter of family honor. Despite her father's objections, Hui Xiaozhang married her lukchin classmate, and for this her father disowned her. The last time I talked to her, in 1992, she had not been back to visit her family in China since her departure for Bangkok in 1935.

The Tongyangxi *or "Little Daughter-in-Law"*

"No one ridiculed me when I gave my daughter away. If I had given away my son, I would have been a laughingstock." The chinkao man who said this to me had given away his newborn daughter as a little daughter-in-law in China in 1941. A tongyangxi was a girl sold or given away to be raised by her future in-laws. This was a common practice in southern China in pre-revolutionary times (A. Wolf 1975:95–96; Wolf and Huang 1980:233–234). A little daughter-in-law bore the double stigma of being abandoned by her natal family and bringing no dowry to her husband (M. Wolf 1968:40). Since all she brought was her potential productive and reproductive labor, she was commonly treated more like a maid than a family member.

A gentry family would want to have as many sons as possible, for more sons were thought to bring more happiness. Among the very poor, however, sons, except for the eldest, were also sometimes sold or given away. The eldest son was almost always especially valued as the family's "root of life" because of the significance accorded his seniority as the first heir of his generation. Giving away or selling a junior son might provide a better chance for both the junior and senior sons to survive.

Nevertheless, a family would only rarely admit publicly to having given away a baby boy, for this was considered unfilial behavior toward family ancestors. The father, in particular, would suffer humiliation if he gave away a potential heir. The chinkao man's statement about being a laughingstock expressed this cultural valuation.

Families with no biological son frequently adopted a boy and raised him as an heir. An adopted son was expected to support his adopted parents, marry, and sire a son of his own, thus continuing the family line.

In addition, superstition played a part in the adoption, as it was often believed that by adopting a son the couple would now be able to conceive their own biological son (M. Wolf 1972:172; also see Wolf and Huang 1980:242–243).

In contrast, giving away a daughter was a way to rid the family of an eventually "useless" member. A Chinese saying, "a married-out daughter is like spilled water" (*jiachu qu de nü pochu qu de shui* [M]), expresses the cultural evaluation of a daughter's worth. A poor family could take on a little daughter-in-law to work for the family while she was growing up, then marry her to their son, so that eventually she could bear children to carry on the family line (M. Wolf 1972: 172–173). A small number of little daughters-in-law were sent to Thailand to live with husbands they had never seen before. For example, a chinkao woman said that she was adopted at age three and sent to Thailand to join her immigrant husband when she turned seventeen. This way her husband did not need to interrupt his work, and the family saved the cost of a round-trip ticket.

Giving a daughter away stigmatized the daughter, but not the family. Born in 1915, Jin Nainai was the eldest daughter of a very powerful gentry family. All three of her younger sisters had been given away as tongyangxi. She recalled, "My grandmother said that one granddaughter was enough. My mother could not say anything against my grandma because others looked down on a rich family with too many daughters." By reducing the number of girls, Jin Nainai's grandmother minimized the family's risk of social stigma. Gender politics motivated a senior woman to manage junior female family members in the interests of the patriarchy. Jin Nainai's seniority as the eldest daughter exempted her from becoming a tongyangxi. Class privilege enabled her to enjoy better food and clothing than did many boys from poor families, but as a female, she suffered from gender inequality.

The eldest daughter in a poor peasant family, however, would not share the privileges Jin Nainai enjoyed. Ayi, born in 1929, had five brothers and four sisters. Her widowed mother did not give away any of her sons, even though three of the five were stepsons, but Ayi and all her sisters were sold or given away. Impoverished by a famine, her future in-laws resold Ayi to a merchant, who brought her to Thailand to work as his servant. She was first a tongyangxi in China and later a maid in Thailand.

A son's seniority is valued more highly than a daughter's, and the seniority of a gentry family's daughter carries greater privilege than the seniority of a daughter from a poor family. It is the different cultural values invested in the categories "son" and "daughter," in addition to class differences, that made the little daughter-in-law practice prevalent.

Although the little daughter-in-law configuration is no longer practiced in Thailand, the social stigma attached to it remains strong. The reluctance of several women to talk about their tongyangxi past, considered proof of low socioeconomic status, reveals the complexity and diversity within the Chinese Thai community and provides us with an insight into its social hierarchy: men have higher status than women, and women with arranged marriages are considered superior to tongyangxi.

Liangtoujia *or "a Family on Both Ends"*

Sipping tea late one afternoon, Zhu Xiansheng, a businessman, explained to me that having one wife in China and one in Thailand—a practice known as *liangtoujia*—was an arrangement based upon a "heaven-born rule" (*tianjing diyi* [M]). He formulated it roughly as follows: by sending remittances back to his natal family in China, with whom his first wife and children lived, he fulfilled his economic obligation and was therefore entitled to have an additional wife and family in Thailand. When I asked whether his wife could have another husband in China, he replied, "No. I married her already." In other words, to have "a family on both ends" is an exclusively male privilege.

Liangtoujia was primarily a class-based practice among better-off Chinese immigrants in Thailand and other Southeast Asian countries (Willmott 1967:42). In 1940 Ta Chen described the process by which a migrant man could engage in it.

> The first few years of his stay abroad are devoted to earning a living and if possible preparing the way for economic independence. As soon as income exceeded his modest wants he sends money—in small amounts at first, but at frequent intervals. Normally, unless it belongs to the very poorest class, the family will lay aside part of the remittances toward the cost of his prospective marriage. Normally, also, the emigrant returns after a few years to be married to a girl selected for him by his parents. Soon after this marriage he will return to the Nan Yang, either to take new employment, or more often, to take his place again where he left off. Thereafter, he will visit his parental home, which is also his home and that of his wife, at intervals. . . . More often than not it is during this period, especially if he succeeds in establishing some small business of his own, that he will take a second wife. . . . (1940:140)

Transnational mobility, with long periods of separation from wife and family in China, together with economic upward mobility, enabled an immigrant to establish a transnational polygynist family. Ta Chen regarded a liangtoujia practitioner as a wealthy man who participated in a "dual family system." Unfortunately, Chen did not explain how this dual system actually operated (ibid., 140–143).

Most liangtoujia practitioners I interviewed lived with the wife and family in Thailand and only occasionally visited the family left back in China. Only one man I knew, a Chinese herbal doctor, had brought his wife over from China to join him in Bangkok. He did this because he needed "an assistant who could read Chinese." He was the third generation in his family to dispense Chinese herbs to cure female infertility. He regarded his specialized herbal treatment as a trade secret, therefore it was much safer to have his wives work with him, rather than outsiders who might learn his formula and become competitors. When I visited his clinic, the first wife was processing orders in the pharmacy while his second wife, a lukchin, worked at the reception desk, and the doctor sat at his desk surrounded by his patients. The three worked together as a medical team.

Each wife—in Thailand and in China—contributed her labor and skills to the polygynist family, and this inevitably demanded a great deal of emotional work. The Chinese wife left behind in the village was sometimes asked to raise a son or sons born to the wife in Thailand as her own in addition to carrying out all her other responsibilities for her husband's natal family. The wife in Thailand had to give up her son to be raised by strangers. Transnational polygyny not only absorbed the wives' productive and reproductive labor but also created enormous emotional stress for these women.

Remittances served as the crucial bond between the polygynist in Thailand and his wife in China. He might feel no attachment to her but would still consider it his duty to meet this economic obligation. Thus Qian Bobo fled for Thailand three days after his wedding to escape the marriage his parents had arranged for him. Although he never went back to visit his wife, he sent her regular remittances for fifty years. The remittances were considered the price he paid for leaving his wife in China behind; for the wife in China, the money symbolized her absent husband. She lived with her in-laws, took care of them, worked on the farm, and adopted a son in the hopes that he and his future wife would take care of her when she grew old.

The three primary forms of remittance, practiced not only by polygynists but by almost all migrants, were the "safe arrival remittance" (*pingan pi* [M]), the "remittance for supporting the family" (*zhanjia pi* [M]), and the "New Year's remittance" (*guonian pi* [M]). The first remittance was sent only once, to inform the family that the migrant had arrived safely; the second one was sent periodically; and the third was sent annually for Chinese New Year. The remittance was customarily sent with a letter written on a thin pink sheet of notepaper about four centimeters wide and no more than seven or eight centimeters long.[13] A remittance, then, was a special form of communication, for it embodied not merely money but also the message that the husband was still alive, and still thinking about his wife and family back in China.

Letters were a major form of communication between a couple and were often shared with family members and neighbors in China. Since many couples did not know how to read and write, they needed to enlist the services of professional letter writers or literate friends. This problem often made communication very infrequent.[14] Even if a couple could write to each other, the immigrant's job mobility and ongoing wars (in China and in Thailand) made frequent contact difficult.

Not all polygynists dutifully sent remittances. Some earned too little; others spent most of their income on gambling or opium and were hardly able to support their family in Thailand.[15] Jianjun, a young Chinese man I interviewed in Shantou, China, told a story about his stepgrandmother Yang. In 1930, at age eleven, Grandma Yang immigrated with her mother to join her father in Siam. She married Jianjun's grandfather, Kuo, who concealed the fact that he already had a wife and four children in China. Later, Grandpa Kuo became an opium addict, leaving Grandma Yang to support him and their four children. On his deathbed he asked Grandma Yang to "please go back to *tangshan* [M] (China) to find my family." It took her ten years to pay off his debts. Then, in 1991, when she was 72, she traveled to Shantou and found his family. Her arrival caused a sensation: having never heard anything from Grandpa Kuo, everyone assumed he had died long ago. Grandpa Kuo's wife in China had raised four children on her own and had died a decade earlier. These two wives, who never met each other, were nonetheless inextricably linked by a polygynous marriage, in this case a secret one, and both had their lives profoundly altered by the constraints of family gender politics stretching across transnational space.

Most women, especially those who had young children, remained in China even if they did not receive remittances. A childless wife, however, might travel to Thailand to look for her husband. Achan Chanwaeng, a professor of English I came to know in 1988, told me about her grandmother Ling. Grandma Ling, having heard nothing from her husband for many years, finally found him in Bangkok but discovered that he had a Thai wife and three children. The Thai wife was socially recognized, but Grandma Ling had no social standing in Thailand. Unable to speak Thai and with no relatives nearby, she ended up working as a servant for her husband and his second wife in exchange for room and board. Immigration and cultural disruption clearly negated her position as the major wife in a polygynous family.

Occasionally, however, a wife's resistance disrupted a polygynous marriage. In Shantou a man told me a story about how his uncle was forced to renounce his polygyny. This uncle had married a lukchin schoolteacher in Thailand without telling her that he also had a wife in China. When she discovered the truth, she told him that unless he divorced his wife in China, she would divorce him. The uncle did not want to give up his marriage in Thailand, so he promised his wife in China that he would provide her with remittances for the rest of her life if she would agree to a divorce. The wife in China was willing to forego all financial support from her husband, but begged him to let the marriage exist in name only, for she needed the institution of marriage to save face in her village. Finally, the uncle traveled back to China and, through a shrewd legal maneuver, divorced her against her will. When this happened, she locked herself inside her house and burned everything that reminded her of her ex-husband. All the relatives in China condemned the uncle for having "no heart" and for "deserting" his wife who had patiently waited for him and served his natal family for decades.

These two narratives—Grandma Ling coming to Thailand to look for her husband and the uncle who went back to China to divorce his first wife—emphasize the same theme from a different angle: both immigrants and the family members they left behind are deeply affected by transnational migration and by different but interlocking disciplinary regimes.

In most cases that I encountered, the wife in Thailand accepted the transnational polygyny, even when she discovered it only after her marriage. Transnational polygynists were, generally speaking, less guarded in talking about their two families than were men whose two wives both lived in Thailand. The geographic distance and separation between the families seemed to reduce tension and conflict. A few women even felt sympathy for their husband's wife and family in China and sent remittances on his behalf. When massive Chinese immigration to Thailand ended in 1949, the practice of liangtoujia sharply declined.

Departing from China marked the beginning of a gendered division of labor between the migrant and those left behind: the son would send remittances back from abroad while the daughter-in-law, the widow of a living one, took care of the family in China. Most migrants saw migration not as an individual choice but as part of a family strategy involving a wide range of interests and concerns. Often marriage was used as a mechanism to bind a migrant man to his family and his birthplace. Poor families raised a little daughter-in-law for their overseas son; better-off families arranged marriages. The migrants and their families still attempted to function together despite being physically separated.

If not for Chinese labor migration, large-scale interethnic marriage between Chinese men and Thai women might never have come to pass. Indeed, Chinese transnational migration has affected not only the Chinese Thai and the people they left behind, but also the people they live with in Thailand. And while marriage was used to facilitate or constrain labor migration, migration also helped generate innovative marital configurations, such as liangtoujia.

The worth ascribed to migrant men and women because of their labor value changed over time. For centuries Chinese migration flourished because male Chinese laborers—but not female laborers—were valued by Siam's monarchy. Before large-scale female immigration started, a few daughters of Chinese merchants found that they had acquired new worth and desirability in Siam. But this attribution of value, which led to interethnic marriages between Chinese women and elite Siamese men, was short-lived. Once large numbers of Chinese women began immigrating to Siam, a Chinese woman's worth declined precipitously. Just as a Chinese man and a Chinese woman were disciplined differently according to their gendered worth, the Thai state stripped a Thai woman of her citizenship if she married a foreigner, but applied no such regulation to Thai men.

Assimilation theory fails to take into account the politics of interethnic marriages and thus cannot explain why so few Chinese women had them. The convergence of several regulating forces—each exerting its own form of discipline—simultaneously enables and constrains migration and marriage, so that chinkao men and women work both for and against competing regulations. Only when we take women's experiences and gender politics into account can we begin to understand how gendered citizenship and cultural identities are produced.

4

Middle-Class Chinese-ness,
Nei/Wai Politics

The most serious mistake a man can make is to choose the wrong occupation; the most serious mistake a woman can make is to marry the wrong husband (*nan pa rucuo hang, nü pa jiacuo lang* [M]).

—Chinese maxim

FONG LAOBAN WAS three years old in 1917 when his mother brought him to Siam to join his father. He recalled, "My father worked as a cashier until midnight nearly every night. His boss usually gave him one *sadang* for his evening meal [at that time 2,000 sadang equaled approximately one dollar].[1] My father never spent that money on food. Instead he drank two cups of cold water, then went to bed." But despite his best efforts, the father was never able to lift his family out of poverty. It was Fong Laoban who finally fulfilled his father's dream by becoming a successful entrepreneur, the president of a thriving printing firm.

This kind of success story, repeated in numerous other Chinese migrant contexts over the centuries, has reinforced an ethnicized image of the Chinese as "diligent, frugal, and business-oriented." The ethnic Chinese in Southeast Asia have long been depicted as the "trading minority" (Wertheim 1965), their typical representatives being "the commercial man" (Heidhues 1974:8–29) or "the middleman" (Ingram 1971:211). In Thailand, both ethnic Thai and Chinese have taken commercial orientation and business success as major criteria of being Chinese (Boonsanong 1971:66; Szanton 1983:109). Thus *khuam pen chin* or "Chinese-ness" is not only an ethnic category but also a class category, connoting middle-class status regardless of whether the subjects are middle class or not.

This chapter addresses a complex interaction between state regulations

"The China-Siam Trading Co., Ltd."(By permission of the National Library, Bangkok.)

regarding occupations and various cultural constructions of class, gender, and ethnicity. In the nineteenth century, Siam's kings favored Chinese labor migrants, but by the early twentieth century, an era of emerging nationalism, the Chinese encountered unprecedented occupational and business constraints. Nevertheless, Chinese entrepreneurs used their accumulated economic capital to forge class-based alliances with the new Thai elite, and Chinese laborers used Chinese association networks to evade state regulations. These class-based alliances and ethnic-based networks help explain the historical process which formed the Chinese Thai middle class.

In this chapter I also suggest that middle-class Chinese-ness is intertwined with the cultural construction of masculine and feminine identity. By performing housework as well as income-producing activities, chinkao women overcame even greater obstacles than chinkao men in achieving socioeconomic upward mobility, but their economic contribution remains unacknowledged. In contrast, although chinkao men took their breadwinner role seriously, the few who transgressed nei/wai boundaries by doing domestic work felt obliged to hide it in order to preserve their masculinity.

Ethnicized Occupations

In her article "How did Jews become white folks?" Karen Sacks describes the belief that Jews were naturally "smart" and that their individual successes were "reinforced by a culture that valued sticking together, hard work, education, and deferred gratification" (1994:78). In the United States, Jews were often considered inferior because "real" Americans were of Anglo-Saxon ancestry. After World War II, Jews gained social and economic mobility and became "whitened." The GI Bill allowed male Jews and other Euro-American men to attend college, and the FHA/VA mortgage programs and other forms of affirmative action made it possible for them to buy homes and become professionals, technicians, salesmen, and managers in the economic boom of the late 1940s and the 1950s. In contrast, African American men and women were denied the same postwar opportunities for education, housing, and employment by institutionalized racism. These "racially skewed gains," Sacks comments, "have been passed on across the generations, so that racial inequality seems to maintain itself 'naturally,' even after legal segregation ended" (ibid., 98). The differences in socioeconomic mobility of Jewish Americans and African Americans needs to be understood in relation to structural inequality and the cultural logic of racism in the United States.

The same is true for our understanding of class formation, ethnicized occupations, and structural inequality in Thai society. Although the corvée system in Siam was finally abolished in 1905, the effects of the previous ethnicized occupational practices did not immediately disappear. Siamese continued to work mainly in agriculture and government services, and Chinese immigrants continued to work mostly as coolies, miners, fishermen, commercial farmers, and entrepreneurs.

Luang Phibun Songkram, Thailand's prime minister from 1938 to 1944 and again between 1948 and 1957, promoted Thai nationalism and "Thai-ification." The state restricted alien ownership of private enterprises, limiting the number of businesses that could be owned by Chinese immigrants and their descendants (Keyes 1987b:74). In July 1938, Luang Wijit Wathakan, who was regarded as "the architect of Thai nationalism," gave an address in which he compared "the Jewish problem" in Germany to "the Chinese problem" in Thailand and implied that the "Nazi solution might be applicable" to Thailand (Skinner 1957:261). Chinese migrants, who were once regarded as the goose that laid the golden egg, were now depicted as outsiders, the source of Thailand's problems. Scapegoat rhetoric ("scheming Oriental Jews" or "treacherous Chinese communists") was used to bolster Thai nationalism. Various laws were passed to restrict Chinese trade, and Chinese immigrants were barred from entering many occupations, including those of barber, taxi driver, metalworker, and butcher (ibid., 262–264). They were also prohibited from manufacturing certain products, such as salt, charcoal, and umbrellas, and from operating private wharves and commercial fishing businesses (Coughlin 1960:135–143; Landon 1941:215–260; Skinner 1957:355–356).

Until this time, most Chinese immigrants were citizens of China, but in response to the new regulations, some chinkao changed their citizenship to Thai. Some used the name of a wife or child who was a Thai citizen to register businesses. Others simply bought business licenses outright from Thai citizens or bribed Thai officials to look the other way (Coughlin 1960:136). Such maneuvers made it possible to obtain permits and licenses or to receive "government contracts and purchase orders" (Riggs 1966:253; Skinner 1958:191–192); they could also provide protection from police interrogation, extortion, or arrest. "The big fish eats the small fish, and the small fish eats the shrimp," was how Mali Bobo described the conflicts between Chinese and Thai as well as the competitive relationships within each ethnic group.

The consequences of Thai-ification, as Skinner points out, "go far beyond the facts of limited Chinese retreat, sporadic Thai advance, and increased corruption. Of greater significance than any of these is the alliance which it stimulated between Chinese merchants and the Thai ruling class" (1957:360). By the end of 1952 it was estimated that hundreds of government officials and other members of the Thai elite were either fully "cut in" on Chinese businesses or serving on the boards of Chinese firms in a "protective" capacity.[2] Some government officials and elite class members who participated in the official anti-Chinese rhetoric also made alliances with entrepreneurial Chinese elites, motivated at least in part by opportunities for private gain.

This development recalled the partnerships forged between Siam's kings and Chinese merchants in the nineteenth century; but where the nineteenth century alliances involved a certain celebration of Chinese-ness, in the mid-twentieth century Chinese-ness had lost much of its worth. Despite regarding the Chinese as inferior, the Thai elite tolerated them in order to serve their own purposes. The alliances between Thai political and military leaders and the economically influential Chinese entrepreneurs demonstrate complex interactions between class, ethnicity, and fraternal culture.

The Thai state's ethnic policies and nationalistic rhetoric were intended to provide all ethnic Thai with more favorable economic opportunities, but in practice working-class Thai, who rarely held government positions, seldom gained any benefits. For centuries they had been shut out of commercial activity. Most continued to work in subsistence agriculture. In contrast, most Chinese immigrants, without access to land, were excluded from peasant production and thus took up wage labor. Excluding Chinese from certain occupations did little to stimulate Thai commercial enterprises (Ingram 1955:218).

Unlike the Chinese entrepreneurs, most chinkao did not have the money to buy protection and were forced to find other ways around the new occupational regulations. A Chinese aphorism, "at home you depend on your parents, away from home, you depend on your friends" (*zaijia kao fumu, chumen kao pengyou* [M]) succinctly depicted their circumstances. Chinese associations—historically organized according to a common dialect, birthplace, clan, surname, or even occupation—now became crucial. Newly arrived immigrant laborers might be given a job and a place to live simply because they shared the same "origin." Through fictive kinship ties—expressed in terms of address such as uncle, auntie, elder brother, or older sister—they forged connections and built trust. Besides providing their working-class members with loans, jobs, and information, these associations and informal networks offered the Chinese entrepreneurs a pool of more familiar laborers.[3]

In *Southeast Asia's Chinese Minorities*, Mary Heidhues (1974:13) notes that in Bangkok of the early 1950s, bankers, gold and jewelry retailers, rice merchants and exporters, and rice-mill laborers all came disproportionately from among Teochiu speakers; Hainanese specialized as ice-plant proprietors, hotel owners and workers, sawmill operators, and general laborers; Hakka were unusually active as silversmiths and newspapermen; Cantonese worked as machine-shop proprietors, machinists, and auto repair men (also see Skinner 1957:315–319). This demonstrated both the unity and diversity within the Chinese Thai community. Chinese-ness could at that time be called upon in a broad sense—as in the exclusion of Thai individuals from any of these associations—and also in a narrower, local sense, to make sharper divisions according to dialect, occupation, and so forth. Thus, Chinese-ness was weighed on many different scales, and invested with multiple layers of cultural significance. Several chinkao pointed out that one unexpected outcome of Thai-ification was to funnel even more chinkao into the commercial and business world: those who lost their wage labor jobs found new jobs in commercial enterprises, and some of them eventually became independent entrepreneurs.

In the late 1950s Prime Minister Sarit Thanarat turned away from Luang Phibun's program of creating state-owned enterprises and passed

Hainanese Chinese, instead of Teochiu or Hakka, specialized in operating sawmills. (By permission of the National Library, Bangkok.)

laws that made capital investment in private enterprises attractive to domestic and international investors (Keyes 1987b:77). He brought the country firmly into the American camp and promoted strong economic development with less focus on exclusively Thai-oriented policies. Chinese Thai entrepreneurs took advantage of the more favorable investment climate to diversify their holdings and strengthen their position within commercial and industrial circles, further reinforcing the notion that their business success was due to being Chinese.

Throughout the 1960s, as Thailand experienced an economic growth rate that was probably the highest in mainland Southeast Asia, some chinkao and lukchin rode an economic wave that was unavailable to most working-class Thai. The same thing happened again during the boom years from the mid-1980s through late 1997.

By the 1970s, as an increasing number of Chinese laborers grew old or moved up into the middle-class, urban enterprises—including those in the sex industry—began recruiting workers directly from the countryside. Landlessness, high poverty rates in rural regions, and the lure of city life led large numbers of Thai farmers to migrate to Bangkok in search of jobs. At the same time, an increasing number of educated lukchin professionals, who had Thai citizenship, Thai surnames, and spoke fluent Thai, began taking government jobs. Also, people from different ethnic backgrounds began working in businesses on the basis of merit instead of a shared "origin." The occupational boundaries originally drawn along ethnic and dialect lines began to blur.

Jamie Mackie has noted that the Chinese entrepreneurs who are prominent in Thailand today are mostly descendants of poor peasants from Fujian and Guangdong who came to the region as coolie laborers, mainly between 1860 and 1930 (1992a:163). Early advantage in business is one of the key reasons why the Chinese were better placed than others to seize the business opportunities that arose during boom times (ibid., 162–163). Today, business leadership rests largely in the hands of the Chinese Thai,[4] and Thai entrepreneurs have lagged far behind despite government aid in the form of protectionist and discriminatory regulations (ibid., 162).

The Chinese Thai, as a group, remain vulnerable to the Thai state's changing ethnic politics, but Thai political power and Chinese economic power are more closely intertwined than it may at first appear. While the Thai elite has used political power to enrich itself, the Chinese Thai have used their economic power to influence Thai politicians, with the general result that the rich get richer and the poor get poorer.

Gendered Occupations and Upward Mobility

The chinkao men in this project achieved greater economic success and more upward mobility than the chinkao women largely because of the structural advantages granted to men within the patriarchal family and society at large. With rare exceptions, men alone could inherit family businesses. Mu Bobo was born in 1917 and immigrated at the age of fifteen. He was the sole heir to his father's noodle factory; his sisters did not receive even token shares of the family business. In addition, there was an unspoken but clearly understood rule that a wife should work for the family business. A wife's labor reduced operating expenses and lowered risk, which enabled her husband to amass profits that were then reinvested to expand the business. Thaokae Zi, who immigrated at age twelve in 1937, became a polygynist after he had established a successful electronics shop and a real estate office. His major wife, who spoke both Teochiu and Thai, was in charge of the electronics shop. His minor wife, a young ethnic Lao (*khon isan*), did more outside administrative work related to his real estate business. The two wives worked separately in different family endeavors, with Thaokae Zi situated in charge of both.

Thaokae or "boss" is a gender-specific term that can refer only to a man. A thaokae's wife may well run the family business, but she usually positions herself as her husband's "inside assistant" (*neizhu* [M]). She is referred to as *thaokae nia*; although she also has considerable power, her identity and status derive from her husband. While complementary working relations between a husband and wife are recognized, the gender-based hierarchical order is reinforced.

A chinkao man made the best use of any opportunity that came his way, including using his wife's labor, but his wife usually chose her occupation only after factoring in the demands of her children, housework, and her husband's job. Most chinkao couples organized their income-producing labor in one of four ways.

In the first type, the husband engaged in income-producing work while the wife was restricted to piecework and non-income-producing housework. Piecework—sewing, rolling cigarettes, washing clothes, selling homemade food, making the paper objects that are burned as offerings to deities, and so on—was common because of its flexible demands on time. Some women also performed other kinds of casual labor. For example, when there was no running water in Bangkok, carrying buckets of water on a shoulder pole was considered a kind of "women's work" (*ngan khong phuying*). Song Mama remembered: "To help my father support the family, my mother would carry water from a well for a rich family to earn money. For a hundred trips back and forth she made 25 sadang." Women in this group toiled in the most exploitative sector of the economy; nonetheless, piecework gave them some flexibility in deciding how much work they could take on and when they would do it. Piecework was only intermittent and poorly compensated, but it provided a woman with cash to supplement her husband's income or to use as pocket money.

Two characteristics of piecework—that it is "trivial" and often done at home—mark it as women's work. If a chinkao man did piecework, his masculinity was immediately called into question. In contrast, piecework could actually enhance a chinkao woman's feminine identity because she was seen as contributing to the family in a way that did not compete with her husband's breadwinner status, and was thus conforming to her role as an inside assistant.

Women in this category usually worked at many different jobs during different periods in their lives. Mei Nainai, the woman who brought her adopted son with her to Thailand and left her biological daughter back in China, became a noodle vendor when her husband's health began to fail. For ten years she did housework and cared for her husband in the morning and then sold noodles on the street all afternoon and into the evening. Ayi, who was first a little daughter-in-law in China and later sold to work as a maid in Thailand, toiled her whole life for room and board. She was allowed to do piecework in the evening to earn pocket money after she finished her daily chores.

In the second arrangement, a husband and wife each worked separately for a salary. Men often had to hold two or three jobs at once, especially at the beginning of their careers. For almost fifty years Jiang Bobo worked at a bank during the day, then wrote and edited the local Chinese newspaper at night. He said, "My life is work, work, and work."

Even though their labor was much less celebrated, the women in this category had marketable skills—as schoolteachers and nurses, for example. Hui Xiaozhang, Jin Nainai, and Yu Mama chose to become teachers. They had come from wealthy families, and in China none would have needed to work, but in Thailand they had to earn a living. Jin Nainai migrated to Malaysia to escape an arranged marriage and later married a Chinese teacher there. When Japan invaded Malaysia during World War II, she immigrated to Thailand with her newborn baby, but her husband stayed behind to fight. Recalling the hardship she had suffered, she showed me a jade ring that she wore on her right hand:

> I sold all my jewelry except for this ring. My mother sent me this ring after I came to Thailand. My mother told the person who brought me the ring not to let anyone know this, because she was afraid that it would make me lose face. Instead of sending remittances back to her, here I was accepting a ring from my mother. I told myself no matter how poor I became I would never sell this ring. [At this point she cried and could not go on.]

Like many chinkao women, Jin Nainai had to work long hours, foregoing sleep and ignoring her own needs: "When the babies were small, I slept only three or four hours a night. Sometimes I was so tired, I fell asleep with my pen and my students' homework in my hands."

These women took their jobs very seriously. In the 1950s Hui Xiaozhang, the only woman in her county to attend college, was appointed principal of one of the best private Chinese primary schools in Bangkok. Because politics was believed to be a man's affair, Hui Xiaozhang explained to me, being female worked to her advantage. Her political savvy was constantly underestimated, and she was able to camouflage the maneuvers inherent in running a Chinese school in an anti-Chinese atmosphere. Nonetheless, she still had to overcome many obstacles—including death threats from rightist zealots—to raise funds and recruit students to keep the school afloat. In

A group portrait of the teaching staff at the "Bangkok Poor Children's Home" (1948). (Given to the author by one of the teachers.)

1992, at eighty years of age, she was still serving as an adviser to the school three days a week. "This school is my baby," she exclaimed.

Although teachers worked at school, outside the immediate family, chinkao regarded teaching as taking place within the Chinese community and hence as part of the inside domain. And although teachers worked less flexible hours than they might in a family business or doing piecework at home, teaching was considered a good job for women.

In the third division of labor, husband and wife worked together carrying out different but coordinated tasks in a family-owned enterprise, with their preexisting skills determining how they divided up the work. Trained as a nurse in China, Yan Mama first worked in Tianhua Hospital, Bangkok's first Chinese hospital. But after her husband, Gong Bobo, set up a textile factory, she left the hospital to devote herself to the family business. Gong Bobo took charge of the factory because he was considered head of the family and also had experience in the textile trade.

Both men and women learned new skills and technologies in the process of establishing and maintaining a family firm. Self-made businessmen, like Fong Laoban and Thaokae Zi, learned new business skills from practical experience rather than in school. Wang Mama taught herself to speak English, and long after her retirement, she was still proud of her accomplishment: "I sold things to the foreigners," she said. "No problem. My daughter (a college student) could not do better than I."

Husbands and wives had to work closely together as business partners to advance the family's economic interests, but this often generated tension between them as spouses. Yan Mama had many ideas about how to operate the business and how to invest profits, but Gong Bobo often dismissed her suggestions out of hand, frustrating her and upsetting their conjugal relationship. Yan Mama once mused, "If I could do it over again, I would never work with him."

In the fourth type of arrangement, the woman became the family's primary economic provider. Structurally, a man was expected to support the family, but in practice he might not be able to do so. At age three, Song Mama immigrated to Thailand with her mother to reunite with her father. When she was sixteen, her mother married her off to a man who turned out to be a brutal alcoholic. "When he drank," she said, "he would destroy everything." If Song Mama refused to have sex with him, he would strangle her and threaten to choke her to death. "Each time before I was going to give birth, I bought a bottle of soy sauce and a sack of rice so I could have something to eat after the birth. . . . I made porridge for my baby [meaning she was so undernourished she could not produce milk for her infant]." Her husband rarely brought home any money. Her marital life became a long agonizing battle to pull herself and her fourteen children out of grinding poverty punctuated by episodes of sadistic violence. Finally, despite her Catholic faith and the daunting prospect of raising fourteen children, she divorced her husband: "I asked my children if any of them wanted to go and live with their father. No one would go," she said.

With a modest loan she opened a tiny grocery store that sold mostly small items such as tea, soft drinks, cigarettes, candies, pencils, and small cups of alcohol—merchandise that often sold for only a few baht. She smiled at every customer, even those who spent only a baht or two: "I am grateful to all my customers. They come to buy things from me. Without their help, I cannot have the shop."

Song Mama opened early and closed late, working from 4 A.M. to 11 P.M. seven days a week to take advantage of the business from taxi drivers and nearby night-shift workers in addition to her regular customers. Her shop faced the street; looking out, one saw only endless haze and blue smoke constantly floating through the air. Traffic police wore white surgical masks to protect against the choking exhaust fumes billowing from the cars, buses, motorcycles, taxis, and three-wheeled *tuk-tuks* jammed along the narrow roadway. Sometimes the traffic's roar made it all but impossible to hold a conversation. However, none of this seemed to bother Song Mama. Since she was the primary shopkeeper, she often did several things at once, simultaneously making change for one customer, exchanging pleasantries with another, and scanning her aisles for shoplifters. Astonished by her workload, I asked her when she found time to unwind. She said her most relaxing time was when she traveled from Bangkok to a Malaysian border town to buy $400 worth of duty-free goods (the maximum allowed per visit)—a sixteen-hour train ride!

Because the grocery's success was crucial to the family's well-being, Song Mama's children helped out after school and work. Despite her encouragement, however, none of her sons wanted to inherit the business: "They want to sell big things and make big money. They complain that the job is too 'minute' (*chukchik*)." Only one daughter helped her to run the shop on a regular basis.

Song Mama bought condominiums for several of her children but continued to live a very frugal life herself. When she needed cigarettes, for example, she would ask her child, or a neighbor's child, to go and buy her three or four, but never a whole pack. I asked her why she didn't stock her own brand in the shop. "This way," she answered, "I will not smoke so much and waste money." Smoking was one small pleasure she allowed herself, but even here she chose the middle way, saving money by deliberately making smoking inconvenient.

Despite her economic accomplishments, and in stark contrast to the male entrepreneurs I encountered, Song Mama never spoke of her success as a breadwinner. Instead, she described herself as doing a "man's job out of necessity," the consequence of having married the "wrong" man. But she also said to me, "If children have no father, it is okay. But if they have no mother, it will be a disaster."

Yu Mama also became the primary provider for her family. Her husband started gambling and drinking heavily after his father's business went bankrupt. Besieged by people to whom her husband owed money, Yu Mama was so humiliated that she contemplated suicide. Finally, she made it public that she had nothing to do with his debts. In order to make more money by working longer hours, she hired a live-in Chinese domestic worker, a new widow with a teenage son, to care for her four children.[5] This way Yu Mama could teach both during the day and at night school. When she had a newborn child, Yu Mama had to rush home to nurse the baby and then hurry back to school: "I was teased for being a wet nurse." She worked as a private tutor on weekends and during semester breaks to earn extra money; she also published short essays in a local Chinese newspaper. Although struggling doubly hard to support her family, it was necessary, for, as Yu Mama said, "I am my children's father and mother" (*dang ba you dang ma* [M]).

The lives of chinkao women have been transformed perhaps most dramatically within the world of work. Before immigration, most of them worked in the fields; conducting business or earning money from an income-producing job was considered men's work. But after these women came to Thailand several factors—economic necessity, freedom from control by a mother-in-law, and the Thai acceptance of women working in small businesses—created opportunities in economic endeavors that had been unavailable to them in China.

Collectively, however, chinkao men achieved a higher degree of upward mobility. Six of the eight chinkao men I interviewed were wage earners when they married (Mu Bobo inherited a family business and Thaokae Zi established his own electronics shop). By 1992, or at retirement, five of the eight men owned a family business. The three others were still employed within the same general job category but had advanced to more lucrative senior positions.

In contrast, not one woman in this project inherited a family business. At the time they married or joined their husbands in Thailand, only one of the nine (Wang Mama) worked in a family business; three were teachers, one was a nurse, and the remaining four did piecework. By 1992, or at retirement, only Song Mama, a former pieceworker, had become the owner of a business; Yan Mama, the former nurse, worked with her husband in their family-owned textile factory. Of the rest, only one of the three teachers was promoted; the remaining five held jobs similar to the ones they acquired when they first started working.

The Gendered Division of Domestic Work

Chinkao men do perform certain kinds of domestic work, but such work is feminized and devalued. They spent most of their time and energy on income-producing work, especially when struggling to establish a career or find a good job. Ideologically, they were not encouraged to cross the boundaries between income-producing work and domestic work.

Compared to their wives, husbands spent much less time with their children. A father who cared for his children often expressed his devotion through the culturally constructed role of the "strict father" (*yan fu* [M]). Husbands often decided which school their children would attend or which occupation they should aspire to. After his eldest son died because he was too poor to pay for treatment, Fong Laoban decided that all his remaining children should become doctors. To help his youngest daughter get over her fear of blood, he forced her to cut the heads off chickens. To prevent one son from neglecting his studies because of his girlfriend, he took him to visit a nude bar; "I told him 'Now you have seen everything. You should not be so curious about women.'" Then, to "frighten him away from sleeping with prostitutes," Fong Laoban took him to visit a leprosy hospital. He believed it was this strict discipline that led three of his four children to become physicians: one was a heart surgeon in the United States, another a neurologist in Taiwan, and the third an internist in Bangkok.

In comparison, chinkao women disciplined their children not only in the important matters, such as those overseen by the husband, but also in the most minute activities. I was told repeatedly that the most difficult time for a wife was the first fifteen years after her marriage, when she had to struggle with work, children, and the household chores. Childcare was extremely demanding. Most chinkao I knew had at least three or four children, and none of them had in-laws who lived with them. Several pointed out that the one advantage of living in China was that the in-laws could keep an eye on the younger children. In Thailand women had to perform both income-producing work and domestic labor. Wang Mama, the woman who taught herself English, gave birth to four children in five years. For nearly seven years, after running the store all day, she got up several times every night to feed and care for her babies, "Sometimes I was so tired that I forgot to brush their teeth after I fed them. All my children's teeth went bad."

Monitoring the children's homework also often fell upon the women's shoulders, regardless of how busy they were. Yu Mama, whose husband became a gambler and an alcoholic, said: "I was a teacher, but I had no time to check my own children's homework. While I did the washing, I asked my children to tell me about their homework or read to me. . . . My children are good. They did not want me to worry about them. I always told them that they need a skill. If I had not had a skill, this family would have been finished a long time ago."

As for housework, most chinkao women did the routine and daily housekeeping while their husbands did nonroutine, occasional tasks such as electrical repair or furniture moving. In the survey of forty chinkao households, 90 percent reported that the wife did most of the cooking, cleaning, and washing; the remaining 10 percent said that both husband and wife shared these tasks. It is possible, of course, that a few men performed housework but did not feel comfortable acknowledging it. Jin Nainai, for example, said that whenever her late husband mopped the floor, he always made sure the door was closed so that no neighbor would see him doing "women's work."

Some chinkao women had a low opinion of a man's ability to do housework. For instance, Yan Mama, who worked together with Gong Bobo in a textile factory, compared her husband's hands to "duck's feet," as if his fingers were stuck together and therefore useless for doing housework. Actually, Gong Bobo was quite a skillful gardener. But from his perspective, which was shared by the chinkao in general, keeping a garden was an "art" while housework was "insignificant women's work." When he performed any domestic task—for example, buying fresh fruit at the market on his way back from morning exercise—Gong Bobo regarded himself as "helping" (*chuai/bangmang* [M]) his wife.

Chinkao women also often said "helping" rather than "sharing" when they described their husbands' participation in housework. For example, Jin Nainai: "My husband often helped me cook rice and prepare dishes." Or Hui Xiaozhang: "He helped me do the shopping and pay the bills." This use of "helping" indicates how housework and childcare are feminized within a patriarchal logic. The characterization is similar to what Arlie Hochschild found in households in the United States: American husbands almost never talk about feeling "lucky" that their wives do housework, whereas wives feel "lucky" whenever their husbands pitch in (1989:203). The notions of help and luck betray a common theme: a wife should be grateful when her husband joins in the housework. In contrast, I rarely heard chinkao men say they felt lucky that their wives shared the workload in a family business.

Wang Mama was often impatient with her husband Deng Laoban: "When he finishes eating a bowl of rice, he waits for me to serve him more. My daughter-in-law commented that my husband was as helpless as her baby son." Yet this "helpless" husband meticulously cleaned his Mercedes-Benz every weekend. Apparently, Deng Laoban could choose to perform certain "manly" tasks, leaving Wang Mama no choice but to do everything else.

Coping with an increased workload generated from both nei and wai (inside and outside) domains, women used the term *yijiaoti* [M] to describe how they got their work done. I was told that yijiaoti originally meant doing three things simultaneously at a funeral: carrying the coffin, crying for the dead, and spreading paper money on the road. Now it describes doing several things at once in any context. In 1991, for example, at the age of sixty-four, Cao Mama literally ran back and forth between her house and her parents' house to take care of her partially paralyzed husband and her bedridden ninety-year-old parents. Every evening after dinner she soaked her aching feet in a wooden tub and chanted the Buddhist Suffering Scripture, occasionally glancing up at the TV screen when she heard her children comment on a program. Even when her body was exhausted, Cao Mama still did three things at once.

When the family was better off or the wife grew old or got sick, some chinkao families hired Thai or Lao domestic workers.[6] What had been non-paying domestic work for the wife now became an income-producing job for the maid, who in turn often used her wages to support her own family in a distant village, while her mother or grandmother replaced her as caretaker. Having a domestic worker living, working, and sleeping in the house brought with it the tensions of a new power relationship between two women of different classes and ethnicity, and this tended to absorb any previous conflict between husband and wife over housework. The chinkao wife had to learn to speak at least some Thai in order to supervise the maid, who performed such routine tasks as washing, ironing, cleaning, and preparing food. The wife often continued doing most of the cooking until the maid learned how to prepare Chinese dishes. Even when she had domestic help, her success as a "good" wife would still be measured by whether meals were carefully prepared, the family members suitably dressed and well fed, and the house neat and clean.

Segregated Socialization

Many chinkao couples lacked the time, money, and inclination to go out together for recreation, especially early in their married life. Mei Nainai said she and her husband had gone out alone together only once in all the years they had been married, and on that occasion they became separated in a crowd and spent hours trying to find one another, thus engendering a longstanding family joke.

Echoing the segregated socialization they had experienced in China, where public interactions between men and women were discouraged, the majority of chinkao couples I knew did not participate in social activities together. In the survey, eighteen out of forty (45 percent) stated that they never went out together as a couple. Doing so was considered much less important than going out with the family: a slight majority, twenty-one of the couples (52.5 percent) reported that they went out together with their children to attend weddings, funerals, or for worshiping their ancestors on Qingming Day (if their parents had died in Thailand). Only one couple said that they went out together frequently. Again echoing their practices in China, the rate of cross-gender friends was very low: a majority of both men and women (80 percent) reported that they interacted mainly with same-sex friends of the same ethnic background. In other words, not only did wives and husbands often socialize separately, but also women usually socialized with other women and men with other men.

The usual places for socialization were also gender-specific. I observed that chinkao women interacted with relatives, friends, and neighbors in their shops, kitchens, living rooms, at temples, or on the street. The men, in contrast, regarded social dining and drinking in bars and restaurants as necessary for doing business, and on these occasions they shared a broad range of information. Sometimes the meals were considered incomplete without a visit afterwards to a brothel. When the businessman acting as host paid for the meal and the brothel visit, he reaffirmed his power vis-á-vis his male colleagues. Guests who hesitated about going along were often persuaded to participate by group pressure, the desire to strengthen business ties, or the local attitude that male philandering is "a common matter." Ironically, while visiting a brothel has become socially acceptable for men, an ordinary street-corner conversation between a man and a woman can easily cause gossip or create suspicion that something is "going on."

Segregation into separate discursive and spatial realms favored the direct masculine display of economic success while limiting women to indirect and self-effacing expressions. More important, such male-oriented social networks excluded chinkao women as well as ethnic Thai.

Class Identity

Among entrepreneurial chinkao men, donating money was a key strategy for converting economic into social capital. It was well understood that a generous donation could be exchanged for a prestigious position or an honorable title. Mu Bobo, who inherited the noodle factory, donated large sums to different charities, especially to an orphanage he had established in Bangkok. In return, Thai society and the Chinese Thai community honored him. In the two "picture halls" of his personal museum, a three-story monument to his success, were hundreds of framed photographs of Mu Bobo posing with Thai royal family members, military leaders, and various politicians from Thailand, Beijing, and Taiwan. By demonstrating his high social status and "good reputation," the pictures were intended to further promote his family businesses. Although he made generous donations, Mu Bobo still valued "careful calculation and strict budgeting" (*jingda xi suan* [M]). He would not, for example, spend the money to buy himself a weekly planner. Instead, he recorded his daily appointments on used envelopes he had turned inside out. This might reflect his habitual thriftiness in handling money: buying a weekly planner was considered an unnecessary waste of money, but making a charitable donation was a strategy for accumulating social capital.

Fong Laoban, the owner of a printing company, shared this notion of frugality. He and his minor wife invited me to visit their vacation home outside Bangkok. One morning, trying to find something for breakfast, he haggled with a street vendor, saying, "Your soybean milk costs two baht [5 cents] more than in Bangkok!" When the vendor would not lower his price, Fong Laoban refused to buy. Later that day we went to look at a parcel of land for sale. He walked once around the lot, which was offered at two million baht (about $80,000), talked to his wife for a minute, then told the owner, "I'll take it." He did not bother bargaining for a better price. In his view, buying an "overpriced" bowl of soybean milk was a waste of money, but buying a piece of land was an investment. This reminded me of the story Fong Laoban had told about his father filling up his stomach with water rather than spending his meal money. For his father, such thriftiness was an attempt to survive and to save enough to lift his family out of poverty. For Fong Laoban, the apparent thrift was really an example of sophisticated money handling: money spent to make more money is a good investment, but wasting even a minuscule amount of money is simply bad management.

Owning a family business, paying the bills, making donations, and acting as host to a group of men at a business dinner are all seen as appropriate expressions of masculinity. Not "wasting" money on something that is overpriced or unnecessary, or provides only fleeting pleasure, such as a cigarette, illustrates the other side of this economic strategizing, which is equally valued by chinkao men and women. Despite the fact that thriftiness is a stereotype that the Thai associate with ethnic Chinese, this construction of frugality resonates strongly among chinkao.

If a wife earns more money than her husband or controls the family income, her husband's masculinity may be questioned, but being frugal rarely threatens middle-class Chinese masculinity. Controlling the family income is connected with being a "man" and being an authoritative figure within the family. Wang Mama was integral in expanding her family's grocery store into a department store, and she also took care of her husband and children at home, but she received only a monthly salary, from which she had to pay family expenses: "I worked in the shop for more than thirty years, half of my life. When I worked, I hardly ever had a day off. Sometimes I even did not have time for a meal. But I was only paid a salary. The shares in the business were divided between my husband and his brothers [together they owned three department stores]. Now I am retired, but I've ended up with no money. My husband asked my children to give me money, but I don't want to take money from my children's pockets."

Although Wang Mama regarded herself as her husband's inside assistant, performing tasks he would not or did not have the time to do, she also wanted recognition for her work. Her husband took her labor for granted simply because she was his wife, and he asked their children to give her pocket money because she was their mother. Wang Mama was seen through a patriarchal lens as a wife and mother instead of a breadwinner.

Having access to income-producing jobs did allow chinkao women to do certain things they had never done before. A few even sent remittances back to their natal families in China. Some did so secretly, to avoid conflict over violating the conventional notion that women should forget their natal family members after they marry. Others did it despite their husbands' objections. Yan Mama said: "When I went back to work [after giving birth], I said to hell with him. I no longer needed to beg him for money or ask his permission to send remittances." She put her salary in a bank account and drew on it to send remittances and parcels to help her younger sister cope with food shortages in China in the late 1950s and early 1960s. Likewise Cao Mama, at the request of her relatives in Shantou, sent small amounts of money, ranging from 200 to 1,000 baht ($8 to $40), to help build a village school: "It expresses my heart and gives face to my relatives." The ability to send back remittances or donations was a way for these women to express their feelings and demonstrate their class status to their kin in China.

———

In contemporary Thai society, the Chinese Thai are considered middle class. They have been valued and marginalized at the same time: valued for their productivity, knowledge, and business skills, but subtly and sometimes overtly discriminated against for being Chinese. Although the Chinese Thai have collectively achieved greater economic upward mobility than many ethnic Thai, categorizing them as the "trading minority" or "middle-class Chinese" is a gross oversimplification. Such categories fail to acknowledge the existence of working-class Chinese and middle- or upper-class Thai. Nor do these terms accommodate the marginalized experiences of the middle-class Chinese. Depicting the Chinese as "natural-born" entrepreneurs also devalues the economic activities of the Thai and obscures the power relations between the Thai state regime and ethnic Chinese. The Chinese Thai are the by-product of time-specific regulations of ethnicized occupations, and their identity is being shaped by various forces—economic, political, local, and global—that are brought to bear on them. They have been used to produce wealth and to generate revenue for the state, and they have also reproduced the class inequalities of Thai society in themselves.

Immigration encourages and in some ways forces chinkao women to cross nei/wai boundaries. The women encounter new demands and new opportunities while still having to conform to the construction of femininity placed upon "good" mothers and dutiful "inside assistants." Chinkao women keep finding themselves located in an ambiguous and contradictory position: they have to conform to conventional gender roles even though their own sense of themselves is changing as they increasingly engage with income-producing jobs. Just as the Thai state's historic regulation of Chinese labor and occupations set the stage for their commercial success, more recent changes in family gender politics now shape the gendered characteristics of that success.

Chinkao men's conventional breadwinner role meshes well with the new expectations they have encountered in Thai society. As one effect of Chinese fraternal culture, men have been able to use exclusively male networks to achieve greater socioeconomic mobility and to convert their economic power into a much wider range of capital than chinkao women. The injunction not to cross nei/wai boundaries is the most visible constraint men experience regarding the division of labor. The few who did perform "women's work" felt obliged to disguise it or keep silent about it.

Thus a striking parallel emerges: the men downplay their domestic role while the women downplay their breadwinner role. The cultural construction of masculinity and femininity masks women's contributions to the economic enterprise by naturalizing men as breadwinners and women as nurturing mothers and inside assistants. The seemingly natural ethnic-based entrepreneurship and conjugal division of labor among chinkao suggests that cultural identities are produced not only by the state's ethnic politics but also by family gender politics embedded in even the least significant socioeconomic activities. Among chinkao, the cultural meanings and ideological significance invested in nei/wai have remained relatively static, lagging behind the transformations taking place in practice. In other words, despite the women's rapid adaptation to the new environment, the transformation of family gender politics has moved at a much slower pace.

5

Changes in Sexual Practice: "Same Bed, Different Dreams"

The Thai language is rich with expressions on men's unfaithfulness. Men can stray or *nok jai*. They can have "another woman" or *mee puying uen*. They can have a mistress or *mee mianoi*. But they can never, never *mee choo*, or commit adultery, because, linguistically, this expression is used only when a married woman has an extramarital affair.

—SANITSUDA EKACHAI, "Adultery is for women only"

A FTER THE FIGHT with her womanizing husband, whom she compared to a promiscuous rabbit, Guoyi Mama said, "Don't think I make him lose face. He does not have any face to lose." For years she and her husband had been "sleeping in the same bed but dreaming different dreams." After she discovered her husband's affair with their Thai maid, however, Guoyi Mama moved into her own bedroom. She distanced herself from her husband while continuing to hold on to the social, economic, and familial benefits the institution of marriage provides. Her response—firing the maid and sexually detaching herself from her husband—reveals how ethnicity, sexuality, and class came together in her decision to remain in a troubled marriage rather than seek a divorce.

Among the chinkao, divorce is usually seen negatively because it splits up the family and the family business, if there is one. A divorced woman will lose her hard-won middle-class status and risk diminishing a social network she may have spent a lifetime building up. Therefore, some wives endure their marriages for "the sake of the children" (*henkaeluk/weile haizi* [M]) and their own economic security.

Endurance (*otthon*) is valued in both the Thai and Chinese Thai communities, and it is a key teaching of the Theravada Buddhism that perme-

74

Among the many decorations in this chinkao home was a wall hanging entitled "Endurance." (Photograph by the author.)

ates the Thai social order. A good Buddhist is expected to tolerate suffering. The Chinese character for endurance (*ren* [M]) is formed by combining two words: the upper part of the character means "knife blade" and the lower part "heart," implying that one should endure even a knife in one's heart. In the chinkao homes I visited, I often saw wall hangings with aphorisms extolling endurance—"Step back one step, the future will be brighter; endure a little bit, the road for maneuvering will be broader." Endurance is understood as a central means of overcoming obstacles to a better life.

Chinkao men and women apply the notion of endurance differently. Men most often think of it in the context of hard work and the struggle to establish a business or sustain a job. Significantly, they often see extramarital sexual liaisons as a "reward" for their endurance—a notion that intersects with the cultural emphasis on the male breadwinner's role and male sexual privilege. Women, on the other hand, commonly apply the notion of endurance in the context of work and childcare, but they also use it to describe putting up with their husbands' philandering. Women aged seventy and older, in particular, considered such endurance the primary virtue of a good woman. An elderly widow whom I had met doing the household survey told me that she had breast-fed the baby her husband and his minor wife had abandoned and explained her actions as follows: "Buddha gives a fair judgment based on each person's behavior—plant melons and get melons, sow beans and get beans." She regarded the fact that her husband came back to her, and that she outlived him, as the reward for her endurance.

But being a "good" woman and an "enduring" wife need not be entirely passive. In practice, even as they claimed to simply be enduring their troubled marriages, some women—like Guoyi Mama—found subtle and informal ways to maneuver within the patriarchal system. Refusing to sleep with a philandering husband or adopting an abandoned infant can be read as culturally specific forms of resistance.

Nei/Wai Sex

Chinkao men often boasted with other men, sometimes with women present (though not women from their own families), about their extramarital sexual encounters in various settings, even as a topic for passing the time while stuck inside a car during a Bangkok traffic jam. At a dinner party I attended, a chinkao businessman over seventy bragged that many young girls working in his factory wanted to be his minor wife. "I have nothing to attract them except money," he said without irony. "They want a lifetime meal ticket."

Unlike the men, however, no chinkao woman ever talked to me about having an extramarital affair. Several factors may have contributed to this. Legally, a husband can divorce his wife for adultery, but the reverse is not true. So women would risk much more by admitting to having had an affair. However, their silence does not mean that they never had extramarital affairs. In addition, most of the chinkao women I interviewed were grandmothers—as Hui Xiaozhang, the school principal, said, "already sallow-faced old ladies" (*huanglianpo* [M]) no longer physically attractive to men. In some communities, being old ladies might have the opposite effect, freeing them to speak more bluntly than younger women. But for chinkao women like Hui Xiaozhang, middle-class respectability would rule that out.

While the women were silent about their own extramarital affairs and conjugal sex, they complained loudly about their womanizing husbands. On the one hand, they appeared to accept the notion that it was a "man's nature" to need sex more than a woman. On the other hand, they resented it and complained vociferously about a husband who promiscuously sleeps around *outside* the home. The term *waimian* [M] (outside) is applied to a wide range of men's extramarital sexual practices: seeking a single act with a sex worker, having an affair, keeping a mistress, or taking another wife. This notion of "outside" is juxtaposed with an unspoken but deeply entrenched notion of sexuality "inside" the family. Understanding nei/wai is crucial for understanding the chinkao's sexual behavior.

At the same time, both chinkao men and women remained silent about conjugal or "inside" sex, treating it as a private matter. But the women would share information about reproduction, such as how to increase the odds of bearing a son by eating certain foods or observing certain practices. A few women vaguely referred to sex as "troublesome"; some even implied that it was a kind of labor.

"Seeking pleasure and happiness" (*xunhuan zuole* [M]) was mainly used to describe a man's outside liaisons. Within the Thai moral code female sexual organs are positively associated with childbirth and negatively associated with female sexual pleasure (Harrison 1999:168). Many chinkao also believe this. In addition, some chinkao believe that sexual excess leads to illness, because semen is a crucial part of a man's *qi* or life force.[1] In classical Chinese fiction, a "chaste polygamist" had to be modest, using sexual intercourse mainly for the purpose of procreation (McMahon 1995:150–151). However, pursuing sex for pleasure has become a familiar practice among chinkao men, in part because of the widely held Thai folk belief that it is "healthy" for a man to indulge in sex rather than restrain himself, and in part because of the pervasiveness of Thailand's sex industry.[2]

But as Chris Beyrer points out, the women's attitudes are very different when it comes to their own sexual pleasure:

> Every one of these women was shocked when my friend [a Western researcher] mentioned that she and her husband had a satisfying sexual relationship. What did she mean? That her husband was satisfied? No, she explained, she meant that she was satisfied; her husband was a generous partner. She had orgasms. *Orgasms*?! Impossible. Women couldn't have orgasms. . . . (The Thais present were all educators, physicians, or pharmacists.) . . . But the daughters of these women might tell you a very different story . . . young women who want to be a part of their husbands' erotic lives, not just dutiful and sexless mothers of children. (1998:124)

Since both Thai and Chinese cultural logics disconnect sexual pleasure from femininity and motherhood, reproduction-oriented inside sex is considered superior to pleasure-seeking outside sex. Guoyi Mama was angry with her husband not only because he had extramarital sex but also because it took place inside her home. Visiting a sex worker might be tolerated, but sleeping with the maid at home—and thereby violating inside/outside sex boundaries—was deemed a greater insult to the wife. Guoyi Mama's response illustrates how the cultural construction of endurance allows both an acceptance of male sexual privilege and resistance to it, creating a tension between silence and discourse, complaint and compliance, and action and passivity.

Most women resisted their husbands' exercise of sexual privilege in subtle, sometimes nearly invisible, ways. For example, although Yan Mama, who earlier referred to her husband's hands as duck's feet, made sure that Gong Bobo was properly fed and dressed appropriately in public, she rarely initiated conversations with him. She maintained the public image of a good wife while privately distancing herself from him. "We have nothing to talk about," she explained. "He makes me impatient." She often, however, spent hours talking on the phone with her friends and fellow church members. To make sure she would never miss a call, she installed a second telephone line at home even though only she, her husband, and a domestic worker lived there. Gong Bobo once bitterly joked that Yan should become a "nun" because she was so warm to everyone except him.

One evening while Yan Mama and I were talking, we were interrupted by a telephone call from Wei Jie, a lukchin who had just discovered that her husband had been secretly keeping a mistress. In the following telephone conversation I heard Yan Mama say:

> You should not take it too seriously. This kind of thing happens in almost every family. It is not important enough for you to worry about it like this. . . . When it happened to me, at first it seemed so important that I seriously considered committing suicide, but then I finally realized it was not so important. . . . What did you tell your children? . . . You have such good children. . . . If you did not have any children, you might consider getting a divorce. . . . This probably happened because your husband didn't have anything to do. You are too capable, and he felt left behind. . . . You should learn to forgive others. . . . If you cannot forgive him, just imagine that he is another person, not your husband.

By imagining a husband as a stranger, an aggrieved wife could create enough space for herself to endure the marriage for the sake of her children. At one moment Yan Mama seemed to see Wei Jie's husband as a naturally active agent of sexuality and the breadwinner. Then, in the next moment, she asserted that Wei Jie was too capable and that this may have bruised her husband's ego and prompted his affair. A "man's nature," therefore, was actually being linked to socioeconomic activities and gender roles.

A few chinkao women, such as Hui Xiaozhang and Jin Nainai, said that they were "fortunate" because their husbands did not have affairs. Indeed, not all chinkao men had affairs or visited brothels.[3] But the fact that these wives considered themselves lucky is significant. Men never talked of feeling fortunate or lucky that their wives did not have extramarital relations. In fact, they took their wives' fidelity for granted, just as they took their domestic labor for granted.

In everyday discourse, a woman who maintains her troubled marriage for the sake of the children generally gains more respect in the community than a divorcée. Song Mama was the only chinkao woman in this project who divorced her husband. Indeed, many prefer to wait for widowhood and a new life in their remaining years because a widow's social status remains unaffected by a husband's death. Nian Lamei, a female lukchin author, captured this attitude in a short story called "I'm Happy My Husband Died" (1991:11–12). Yu Mama shared feelings similar to the happy widow in this short story. After her husband passed away and her children graduated from college, Yu Mama traveled to China, Taiwan, the United States, and Europe to visit friends and relatives and to see places she had always wanted to see. Much of her late-blooming happiness came from releasing a lifetime's accumulated resentment while tapping into the status provided by widowhood.

While both chinkao men and women maintain a shared silence about conjugal sexuality, they speak about men's extramarital affairs in distinctly gendered voices, voices characterized by male boasting and varying degrees of female compliance and complaint. The cultural construction of endurance, informed by nei/wai family gender politics and expressed in shared but distinct strategic discourses and silences, reveals not only that male sexual privilege is naturalized, but also that it is deeply embedded in socioeconomic activities. Endurance—the effort to balance sometimes conflicting strategies involving class respectability and the rewards of economic success—embodies all the tensions women feel about accepting or resisting asymmetrical gender regulations and male sexual privilege.

Cosmopolitan Polygyny

Legal polygyny was abolished in China in 1929 and in Thailand in 1935, but this changed only the letter of the law. Skinner attributed polygyny among Chinese in Thailand to being "Chinese traditional." He assumed that the younger generation would tend to look on polygyny less favorably (1958:54). By this logic, polygyny would gradually disappear as old Chinese immigrants died and subsequent generations assimilated, embracing a "cosmopolitan-modern" identity.

Almost half a century after Skinner's research, however, the practice of polygyny persists. Thaokae Zi, who assigned different jobs to his two wives, certainly qualified as a cosmopolitan-modern man according to Skinner's criteria.[4] He spoke Teochiu, Thai, Mandarin, and even knew some simple phrases in English and Japanese. Moreover, he was an accomplished photographer and a prize-winning novelist. He also rejected the "Chinese traditional" polygynist lifestyle by physically separating the two families, instead of having them live under one roof.

Yet Thaokae Zi conformed to conventional Chinese gender politics by longing for a son. He said, "My [major] wife is a kind and honest person with great tolerance. But she gave me five daughters. I waited and waited one after the other. A son never came." Thaokae Zi's desire for a son was doubtless sincere and may have been the reason for his taking another wife, but that is scarcely the only reason for practicing polygyny. Fong Laoban, the printing firm president, already had three sons before he became a polygynist.

Clearly, polygyny is not about being "traditional" or "modern"; it is about gender inequality. Marrying more than one wife enhances a man's masculinity, at least among other men. While Thai law decrees "one husband, one wife," practice dictates one husband, many wives. Polygyny symbolizes a man's wealth, status, success, and "charm."

To have an unregistered "customary marriage" is a common strategy among polygynists, although the Family Registration Act of 1935 states that only registered marriages are legal (Napaporn 1989:206). Nonetheless, customary or ceremonial marriages carry no social stigma because the wedding ritual is commonly considered more important than the act of registration. In 1987, for example, only 55 percent of marriages by women between the ages of fifteen and forty-nine had been registered (ibid., 205).[5]

Deciding whether or not to register a marriage often requires careful deliberation. Thaokae Zi registered his first marriage, at the insistence of his major wife and their adult daughters, only after taking a minor wife. The children of a lawfully registered married couple have the legal right to inherit property from the father. To compensate for *not* registering the second marriage, he complied with his minor wife's request that he deposit money in her bank account and put their residence into her name. As a cosmopolitan polygynist, he had to manage a range of difficult tasks and continuously negotiate with two wives and two sets of children in order to maintain his class respectability and polygynist status.

In the classic Thai story *Khun Chang Khun Phaen*, the term *chaochu* is used to characterize an heroic man who is a master of magical arts in warfare and in love.[6] Today the chaochu image, which emphasizes a man's skill at charming women through clever and witty conversation, embodies Thai masculinity. It has been openly embraced by men of all classes, up to and including a former prime minister of Thailand, Sarit Thanarat. Although Sarit made prostitution illegal in 1960, in an effort to improve Thailand's image in the West, he himself had numerous mistresses.[7]

The Sex Industry and Its Impact

Although the history of indigenous Thai prostitution can be traced back to the fifteenth century, it was not until the mid-1960s that prostitution became widespread (Muecke 1992:892).[8] At that time the Thai state began promoting sex tourism in the hopes of improving Thailand's economy.[9] Thailand provided "rest and recreation" centers for U.S. military personnel during the Vietnam conflict (Truong 1990:81–82).[10] After U.S. troops withdrew from Vietnam, Thailand's sex industry was reoriented toward a wider international market. From 1977 to 1986 the sex ratio of tourists averaged 2 to 1 in favor of men (ibid., 173). Sex package tours were marketed in the Netherlands, Norway, West Germany, the United Kingdom, the Middle East, and elsewhere throughout the 1970s and 1980s (ibid., 177). To this day the red-light districts of Bangkok, Phuket, Chiang Mai, and Pattaya attract sex tourists from all over the world. The growth of the tourist industry in Thailand has been phenomenal, with income from tourism rising from approximately 200 million baht in 1960 to more than 37 billion baht in 1986 (ibid., 163). By 1995 tourism had replaced agriculture as Thailand's largest source of foreign exchange. In 2002 10.8 million tourists came to Thailand and spent US $7.7 billion, amounting to 6 percent of the country's gross domestic profit (Mydans 2003).

The size of Thailand's sex industry is a much-contested issue. In 1980

Tawan Mai magazine used police statistics to estimate that out of a total population of about 55 million, more than 400,000 women worked in the sex industry (Bamber, Hewison, and Underwood 1997:50). Another source estimates that there are "80,000 to one million women working as prostitutes, plus perhaps some 20,000 girls under the age of 15" (Muecke 1992:892). In 1996, according to epidemiologist David Celentano, "the AIDS epidemic has made prostitution less popular, but business is still thriving. . . . Eighty-five percent of all men over the age of 16 have visited prostitutes, down from 96 percent in 1993" (*Johns Hopkins Gazette* 1996). Regardless of the exact number of sex workers, the size of Thailand's sex industry is impressive.

As demand has increased over the past few decades, chinkao entrepreneurs, predominantly Hainan Chinese, have rebuilt Thailand's sex industry by renovating old-fashioned brothels into modern massage parlors and bars. These previously impoverished peasants, who had been too poor to visit a brothel in China, now became brothel owners. Perhaps drawing upon their own experience of having participated in ethnicized occupations and being marginalized because of their ethnicity, they tailored sexual services to the ethnic backgrounds of their domestic and foreign customers, meeting culture-specific fantasies and desires.

In the mid-1980s brothels disguised as teahouses became very popular

Chaophya 2 Bath & Massage. One of many establishments where sexual services can be purchased (2002). (Photograph by the author.)

among Chinese Thai men (Wathinee and Guest 1994:39, 41, 45). I learned about this personally one hot afternoon while walking near Bangkok's Chinatown. I was thirsty and happy to see a teahouse nearby. But the moment I entered, a middle-aged woman, presumably the proprietor, began waving her arms and yelling at me, motioning for me to leave. Although I could not understand her Teochiu dialect, I quickly realized that this "teahouse" was there for men to purchase sex, not for me to purchase tea. This experience brought home to me how brothels exist in a variety of different forms, each catering to the specific tastes of their particular clientele.

The sex workers who served the ethnic Chinese tended to be light-skinned Thai women, mostly girls from northern Thailand. Many establishments that target white Westerners (*farang*) feature Thai women with darker skin, in recognition of a longstanding erotic preference. Other Western-oriented services include sex shows, call girls, and specialists in oral sex (Manderson 1995:305–329, 1992:451–475). Japanese tourists can purchase Japanese-style sex baths. Middle-class Thai or Chinese Thai can visit "curtain hotels" (*rongraem manrut*), where a couple drives up and parks in a numbered parking space outfitted with a curtain, so that they can walk directly from their car to a hotel room without being seen. Working-class Thai men can take advantage of low-priced sex services at inexpensive brothels, including ones disguised as barber shops or restaurants.

A "curtain hotel" (2002). (Photograph by the author.)

Young virgins are provided for Chinese customers in deference to the Chinese folk belief that sleeping with a virgin will drive away bad luck and enable an old man to regain his youthful vigor (Matsui 1989:65). Local Chinese newspapers print listings for Chinese clubs with assorted "star singers" that include pictures and even details about a performer's age, height, and weight. Mandarin-speakers can visit nightclubs where the entertainers include undocumented Chinese women. Customers hang a garland of flowers with currency attached around a singer's neck after she finishes a song. Later the performer may join the customer at his table, and he will offer to buy her food and drink. They may also negotiate the price of a "date," which may or may not include sex. One singer I met lived in a luxury apartment and sometimes earned extra money by bringing preferred clients home to spend the night.

As ever-increasing numbers of men visit brothels, the old Teochiu euphemism for visiting a brothel, "to have tea" (*imcha*), has been superseded by the term "visiting women" (*thieo phuying*). "Much of the Thai population," note Wathinee Boonchalaksi and Philip Guest in *Prostitution in Thailand*, "is directly touched by prostitution, either through working as prostitutes, financially benefiting from prostitution, or paying for the services of prostitutes" (1994:38). Scholars have noted that men's widespread use of prostitutes is a key factor in the prevalence of sexually transmitted diseases in Thailand (Bamber, Hewison, and Underwood 1997:59–60; Beyrer 1998:23–32; Celentano 1996:122, 127).[11] Chaochu masculinity influences sexual practices and discourses both inside and outside the home. As Annette Hamilton points out, "for the Thai male, sex with prostitutes becomes an element of his display of masculinity. However, he can also undertake socially desired proofs of masculinity by marrying a 'respectable' girl" (1997:163). For men in Thai society—regardless of their ethnicity—the boundaries between marital and extramarital sex are quite flexible.

Transforming Chinese Masculinities

When two friends, an older man and a younger woman, offered to give me a tour of a brothel, the man, Su Xiansheng, pulled his car right up to the front door and requested valet parking. This was unusual. In the past when we had gone out together, he would drive around and around looking for free parking on the street. As he proudly led us into the brothel, I realized that he was showing off. Not only was he visiting a brothel, he had brought two women with him!

This process—the change from money-oriented masculinity to what I call economically responsible chaochu masculinity—is expressed in everyday talk and activities. Earning enough money to support the family and to send remittances back to China is no longer enough; they want to become a chaochu as well. In discussing their changed sexual behavior, chinkao men often emphasized their responsibility. This responsibility includes "supporting the family," "earning money," "doing business," and "being head of the family."

Chinkao men often stressed that their extramarital sexual encounters "did not disrupt the family." Not disrupting the family meant no phone calls, no letters, no visits, and, most important, no children from other women, which could lead to a marital conflict or inheritance issue. A few men even underwent vasectomies to prevent accidental impregnation.[12] Wang Mama, the woman who spent her entire salary on family expenditures and ended up with no money when she retired, was surprised to discover that her husband had had a vasectomy *after* her tubal ligation.

Today chinkao men appear to be developing a new version of middle-class respectability. They reinforce their economically responsible "Chinese" version of chaochu masculinity by representing Thai men as irresponsible, because "they gamble, drink, and 'lay eggs' everywhere," but "do not support the family." Actually, such ethnicizing is quite class-specific. By differentiating responsible chaochu from irresponsible ones, chinkao men are in effect denigrating the chaochu masculinity of the Thai working class. What is noteworthy is not whether such assertions are "true," but rather *how* chinkao men use their own economic capital and Chinese cultural identity to marginalize Thai chaochu masculinity.

A Chinese saying—"a domestic flower does not smell as sweet as a wild flower, but a wild flower does not last as long as a domestic flower" (*jiahua buru yehua xiang, yehua buru jiahua chang* [M])—is sometimes used to explain the differences chinkao men perceive between Chinese and Thai women's bodies. The chinkao woman's body, the "domestic flower," is expected to provide regular coitus, children, and family stability, while a Thai sex worker's body, the "wild flower," supplies temporary exoticized sexual experiences. These expressions characterize male chinkao sexual practices and specifically reflect the free movement between the domains of marital and extramarital sex. The men's flexible sexuality, constructed in conjunction with class and ethnicity, reflects the formation of sexual desire in specific cultural practices. For example, Fong Laoban, who haggled over the price of a bowl of soybean milk, proudly stated that he had slept with a Japanese woman, an elite Thai woman, and many young Thai women, and that he could still have intercourse even though he was in his seventies. His chaochu masculinity was articulated through the ethnic background and class status of the women he slept with.

In a conversation about men patronizing brothels, a friend told me she could always tell when her chinkao father had been to one. "How?" I asked. "He always bought things for us," she said, "like fresh fruit or snacks. And he became soft. He was just different," she continued. "I could tell." A chinkao man sometimes used gifts to prove that he was still a "responsible" man despite his outside sexual activities. Wives and children would pretend not to know as long as he did not visit brothels too frequently.

Although some chinkao men boasted about their sexual activities outside the home, others tried to be more circumspect. At a weekend gathering, several friends and I were discussing what constituted being a "good husband" in Bangkok, and one man suggested, "getting home on time." Everyone laughed. It was quite common for men to use the excuse of heavy traffic or having to work late to cover up an affair or a brothel visit.

But when "paper is unable to wrap fire" (*zhi baobuliao huo* [M])—meaning when one's secret, the "fire," inevitably comes out—men often showered their wives with gifts in compensation. The gifts might vary—fruit, jewelry, even a parcel of land—but the purpose was always the same. It was not merely to make up for a discovered indiscretion or to smooth things over with a disgruntled wife, but also to reinforce one's masculine identity as an economically responsible husband, thereby justifying extramarital sexual behavior.

However, Mu Bobo, who displayed hundreds of photographs of himself in his picture halls, never hid his brothel visits from his wife. He believed that his hard work running a successful enterprise and his ability to make big donations earned him the "right" to purchase sexual services. He proudly stated: "I am a free man. None of my wives and children would interfere with my life and ask where I go. Many men would tell their wives a lie if they went out to have fun. I just tell the truth, that I went to 'indulge in dissipation'" (*huatian jiudi* [M]).

In this project, not one chinkao man divorced his wife. A man who divorces his wife to marry another woman is often viewed as one who "drinks the water but forgets the one who dug the well" (*he shui wangle wajingren* [M]). Middle-class respectability constrains chinkao men from seeking a divorce, but not from visiting brothels. Out of different interests and concerns, both husbands and wives choose to maintain their troubled marriages.

It is the chinkao men, more than the women, who have changed their sexual behavior in Thai society. This transformation, a continuous process taking place in everyday activities, includes emphasizing their own class respectability, marginalizing Thai masculinity, ethnicizing women's bodies, commercializing the conjugal relationship, and becoming polygynists by manipulating the marriage laws.

Strategies for Maintaining Cultural Identity

Ethnicizing others is a powerful way to articulate one's own cultural identity. Class-privileged chinkao women ethnicize female sex workers in an effort to conform to the ideal of dutiful motherhood and to safeguard family interests. In comparison, chinkao men, who share sexual privileges with Thai men, choose to ethnicize working-class Thai men. A positive presentation of self becomes a negative definition of the Other. As Stuart Hall points out, "identity is always, in that sense, a structured representation which only achieves its positive through the narrow eye of the negative" (1991:21).

Jin Nainai, the exhausted teacher who often fell asleep grading her students' homework, told me that "prostitutes are too lazy to do real work, they just sell the dirtiest part of their bodies." In Thai society, sex workers—or any women who have sex with men other than their husbands—are labeled "bad women" or "women who sell their bodies" (*ying khaitua*).[13] Jin Nainai called sex workers "barbaric female ghosts" (*fanpo gui* [M]). "Barbaric" means foreign or uncivilized, in contrast to the "civilized" Chinese. By linking the imaginary ghost with barbaric women, she was not only reinforcing ethnic stereotypes but also putting her beliefs into the discourse by marginalizing others.

Although chinkao women often marginalize sex workers, they seldom denigrate Thai men's economic power, for that would seem to endorse their husbands' economically responsible extramarital sexual activities. This does not mean that chinkao women never refer to Thai men as irresponsible. They do, but in different contexts, such as when they warn their daughters not to marry Thai men. Conversely, while chinkao men usually refer to sex workers as sexy and desirable objects, they have no hesitation about marginalizing "irresponsible" Thai chaochu.

It is important to note that this gender-specific ethnicizing does not take place in isolation. Chinkao men and women in effect draw one another into a dialogue to reconfirm their gendered middle-class Chinese-ness. By contrasting, on the one hand, the responsible Chinese man with the irresponsible Thai man and, on the other hand, the faithful Chinese woman with the dirty Thai prostitute, chinkao men and women both rearticulate ethnic boundaries and class respectability from a gendered standpoint.

To protect their emergent middle-class interests, chinkao women had to rework their attitude toward their husbands' sex partners. In southern China's emigrant areas, a minor wife was accepted as a family member and lived in the same house with the major wife, but sex workers were condemned. In Thailand chinkao women reversed this; as they often put it, the husband "can visit prostitutes, but he should not have a minor wife" (*thieo-dai tae maiao mianoi/keyi wan, buneng qu xiaolaopo* [M]). Although they denigrate Thai sex workers, chinkao women have come to prefer sex workers to minor wives.

When Wang Mama discovered that her husband had concealed his vasectomy from her, she ignored it. But when he tried to convince her that it would benefit the family business if he married his "hard-working" mistress, Wang Mama refused. Instead, attempting to disrupt their relationship, she humiliated his mistress in public. She remained in her marriage not because of any attachment to her husband, but because she saw no good alternative. She had devoted her life to bringing up the family and building up the family business. Marriage and family encompassed everything she held dear: her children, work, social network, and class status. So she chose to remain in the marriage and maneuver within it, thus maintaining her hard-earned class status and guaranteeing her children's inheritance rights. I will never forget her telling me that she lived her married life as though she were "conducting a performance" (*zuoxi* [M]).

Like Wang Mama, many believe that a minor wife threatens family interests whereas sex workers are less likely to disrupt kinship ties because there is no "relationship" in the temporary exchange of sexual services for cash. Chinkao women enhance their negotiating position with their husbands by distinguishing a sex worker from a minor wife. Paradoxically, by perpetuating male sexual privilege, the sex industry tends to stabilize families by limiting polygyny.

Immigration to Thailand did not alleviate the subordination of chinkao women to men. Nei/wai family gender politics embedded in kinship, the division of labor, and heterosexuality have not lost their asymmetrical qualities. Rather, the gender inequality embedded within immigration, production, and reproduction is inextricably linked with sexual inequality. Middle-class identity and gender-specific sexual practices are mutually reinforcing.

Chinkao women have often had to struggle doubly hard to cope with the geographic and cultural disruptions of immigration. Besides adding an income-producing job to their nonpaying domestic work, they have had to endure their husbands' extramarital sexual activities. The women, who are being changed themselves, have also had to cope with how their husbands are changing as a result of their upward economic mobility and the integration of local concepts of masculinity.

Part III

The Lukchin
Experience

6

Hybrid Identities

Cultural identity . . . is a matter of 'becoming' as well as of 'being'. It belongs to the future as much as to the past. It is not something which already exists, transcending place, time, history and culture. Cultural identities come from somewhere, have histories. But, like everything which is historical, they undergo constant transformation. Far from being eternally fixed in some essentialised past, they are subject to the continuous 'play' of history, culture and power.

—STUART HALL, "Cultural identity and diaspora"

PEI JIE, who came from a family that owned a prominent movie theater, went against the wishes of her chinkao parents by marrying a Thai man. Several years later, when she went to visit her injured husband after his automobile accident, she found an unfamiliar woman sitting beside his hospital bed:

> I said to my husband, "You have not introduced your friend to me." "I am not his friend, I am his wife," the woman said. I was shocked. I burst out, "Oh, you are the singer," because I suddenly remembered that I had been told, but had not believed, that he had a mistress who was a singer. She said, "No. I am a student from abroad." I felt totally lost. I did not know what to do. My husband asked her to leave. She was very angry. Later she came back with my husband's clothes. She threw the clothing in front of him and said that she would not see him anymore.
> I told my husband that he had to choose between us. He said that she was pregnant, and that he would leave her after the birth of the child. I thought that if I treated him well he would come back to me, but that did not work. [After several years] when that woman had his third child, he still did not divorce her. I could not put up with him any more. I did not tell our children until after I divorced him.

I had met Pei Jie, a senior administrator in an insurance company, at a social gathering sponsored by the Chinese Thai Women's Association, an organization founded in 1986. After her divorce she had worked at two jobs to support her four children, and rarely had time for ballroom dancing, an activity she had enjoyed as a college student in Australia. But now that her children had graduated from college, she had enthusiastically taken up dancing again.

One Saturday night Pei Jie took me to a restaurant where the entire second floor was taken over by dancers. Twelve circular tables had been placed along three sides of the room so that when the participants took a break they could eat and drink. I noticed that there were more women than men, and that some women danced together. Most of the dancers, including the restaurant owner, were second- and third-generation lukchin. While the other women danced with a boyfriend, a husband, or a female friend, Pei Jie danced exclusively with Sua, a handsome Thai man in his late thirties she had hired for about US $6 an hour to dance with her. As they danced, she seemed to be transported back to her college days, and appeared completely unconcerned that dancing with a young man might provoke gossip. Although she was an excellent dancer and older than Sua, she still addressed him as her "teacher" (*achan*). But it was she who decided where to go, how long to dance, and when to leave. The pretense of a teacher-student relationship disguised her real authority.

As I observed the room and watched the dancers, what struck me was the multiplicity of symbols and meanings present in the same space. The Chinese restaurant, decorated with portraits of the Thai royal family, Chinese landscape paintings, and a Chinese altar alongside a Thai Buddha statue, was transformed into a Westernized dance floor. As the couples relaxed during the intermission, some sang karaoke, mostly Thai and southern Chinese folk songs; others snacked on Teochiu and Thai dishes. But the novelty of the scene made any analysis difficult. I felt like I could smell, feel, and taste something new, but it was not something I could clearly articulate in words. My challenge was to find a meaningful way to describe the new cultural practices hidden beneath so many hybrid and fragmented symbols. Perhaps examining a beauty pageant is a good place to start, for it will reveal the new ethnic politics that the Thai state began to promote in the 1990s.

Miss Chinatown

As part of the Chinese New Year's celebration, the first Miss Chinatown beauty contest was held in downtown Bangkok in 1992.[1] According to the organizers, the purposes of the pageant were to acknowledge people who were "Thai with Chinese origin," to "revive Chinese customs," and to "strengthen Thai-Chinese culture." In a roped-off VIP section, distinguished guests included Thailand's vice prime minister, the minister of education, Thailand's air force commander, several high-ranking generals, China's ambassador to Thailand, the presidents of the major Chinese associations, and numerous Chinese Thai entrepreneurs. Thai officials coordinated the celebration; entrepreneurs and Chinatown shop owners sponsored it.

The celebration started with a parade. A marching band playing John Philip Sousa's "The Stars and Stripes Forever" was followed by Chinese dragon dancers, lion dancers, stilt-walkers, acrobats, floats carrying beauty contestants, floats bearing Chinese shrines from temples, synchronized dance teams, and a group of musicians performing southern Chinese folk songs. Parade participants included a wide range of people: five-year-old kindergarten kids and elderly grey-haired chinkao; middle school students and Thai bureaucrats; tai chi masters and vendors hawking fruit.

"The Chinese and the Thai are as close as family members" banner in Nakhon Sawan's Chinese New Year celebration (1992). (Photograph by the author.)

A shop owner makes an offering to the dragon by tying cash to its whiskers (1992). (Photograph by the author.)

Together with the near-continuous explosion of firecrackers and the beating of gongs and drums, the dragon dancers bowed to each shrine set up outside a shop, wishing the owner prosperity in the New Year. To have the exalted Chinese dragon dance in front of a shop, or better yet, inside the shop, would bring good luck in the coming year. Shop owners usually presented the dragon with a *hongbao* [M], a red envelope with "lucky money" inside, to pay their respects and purchase the dragon's protection. Some shop owners offered substantial amounts of money to lure the dragon inside their establishments and ensure a longer and therefore more propitious visit. One banker set up a big table with incense, candles, offerings of food, and a large container filled with water and oranges, two symbols of prosperity. When the dragon arrived, it splashed in the water and playfully swatted at the oranges with its tail.

After the parade, a number of performances took place. The most memorable was a Teochiu opera. Since Teochiu opera had been neglected for decades, few native Teochiu speakers aspired to become opera singers. As a consequence the opera's organizers had recruited Lao performers from northeastern Thailand. Although they could not speak Teochiu, the actors sang the opera by memorizing every word. A new "Chinese culture" was created: Teochiu Chinese watched ethnic Lao performers imitate Teochiu opera.

As I was videotaping the New Year's celebration, four policemen walked in front of my camcorder and saluted a shop owner at the entrance to his store; in return, the shopkeeper gave each one a red envelope. The police officers' visits and the Chinese shopkeepers' bribes formed part of another Chinese New Year's custom in Bangkok: buying protection from the police.

It was the eve of the national election and wall banners declaring "May Prosperity and Happiness Reign in the New Year"—written in Thai but based on the Teochiu pronunciation and signed by various candidates for political office—were plastered throughout Chinatown. Major General Chamlong Srimuang, a lukchin campaigning for prime minister, attended the festival and paid homage to the Chinese goddess Guanyin at Tianhua Hospital. He canvassed the crowd while his supporters passed out flyers printed in Thai and Chinese affirming his moral beliefs. His flyer praised "diligence, frugality, trustworthiness, and modesty" and denounced "drunkenness, compulsive gambling, and avarice." Chamlong hoped to advance his political career by emphasizing his Chinese-ness.

The climax of the celebration was the crowning of Miss Chinatown. More than seventy young girls participated. All of them lived within the 1.43 square kilometers of the Sampantavong district where Chinatown is located. They wore Thai silk outfits, swimsuits, skimpy Western dresses with elaborate lace, or other provocative attire provided by sponsors. The winner and the four runners-up donned *qipao* [M], the classic Han Chinese dress, only slit much higher up the leg than usual. The beauty contest stage became a place where identity and culture could be put on display. The judges were mostly men. I overheard one male judge being teased by his friend, "You better bring along a bowl to hold your drool."[2] The Miss Chinatown beauty pageant echoed nineteenth-century constructions of Chinese-ness in which a Chinese woman's worthiness depended chiefly on her sexuality and ethnicity.

While a Miss Chinatown pageant was unprecedented, beauty pageants are nothing new for the Thai nation-state. The reconstruction of a sense of beauty has been a long-running political project.[3] In 1934, just two years after the monarchy ended, the first Miss Siam beauty pageant was held (Van Esterik 1996:211). It was a defining moment, for the new regime used state-authorized beauty contests to reconfigure "Siamese-ness." Later, Prime Minister Luang Phibun's administration sought to upgrade a Thai woman's appearance while promoting "a Thai economy for Thais." Women were requested to wear makeup, hats, and gloves in order to appear as "modern" as women in Western society (Reynolds 1991:7; Van Esterik 1996:213).

The Miss Chinatown pageant reflected a new kind of ethnic politics: the construction of Chinese identity through exoticized Chinese culture and women's bodies. On national television the Thai master of ceremonies remarked that the beauty contest gave the nation an opportunity to view these "beautiful Chinese women" and to "think about Chinese culture and customs" (*nukthung watthanatham prapheni khong chaochin*). Beauty itself had become a serious matter because the state was using its power not only to rearticulate a new construction of "Chinese-ness," but also to reinvent itself in relation to this new Chinese-ness. So-called Chinese culture and customs were part of the Thai national project of reimagining the Thai nation as a multiethnic, multicultural community. The new Chinese-ness had a distinctly hybrid nature: a Sousa march juxtaposed with Thai and Chinese folk songs; Laotian actors mimicking Teochiu opera; and a commentator speaking both Thai and Teochiu while broadcasting the event. Dragon dances, lion dances, and Chinese shrines were intermixed with women in swimsuits, Thai silk, Chinese qipao, and Western dresses. These hybrid cultural symbols also embodied the Chinese Thai efforts to join in the Thai national project; they were happy to take advantage of their temporarily revalued ethnicity—but only up to a point, because this display did not exist in a regulation-free zone.

The exotic and hybrid cultural symbols had been consciously selected—some by government officials and others by the Chinese Thai themselves—as part of an effort to create a certain type of Chinese subject against the backdrop not only of Thailand but also of the West. Although Teochiu opera is now part of the state-sponsored celebration, it is still regarded as old-fashioned. The same is true for the red envelope of lucky money. Giving it out enables the Chinese Thai to simultaneously reveal their ethnic background and demonstrate their economic power. Yet the act of purchasing protection from symbolic dragons and from beat cops reveals an awareness of two very different kinds of constraints. Symbolically, the dragon represents Chinese cultural logic, while the police represent the Thai state. Chinese entrepreneurs are buying protection from *both* the Chinese and the Thai regimes. Meanwhile, the two symbols are not equally situated, because the Chinese dragon needs permission from the Thai state to perform. The tension between agency and structural constraint lies *hidden* beneath the surface of hybridity.

Boundary Crossings

The intersections between different cultural symbols open up new spaces in which the lukchin can negotiate for power. An increasing number of lukchin women are challenging gendered regulations to a degree that their mothers could hardly have imagined.

In the early 1980s, forty-six-year-old Lu Laoshi asked a male Thai friend to register a fictitious marriage with her so that she and her husband, Geng Xiansheng, could buy a house. (She had lost her Thai citizenship and the privilege of buying property by marrying a Chinese citizen.) Her plan was to register the bogus marriage, purchase the house, and then divorce her fake husband. But her real husband was furious when she told him what she had done. Even though he knew that his wife's only motive was to enable the family to buy a house, he saw it as a terrible insult. How dare his wife have two husbands, even if one was phony! Lu Laoshi had to get an immediate divorce.

In fact, by birth Geng Xiansheng was a Thai citizen. But his Thai mother was so afraid of her only son being drafted into the army that she sent him off to his father's hometown in Shantou, China, and later registered him as a Chinese citizen when he reentered Thailand. Before World War II, this maneuver was a common strategy practiced by Chinese immigrant men and their Thai wives who wanted their Thai-born children to be Chinese.

Just as her mother-in-law had manipulated the immigration laws decades ago, Lu Laoshi wanted to manipulate the Thai marriage registration law for her and her husband's economic benefit. Since polygynists routinely exploited or evaded marriage registration requirements, Lu Laoshi saw nothing wrong with registering a false marriage to serve her family's interests. However, while Geng Xiansheng accepted his mother's legal maneuvering to win him Chinese citizenship, he perceived his wife's scheme as humiliating. His mother's legal game had deprived him of privileges granted Thai citizens, but it enhanced his Chinese identity; his wife's legal game challenged his masculinity and his authority. Geng Xiansheng valued his masculine honor more than owning a house.

Lu Laoshi's legal maneuver challenged the very foundation of patriarchy. A married woman is conceived of as "*pen yao, pen ruan,*" which means that she is "the house and home." Within the category of wife, a major wife is identified as a "big home" (*banyai*) and a minor wife as a "small home" (*banlek*). There is no term for "major husband" or "minor husband" in Thai or in Chinese—there is just "husband." The very categories held up as "natural" are in fact created by the politics of marriage.

Lu Laoshi and her husband obviously had different agendas. Each was acted upon by outside forces and applied gender-specific strategies in dealing with them. Such strategies sometimes pull the spouses in quite different directions. Geng Xiansheng defended his masculine honor and the patriarchal system; Lu Laoshi manipulated the legal system for the sake of her family interests and middle-class status.[4] Lu Laoshi's knowledge of marital law, her newly acquired social networks, and her desire for a middle-class lifestyle motivated her to attempt to cross boundaries, even if she was unsuccessful.

เจ๊ก

From Chinese to Thai to Chek

Achan Paisan's birth mother was Thai. At age six he was sent to Shantou, China, to be raised by his polygynist father's Chinese wife. He returned to Thailand after finishing high school. Achan Paisan, now a university professor, described himself as "Thai mixed with Chinese" (*Thai Pon chin*). The mixture refers to the fusion of his Thai and Chinese "blood" (*luat/xuetong* [M]). He believed that his identity was connected with his blood heritage: "50 percent Chinese and 50 percent Thai."

Identity, from his perspective, is also a cultural performance. He emphasized his ability to act "more Thai" than those who are considered "real Thai." As he put it, "I am more Thai than many real Thai; I am also Chinese enough to say that I am a Thai." He shifted between this behavioral notion of identity and a naturalized biological one, positioning himself both within and outside the categories of Thai and Chinese, but never within the category of "authentic" Thai or Chinese. Clearly, his identity was not clear-cut but conditional.

Other Chinese Thai experience the tension between authentic and inauthentic that Achan Paisan felt. Mali Bobo, whom we discussed in chapter 3, also used competing symbols—claiming Chinese-ness but deflecting its negative associations by marrying a Thai woman. His "authentic" Chinese-ness was disguised by his wife's Thai-ness. Achan Paisan considered himself both Thai and Chinese; a single identification failed to accommodate the actual experience of his cultural membership. At one moment, Thai and Chinese might compete within him, but at another moment one might camouflage the other.

Being Thai is always an ambiguous concept, in part because positive Thai-ness can be articulated only through the negative Other (Thongchai 1994:5). There is no definitively essential quality of Chinese-ness or Thai-ness; both are always relational, negotiable, and continuously transforming. Moreover, as different constructions of identity emerge, one construction does not simply replace its predecessor; rather, at any given moment there are several competing valuations of Chinese-ness—some positive, some negative, and some both positive and negative, depending on the context. In addition, the present constructions of Chinese identity echo those of the past. Identity transformations that began in the nineteenth century for the first generation are continuing for the second and third generations.

To be seen as "Thai" is particularly meaningful for those Chinese Thai who have integrated themselves into Thailand's power structure. One former Thai prime minister, a Chinese descendant, displayed his Thai-ness by decorating his home as though it were a Thai museum, exhibiting authentic art and cultural symbols that many "real Thai" could not afford. His social and economic capital helped him to accumulate cultural capital. Of course, a "real Thai" would have no need to arrange his home in this fashion in order to prove Thai-ness. But for the prime minister, his Chinese ancestry could still cast some suspicion on him. Selectively deploying authentic Thai symbols is a key strategy for disguising a non-Thai "origin"; it creates enough ambiguity to protect the individual from being singled out.

But even emphasizing Thai-ness and keeping silent about a Chinese "origin" does not guarantee success. On 18 September 1996, Prime Minister Banharn Silpa-archa was accused of being an "illegal alien" because his father was believed to have immigrated to Thailand in 1937, five years after Banharn was born. One newspaper editorialized, "The Thai people have to ask themselves why they need a Prime Minister with such a shady background" (Somchai 1996).[5] The opposition also pointed out that in 1979—twenty-five years after Banharn's father had passed away—the old man's nationality, which had previously been registered as Chinese, had been changed to Thai (Somchai and Wut 1996; *Bangkok Post*, 20 September 1996).

Prime Minister Banharn quickly responded that he was Thai by birth because his father had immigrated to Siam in 1907. He also pointed out that aliens were not required to register in Siam until 1936. In addition, as Thai law requires that all men holding Thai nationality must register for military service when they turn seventeen, he then displayed his military registration papers to support his claim.[6] Regarding the change of his father's nationality from Chinese to Thai, Banharn blamed human error and insisted that although he knew of the discrepancy, he could not make the correction because according to Interior Ministry regulations only his father himself could file a complaint to have the mistake corrected, and his father had already died (*Bangkok Post* 20 September 1996). Nonetheless, threatened with the defection of three of his coalition partners, Banharn agreed to resign within seven days to avoid the humiliation of losing his office through a vote of no confidence by the parliament (*Bangkok Post*, 1 October 1996). His "origin"—made complicated by changing regulations and shifting political winds—dramatically altered his political career.

Knowing how to play identity games is a key to success in Thailand's ever-shifting political theater, as illustrated by the case of Major General Chamlong, the politician who visited Chinatown during Chinese New Year. When he was young, Chamlong concealed his Chinese background in order to enroll at Chulachomkhao Royal Military Academy, deftly bypassing the requirement that all Academy students demonstrate that both grandfathers had been born in Thailand. His Thai name, Chamlong Srimuang, provided him with cultural camouflage. However, when he campaigned for mayor of Bangkok in 1985, Chamlong publicized his Chinese name, Lu Jinghe, and declared that his father was a Chinese immigrant and his mother a lukchin; he did this to win votes from Bangkok's large middle-class Chinese Thai population. This was a calculated political risk, but Bangkok's middle-class Chinese Thai responded to his call with enthusiasm, and he was elected. And after winning the mayor's race, Chamlong went back to Guangdong, China, to pay homage to his ancestors.

While traveling to emigrant areas in southern China in 1991, I happened to visit Chamlong's father's birthplace. I was amazed to see that Chamlong's portrait had replaced Mao's at the village Communist Party headquarters. I was told that Chamlong's success "brought honor to the village." By playing on his identity at politically appropriate times, Chamlong advanced both his military and his political career.

In running for prime minister in 1992, Chamlong not only made use of his Chinese identity but also built up an image as a devout Buddhist by publicizing his ascetic lifestyle: eating only one vegetarian meal a day and abstaining from sex with his wife. He also wore a "curious hairstyle half-way between a military crew-cut and a monastic tonsure" (Chang Noi 1997). His public image as a "monk in lay clothing" was a way to challenge other politicians who were known for being corrupt or womanizers (Keyes 1989:121–122). Integrating Buddhism into his politics became a key strategy for reaching out to people throughout Thailand, for Chamlong realized that emphasizing his Chinese-ness in a national election had its limitations. He embodied a series of contradictions: having a wife but no sexual life, being a military leader but living like a monk, emphasizing either his Thai-ness or his Chinese-ness depending upon the circumstances. His identity was subject to the continuous play of identity politics and cultural differences.

Nidhi Aeuisrivong, a lukchin and one of Thailand's leading historians, suggested a few years ago that the formerly derogatory term *chek* should be used to refer to the Chinese in Thailand.[7] He and others have argued that it succinctly articulates the special circumstances or special characteristics of the Chinese who live within Thai society (Chang Noi 1996). At the very least, this reappropriation of chek—now just beginning—represents a new way of constructing Chinese-ness that is in direct opposition to the nation-state's construction of it, while also publicly acknowledging the discrimination that the Chinese Thai have endured. Claiming chek-ness reveals a new awareness of the relations between the Chinese Thai and the Thai nation-state, between the Chinese of the nineteenth century and the present, between ethnic Chinese in Thailand and the Chinese in China, and between Thai and Chinese within Thai society. Whether lukchin conceive of themselves as "Chinese" or "Thai" or "chek" is largely shaped by power relations, the global political weather, and the Thai state's ethnic politics.

Most Chinese Thai that I encountered still found the term chek too painful and negative to reclaim. Nevertheless, many lukchin have experienced a struggle similar to that of Achan Paisan in their attempts to create a flexible identity between the categories Chinese and Thai. Chek or Chinese Thai culture is created through hybridization, an active process of mutual borrowing and differentiation.

———

The Chinese Thai have played a key role in hybridizing Thai culture, but at the same time Chinese culture in Thailand has also become hybridized by Thai culture. While different cultural practices coexist, "new" cultural configurations are often reframed according to the "old" cultural logic.

The conceptual space between categories in this project is hardly an "alien territory" (Bhabha 1994:38). It is "alien" only to those of us accustomed to thinking in terms of dichotomies such as Thai/non-Thai or East/West. Such simple divisions cannot capture the complexities of everyday life. In the spaces between different categories and ideologies, the Chinese Thai selectively draw on their history and their present, engage in ever-changing ethnic politics, and make use of their growing economic, political, and cultural influence.

7

What's in a Wedding?

We need to attend to how places in the non-West differently plan and envision the particular combinations of culture, capital, and the nation-state, rather than assume that they are immature versions of some master Western prototype.

—AIHWA ONG, *Flexible Citizenship*

IN THE SUMMER of 1991 Cao Mama, the chinkao woman in chapter 4 who was so pressed for time that she did three things at once, excitedly told me that her eldest son, Daeng, was going to marry Nawarat. The bride- and groom-to-be came from Chinese immigrant families; both had earned M.A. degrees and held high-paying jobs. Rather than accepting an arranged marriage like their parents had, they had dated first to see if they were compatible and then asked for their parents' approval. Daeng and Nawarat had also decided to live with Cao Mama after they wed. By treating marriage as an individual affair and a family matter, they not only conveyed their respect for their parents but also achieved their goal. This illustrates how subtle marital practices can be. Instead of a dramatic change, modern practices combine with conventional ones. Reworking "traditions" becomes a part of almost every lukchin's life.

Cao Mama invited me to attend her son's wedding. To guarantee that I would be there on time, she also invited me to spend the night before the wedding at her home. Traffic can be so daunting—Bangkok has been called the "world's largest parking lot"—that wedding ceremonies often start before dawn to ensure that particular rituals can be conducted at predetermined auspicious times.[1] That night I joined Cao Mama, her family, and her live-in Thai domestic worker in preparing food, rearranging furniture, and organizing the house for the next day's rituals. Even with more than a dozen people running through it, the house did not seem crowded. It was a comfortable, sprawling three-story home that was brightly lit and had several

One of Bangkok's nicknames is "the world's largest parking lot" (1991). (Photograph by the author.)

bedrooms with air conditioners spaced throughout. That night I shared a room with Cao Mama's eldest daughter Yangping Jie, who had chosen to remain single.

The following chronology of Daeng and Nawarat's wedding, pulled mostly from my field notes, may give us some insight into the complex details of wedding rituals.

3:15 A.M. The alarm clock woke us up. We had only slept three hours.

4:00 A.M. We took four cars to go pick up the bride. Everyone was still very sleepy, but we managed to rouse ourselves. Daeng wore a dark-colored Western-style suit, a white shirt, and a red tie.

4:45 A.M. We arrived at Nawarat's house ahead of schedule, so we waited in the car until 5:15 A.M., the auspicious time for the groom to enter the bride's home. I noticed an inscription written in English on a small plaque attached to the gate of her house: "God Bless Our Home." Well, the bride was not a Buddhist. A crowd of Nawarat's relatives and friends were waiting for Daeng. They forged a human chain by holding gold necklaces and silver belts, symbolizing "silver and golden gates."[2] While enduring friendly laughter and good-natured teasing, Daeng had to hand out previously prepared sealed red envelopes containing lucky money as a "bribe." Some would not let him pass until he had given them several red envelopes. At the door to Nawarat's room more than a dozen people blocked his way, and some revelers who had already received their envelopes rushed back to block his path again. Daeng, by now perspiring heavily, carried a bouquet for Nawarat in one hand and kept pulling red envelopes out of his pocket with the other. When Daeng finally joined Nawarat, a professional photographer who had been waiting there took several pictures of them. Nawarat wore an elegant handmade white silk dress, with a red corsage pinned to her bodice.

Then, we were all served *yi*, a special Teochiu wedding soup consisting of sticky rice flour shaped into small round balls mixed together with two soft-boiled eggs and a dash of red dye for color. I was told that this wedding soup symbolized the wish for a harmonious marriage.

5:55 A.M. We drove back to the groom's home bringing Nawarat with us, along with her dowry and wedding gown. Traffic had started backing up; Yangping Jie worried aloud that the couple might miss the auspicious time for entering the groom's house. Our driver drove as fast as he dared, trying to catch every green light.

6:53 A.M. We arrived twelve minutes ahead of schedule. Nawarat and Daeng stayed in the car until 7:05 A.M., the most fortuitous moment for the couple to enter the groom's home together. While waiting for the couple to enter the house, I was astonished to discover that Cao Mama's entire family had fled. What was going on? I found out later that it was believed that a bride brought "evil spirits" (*shaqi* [M]) with her, who would "*chong*" [M], that is, "clash with" or "attack" people born in certain years.[3] The paradox was that while the marriage was regarded as a happy event, a daughter-in-law was perceived as potentially dangerous; she could disrupt the preexisting family structure.

7:15 A.M. Cao Mama and Yangping Jie led the couple in offering homage in front of more than a dozen different Buddha statues, ranging in size from one inch to more than two feet tall; these were positioned throughout all three floors of the house.

8:10 A.M. Three Chinese rituals took place: paying homage to the gods of Heaven and Earth, to ensure that they sanctioned this marriage; paying homage to ancestors by announcing the couple's marriage to them;

and holding a tea ceremony to pay respect to senior family members and relatives.

8:55 A.M. Chinese and Thai spirit worship. The couple paid their respects to *chaothi/tudi ye* [M], a Chinese house deity, whose shrine sat inside the house facing the front door. Next, the couple worshiped *san phraphum*, a Thai land deity, whose shrine sat out in the yard. The young couple knelt many times, offering prepared food and drinks to various gods and spirits, inside and outside the house. Cao Mama wanted every conceivable protective god and spirit to be well fed and worshiped properly.[4]

11:00 A.M. Nine Thai monks arrived to give the benediction. The bride and groom offered them food and gifts.

12:30 P.M. Our lunch was interrupted by a group of Thai youth who suddenly appeared in the front yard and performed a Chinese dragon dance, complete with drums and gongs, to offer their congratulations to the family. Everyone was surprised. Daeng responded quickly and gave them a red envelope with 400 baht [US $16] inside. "Wow, 400 baht for a three-minute performance," commented Yangping Jie. The Thai youngsters were then asked to leave because the longer they stayed, the more the family would feel obliged to pay. These clever and well-organized Thai youth knew that they would be paid well for their performance because no Chinese Thai will risk any unpleasantness on a wedding day. However, since there had been no public announcement, it remained a mystery how these youngsters knew that a Chinese wedding was taking place.

2:15 P.M. A beautician, who charged 1,300 baht for her services, arrived to prepare Nawarat. The makeup irritated her face, but Nawarat felt obliged to endure it. During that time the other guests and I visited the couple's "new room" (*xinfang* [M]), their bedroom in Cao Mama's house. The room was charming, but jammed full of household goods. The bed was also covered with various items; one that caught my eye was Nawarat's jewelry box: she had over a dozen pieces of gold jewelry. Next to the jewelry box was a silk handkerchief-sized red apron top.

The red apron top was something I had read about but had never seen at a wedding in China. It was embroidered with a pair of mandarin ducks, one duck holding a lotus blossom in its beak, the other holding a lotus fruit, each of which expresses the wish to be blessed with sons. The mandarin ducks symbolized the new couple; "*lianzi*" [M], the lotus fruit, represented "having one child after another." "*Zi*" can mean a child of either sex, but here its cultural connotation was unmistakably for sons, not daughters. The apron's pocket contained fertility tokens: red beans, green beans, dried longan, millet, and rice dyed red. Next to the apron top was a stack of new money. There were about ten bundles of 100-baht bills from Daeng's family and about twenty bundles of 500 baht bills from Nawarat's family.

4:00 P.M. The wedding mass was held at a Catholic church. Daeng wore the same suit and tie, but Nawarat changed into a Western-style white wedding gown with a tight bodice, long sleeves, a floor-length skirt with petticoats, and a veil. She also wore a red heart-shaped necklace.

7:00 P.M. The wedding reception took place at a Chinese restaurant. Nawarat in her white wedding gown and Daeng in his Western suit waited at the entry and greeted the guests as they arrived. There was much eating and drinking, laughter and applause. The bride and groom each made a short speech, then cut pieces of wedding cake to serve their elderly relatives and honored guests. Finally, the bride and groom walked throughout the dining room, thanking people and posing for pictures. It had been a long day for Daeng and Nawarat, and they appeared tired. Cao Mama, on the other hand, was still wildly energetic and seemed to have forgotten the chronic pain in her feet.

A Hybrid Wedding

Daeng and Nawarat's wedding was full of hybrid practices. The Catholic bride and Buddhist groom stood side by side and worshiped Chinese ancestors, paid homage to various Thai and Chinese gods and spirits, and then participated in a Catholic wedding mass. Together with their family members, they carefully wove Confucian, Thai Buddhist, and Christian rites together into a single wedding ceremony. The use of different symbols, which do not stand alone but rather are part of a larger social structure, can empower lukchin and chinkao and help them to accomplish certain goals or to express particular yearnings. Nawarat understood that her husband and her mother-in-law held these Buddhist gods, land deities, and Chinese ancestors and spirits in high esteem. In return, Daeng and Cao Mama participated in the Catholic wedding mass to honor Nawarat's religious beliefs. The act of crossing religious boundaries while simultaneously maintaining one's own beliefs enabled them to engage with an outsider not just in the religious sense, but also within the realm of kinship—where Nawarat was, at least at this moment, still considered an outsider.

Just as Cao Mama and her family crossed religious boundaries to strengthen their own interests, so the youthful Thai dragon dancers crossed ethnic boundaries by playing with a Chinese symbol. What is special in this case is that the Thai dancers initiated the interaction. The dragon dance revealed their knowledge of Chinese culture—how, when, and with whom to play the dragon card, a symbol of good luck and protection, in order to make some money.

We observed in chapter 6 that during the Chinese New Year's festivities the dragon was celebrated and deeply appreciated. Money tucked into the dragon's mouth or tied to its whiskers was a donation that would be redistributed back into the Chinese Thai community. At Daeng's wedding, however, because of the tension between ethnic Thai and Chinese, the meaning of the dragon dance changed. The Cao family viewed this dragon dance as a clever ploy to take advantage of them. Like the Chinatown shopkeepers who felt obliged to pay off the Thai police, they saw it as an extra fee they had to pay for being Chinese.

Nawarat and Daeng made use of both Thai and Chinese lucky numbers in the wedding rituals. For Thai, the number nine is a symbol of good luck. According to Stanley J. Tambiah, the mandala—a Buddhist cosmological concept—is composed of a nine-unit system of geometric points (1976:102–104). Nine is also conceived as the largest number, with ten restarting from zero. Linguistically, nine implies "making progress in all directions" (*kaona kaolang*). In other words, the number nine becomes an embodiment of Thai-ness, evoking a particular kind of imagination. On 31 December 1999, for example, to celebrate the new millennium, a mass marriage ceremony was held in Bangkok. The ceremony started at 9:59 A.M. with a Thai wedding parade. The procession was led by nine antique cars carrying 999,999 baht in cash, and gold worth 999,999 baht, followed by 2,000 grooms. The procession wound its way to the Exhibition Center where 2,000 brides were waiting. Then the 2,000 couples made merit by offering food to ninety-nine monks (Anjira 2000). The number nine was carefully integrated throughout the wedding ceremony: from the starting time, to the amount of money and gold carried along, even to the number of monks present. Although 9:59 A.M. may have been understood as a collectively auspicious time for the 2000 couples, the precise auspicious time for an individual wedding can be determined only by a monk or astrologer who has read the couple's horoscopes.[5] Having wedding rituals take place at exact times is believed to increase the likelihood of a successful marriage, which is why Daeng and Nawarat followed their schedule down to the minute.

When they invited monks into their home to conduct rituals, the Cao family followed Thai rules: they invited nine monks, not four.[6] When Daeng gave *sinsot*, a marriage payment, or "milk money,"[7] however, he used the number four. In Teochiu, the spoken word "four" is a lucky number because it sounds like the word "happiness." Four—two pairs—also symbolizes the notion that "good things come in pairs" (*haoshi chengshuang* [M]). In China, Cantonese speakers use the word eight because four, pronounced in Cantonese, resembles the word "dead." But since most Chinese Thai are Teochiu, four is used as a lucky number across dialect groups because it symbolizes "Chinese-ness." Thus in practice, the use of particular lucky numbers reflects culturally specific knowledge and cultural identity, and is much more than a simple statement about the bride's "worth" or the economic status of the families involved.

Certain tensions—some subtle, some more overt—always exist between the groom's family and the bride's family. One elderly lukchin woman I knew made a point of taking home a bowl, serving dish, and pair of chopsticks from each of her five daughters' wedding banquets. For her, this set of dishes symbolized the family's continued good luck, wealth, and prosperity; retrieving them countered her fear that her married-out daughter would carry the family's good fortune away to her husband's natal family.

In the following, I focus on three specific rites in this hybrid wedding—a Thai Buddhist rite, a Confucian tea ceremony, and a Catholic wedding mass—to reveal the hierarchies between holy men and laity, between men and women, between senior and junior, and also to inquire into how these rites both empower and constrain the participants. Symbols are engaged to evoke certain constellations of meaning, but in practice, these meanings are always only partial and always context-bound.

At the Buddhist blessing ritual the nine monks sat in ranked order in a long row in Cao Mama's living room, each in his proper place—inferior to the Buddha statue on the altar, but superior to the lay people. Facing the monks, the groom sat to the right of the bride because right is considered superior to left. The other participants sat at the end of the row of monks. At the center of this ritual was the altar, facing east. Religious and patriarchal hierarchies determine the seating arrangement, which is a spatial as well as a symbolic expression of the Thai social order.

Sitting on the floor with legs folded in the gender-specific Thai manner (men with their legs crossed, women with both legs folded to the side), the couple and their guests listened to the monks recite holy texts intended to ward off any dangers that might befall the newlyweds. The brief monks' prayers were regarded as essential; they sanctified the bond between the bride and groom, as well as that between their families. After the blessing, Daeng and Nawarat knelt reverently before the monks, bowed their heads, and pressed their palms together. Then they offered each monk a wrapped package containing a robe and daily necessities, including a toothbrush and toothpaste. These offerings are considered a crucial means of acquiring merit that will improve the couple's karma. Asymmetrical hierarchies between monks and lay people are expressed through institutionalized material offerings—a mixing of the cosmic and the social order that is taken for granted at weddings.

Compared with the Buddhist blessing ritual, the Confucian tea ceremony is more secular but no less hierarchical. The tea ceremony is a ritual of filial piety, an expression of family order. Nawarat knelt and served tea to Cao Mama, her mother-in-law; Cao Mama then placed a gold necklace around Nawarat's neck and pinned a pomegranate leaf in her hair. Gold symbolizes prosperity and protection; a pomegranate leaf symbolizes fertility and prosperity.[8] Thus Cao Mama, who had been transformed from an outsider to an insider by giving birth to sons, now passed on these patriarchal values through the pomegranate leaf.

While receiving tea and giving away gifts, the seniors also offered the new couple best wishes, stressing two main themes. The first emphasized the marital bond: "Love each other just a little bit but love for a long time" (*rak noinoi, rak nannan*); or "May you be together until you walk with a walking stick decorated with gold and diamonds" (*hai yuduaikan chonkaethao, chonthu maithao yotthong krabong yotphet*); or "May you be together for a hundred years" (*bainian daolao* [M]). The second urged biological reproduction: "May you have a dozen children" (*hai miluk penlo*); or "May you have a son as soon as possible" (*zaosheng guizi* [M]).

The Buddhist and Confucian rituals took place at home; the wedding mass took place at a Catholic church. During the Buddhist rituals and the Chinese tea ceremony, Daeng, Nawarat, and the others all followed the appropriate rules: they appeared knowledgeable about how to use different body language, and they carefully respected the solemnity of certain spaces. However, in the church, despite being directed by the priest to kneel, sit, or stand, some of Daeng's relatives continued to chat and take photographs—

behavior that reminded me of how most foreign tourists act when visiting a Thai temple.

Daeng, Nawarat, and their family members may have cared little about the original meanings of these rituals, but they intentionally chose them to articulate themselves in relation to others. Through a complex arrangement of hybrid cultural symbols, they legitimized their identities, values, and status both within and outside the family. The wedding rituals also allow the newlyweds and their families to articulate their middle-class thansamai, or modernity.

In *All That Is Solid Melts into Air*, Marshall Berman defines modernism as "any attempt by modern men and women to become subjects as well as objects of modernization, to get a grip on the modern world and make themselves at home in it" (1988:5). The families in this wedding selected cultural symbols that they found structurally and symbolically meaningful. Their articulation of thansamai was informed by their class status, a multiple consciousness, ethnic identities, and the ability to integrate cosmopolitan symbols into their everyday life. Daeng, Nawarat, and their families had much greater cultural and economic capital than many working-class families and therefore more opportunities to adopt cosmopolitan symbols and to consume fashionable goods. Their hybrid cultural taste is inseparable from being Chinese at home in Thailand.

An Interethnic Wedding

Nok, a female Thai friend who worked in a bank, planned to marry Somtop, a lukchin technician who worked at Bangkok's Don Muang International Airport. Somtop was proud of his bride: "Nok has light skin like a Chinese, and big eyes like a Thai. She likes to eat rice, too." Somtop's playful comments were rooted in ethnic stereotypes: Chinese have lighter skin, but unattractive slanted eyes; Thai have darker skin, but larger more attractive eyes. In Somtop's eyes, Nok combined the best of Chinese and Thai features.

Nok's family lived in a poor neighborhood. Their house was small, very hot, and badly ventilated. They could not afford an air conditioner, a symbol of middle-class status in tropical Bangkok. There was no shower in the bathroom; to bathe, they filled a bucket with water. Nok and her sister shared a tiny bedroom. Each time I stayed there, the three of us unrolled mats and slept on the floor. Nok's widowed mother shared a room with her mentally disabled youngest son. She had to work from 4:00 A.M. to 4:00 P.M.

and, unlike Cao Mama, she could not afford to hire a live-in maid. Although she worked as a cook, she was usually too exhausted to fix meals for her own family during the week. Instead, she bought a simple prepared dinner from a street vendor that cost from 7 to 10 baht per person. On special occasions the five of them would spend less than 100 baht for a "good" dinner.

When I spent the night before the wedding with them, Nok, her mother, and her unmarried older sister showed me the dresses and jewelry they would wear the following day. Nok, who earned 4,000 baht a month at her bank teller's job, paid 10,000 baht to rent a fashionable white Western-style wedding dress, and she also bought a Thai outfit—a white silk top and dark blue silk skirt. Nok's mother spent more than a month's salary—3,500 baht—on her own wedding clothes. And Nok's sister purchased two different outfits and also rented the expensive jewelry that she and her mother were to wear. Given their frugal daily life, I was surprised that the family was willing to spend so much of their limited income for a one-day event.

Around 4:00 A.M. on the morning of the wedding, just before he left home to pick us up, Somtop called Nok to make sure that she had packed the red apron top and reminded her to wear a pomegranate leaf in her hair. Nok half-jokingly said that her future mother-in-law was talking to her through Somtop.

At about 4:30 A.M. Somtop arrived in a van and picked us up. Then we drove to Nok and Somtop's house out in one of Bangkok's new suburbs. Although Somtop earned 16,000 baht a month, four times Nok's salary, he needed his parents' financial help in order to buy this new, spacious, three-bedroom house. To reduce expenses, Nok and Somtop and their families were conducting three ceremonies on the same day: a housewarming, an engagement celebration, and the wedding ceremony.

Nok wore her new Thai silk outfit in the morning. Some of her relatives also wore Thai dress. Somtop did not dress up; he wore an ordinary grey, short-sleeved shirt. In contrast to Nok and her family members, Somtop appeared deliberately informal.

After most of the relatives had arrived, the important rituals began. First, the young couple paid homage to the Chinese land deity. Next came the engagement ceremony: Somtop's representative asked for the hand of the bride and presented one gold necklace, two gold bracelets, a pair of gold earrings, and a diamond ring, together with 244,444 baht in cash as milk money. After the bride's representative accepted Somtop's marriage proposal, Nok, who had been sequestered in another room, came out and accepted these gifts. I was told that this amount of milk money was appropriate for a middle-class family in Bangkok. A working-class family usually gave milk money between 50,000 and 100,000 baht. A rich family would give between 400,000 and 800,000, or even a million baht.

At 9:00 A.M., nine Thai monks arrived. A long white string was wound around a Buddha statue, and then stretched through each room of the house before terminating in the hands of all the monks. This white string was considered sacred because the house and the wedding participants received the monks' blessings through it. I noticed that Nok's mother and her relatives were familiar with the Buddhist texts and chanted along with the monks at certain moments; this was in sharp contrast to the Buddhist blessing at Cao Mama's house, where only the monks chanted.

At Cao Mama's house, the monks had been seated at a circular table and offered food. But here the food offering was conducted in the Thai manner: the monks' empty alms bowls were lined up on a long table set up outside in the yard and everyone took turns filling these containers with various prepared dishes, rice, and desserts. When Nok and Somtop went to make their offering, we all stood in a circle to see which of them would be first to grab the serving ladle. Nok did. We all cheered. Symbolically, this means that Nok will hold the upper hand at home and that Somtop will have to listen to his wife.

While the lay people continued offering food and the Thai monks were still waiting inside the house to eat, the young couple began conducting a Chinese ancestor worship ceremony—only a few steps away from where they had just offered food to the monks. I was struck by how easily Thai and Chinese rituals could take place in the same space; it was impossible to tell where one culture stopped and the other began. While the newlyweds had made merit by offering food to the monks, a square table holding Chinese dishes, fruit, tea, and an incense holder had been set up for the Chinese ritual. Now the couple knelt, holding incense sticks in their hands, and bowed several times paying homage to Heaven and Earth, and to their ancestors. The two families mingled together throughout the Thai and Chinese rituals. The participants all seemed familiar with both the Thai Buddhist blessings and the Chinese rituals, which have clearly become part of Bangkok's shared social fabric.

After offering food to the Thai monks, the Chinese gods, and the ancestors, we began eating our lunch buffet of homemade Teochiu and Thai dishes. Suddenly, I noticed that we had divided into two groups: Nok's relatives were sitting on the floor, while Somtop's were seated in chairs. As a

In the foreground the young couple informs Heaven and Earth that they are getting married. In the background wedding guests make merit by giving alms to monks (1992). (Photograph by the author.)

friend of Nok's family, I sat on the floor with her older sister. Since there were not enough chairs for everyone to sit down and eat together, Nok's relatives had purposely left the chairs for Somtop's relatives. This division reflected different cultural habits. Chinkao often complained that it was physically difficult to sit on the floor with legs folded in the Thai manner. They preferred to sit on chairs or stools except when listening to the monks' chanting, because lay people are not allowed to sit higher than monks. Sitting separately, one group spoke Thai, the other Teochiu. It was amazing to see ethnic differences expressed in seating preferences during lunch rather than in the context of conducting rituals.

The Chinese tea ceremony followed the meal. Although this was new to her, Nok appeared to know how to act. The couple knelt and offered tea to their parents and senior relatives. In return, they received red envelopes and advice: "Marriage is like a pair of chopsticks. You need both parties in order to get things done." "A couple is like a tongue and teeth. Each needs the other. However, sometimes they clash. Do not be surprised when they clash. It is part of the marriage package." Endurance, harmony, and compromise were dominant themes in the blessings.

The evening reception took place at a medium-sized restaurant. Nok, in her white Western-style wedding dress, and Somtop, in a Western-style suit, greeted each guest. Around 700 friends and colleagues of the bride and groom attended the reception. Everyone signed the guest book and dropped off gifts. The cost of the gift varied according to the guests' social positions and relationship to the bride and groom. Many contributed cash, understanding that it would be used to help pay for the reception.

After most guests had arrived, the couple proceeded with the Thai Water Blessing ritual, *rot namsang*. The bride and groom knelt close together on a stage. Flower garlands were placed around their necks and two circles of connected twine were placed on their heads. Like Somtop, Nok pressed her palms together in front of her face and bowed slightly, showing respect through hand movements (*wai*). Senior family members and relatives approached the couple first. Each offered a blessing for their lifelong happiness while pouring water from a conch shell over the couple's hands. The sacred water, which had been blessed by the monks earlier that morning, was mixed with lotus petals—the blossom of fertility—and other flowers in elaborate patterns to symbolize the happy union. As the monks' blessing was passed to the couple through the white string at the house, the lay people's wishes for the couple's future happiness, financial prosperity, and healthy children were passed on to the newlyweds through the water. Then a band played popular Western and Thai music. Hiring a band to perform at the reception was another symbol of being thansamai. The band played so loudly that it was hard to make conversation, but most guests seemed to be enjoying it.

Weddings are often one of the most expensive, socially demanding, and status-affirming events in family and individual life. A wedding reception for a middle-class couple usually costs at least US $1,500 and often much more (Bamrung 1999).[9] Today, some big hotels market wedding packages directly to middle-class Chinese Thai. The Grand Hyatt Hotel in Bangkok, for example, offered three different "Chinese Wedding Packages," which included a Chinese menu, a five-tier wedding cake, a wedding registration book, and ice carvings.

Throughout the wedding rituals Nok performed her role dutifully, but privately she told me that she had no intention of being a subservient Chinese daughter-in-law. According to Chinese family gender politics, Somtop, an only son, should live with his parents and take care of them. According to Thai family gender politics, it is the youngest daughter, not a son, who lives with her parents and takes care of them. But Somtop had no desire to follow the "Thai tradition" of marrying into Nok's family, and Nok had no intention of following the "Chinese tradition" and living with her in-laws. Establishing a nuclear family instead of living in an extended family now constitutes being thansamai for many in contemporary Bangkok. Nok regarded her marriage as an opportunity to start living a middle-class thansamai life.

Neither Nok nor Somtop completely followed their culturally specific "traditions." In seeking their own thansamai identity, they worked both for and against cultural regulations with regard to being a filial son and a filial daughter. Nok and Somtop would never have been able to resist both Thai and Chinese family gender politics if they had not been able to call upon the idea and meaning of a thansamai middle-class life. They used hybrid cultural symbols and material goods to articulate their identities, their class respectability, and their ethnic worth.

A Capitalist Super Wedding

In March of 1992 I attended a truly elite wedding: the groom was the fourth brother of the president of Taixin, a powerful business conglomerate, and the bride was the youngest daughter of Bangkok Bank president, Chatri Sophonpanich. This time I did not know either family involved, so I was able to observe only two public rites: the Catholic wedding mass and the evening reception.[10]

This was a marriage between the offspring of two large and extremely powerful capitalist families. In the 1990s Bangkok Bank was Thailand's largest commercial bank and one of the largest in Southeast Asia, with assets of approximately US $40 billion and more than 25,000 employees.[11] As members of the elite class, the bride and groom did not need to rise at dawn and worry about missing their auspicious time. Instead, the police were mobilized to handle traffic. Early on the morning of the wedding, more than a dozen police officers armed with walkie-talkies converged on Chinatown to direct traffic along the route to the Catholic church. The state might not be able to solve traffic problems for Bangkok's eight million residents, but it certainly knew how to arrange green lights for its elite.

The wedding mass began at 9:30 A.M. I was told that there were two timetables: the time chosen for the public to attend the wedding, and the most auspicious time for the bride and groom to begin the rituals.[12] Several immaculately dressed young girls carrying baskets of flowers and a young boy holding a tray with the wedding ring on top led the procession. The bride, in a white Western wedding dress with a long train, entered the church on her father's arm as "Here Comes the Bride" played over the loudspeakers. The groom, his best man, and the male attendants all wore matching white tuxedos and black ties. More than two dozen photographers from six Chinese newspapers scrambled and fought to take pictures of the young couple. The archbishop, a Caucasian and the highest-ranking Catholic official in Thailand, and more than two dozen Thai priests and nuns took part in the wedding mass.

Holy Rosary Church usually seats 500 people, but that day there were more than a thousand present. Those who could not fit inside sat under protective canopies in the church's courtyard, a magnificent garden decorated with archways of fresh-cut flowers. A television crew from Bangkok's Channel Three set up a closed circuit and broadcast the ceremony live on monitors for guests seated outside the church.

The wedding reception began about 6:00 P.M. at the five-star Shangri-la Hotel. Several large carved ice sculptures positioned throughout the ballroom added to the elegant atmosphere. Dozens of hanging baskets filled with tropical flowers adorned the hall. Finally, a fourteen-tier wedding cake, complete with plastic bride and groom on top, was prominently displayed on a table beautifully decorated with fresh flowers. The unusually tall wedding cake symbolized wealth and prestige. While guests mingled and strolled among the decorations, they sampled various gourmet dishes. Colorful tropical fruit carved into flower shapes adorned the serving table. While the fruit and flowers evoked the image of exotic Thailand, the cuisine reflected not only the hosts' hybrid taste, but also what they imagined the very diverse assembly of guests would most enjoy. A string quartet unobtrusively played Western classical music, contributing to the relaxed and pleasant atmosphere. At the same time, guests could watch the proceedings on two giant video screens set up on either side of the ballroom.

The bride appeared in a different white wedding dress, without the long train. She had also styled her hair differently—swept up on the back of her head and held in place with an ivory clasp seven or eight inches long. With her expensive but not ostentatious jewelry, light but elegant makeup, sophisticated coiffure, and flowing dress, she looked, I overheard several guests comment, like a fairy princess. The groom had changed into a basic black tuxedo, white shirt, and black bow tie.

Since more than 6,000 people attended the reception, the bride and groom were dispatched to greet only their most prominent guests. These included Prem Tinsulanonda, the former prime minister and current privy counselor to the king, another former prime minister and a previous vice prime minister, several past and present cabinet officers, China's ambassador to Thailand, the head of the Economic Trade Center of Taiwan, and many well-known Chinese Thai entrepreneurs.

Female guests dressed in various styles of fashionable clothing, while most men wore Western suits. A number of *khunying*—women who had received this honored title from the royal family—were dressed in luxuriant designer gowns fashioned from Thai silk, which symbolized both their elite status and their Thai national identity. A number of Caucasian, Indian, and Japanese entrepreneurs also attended the reception. Many were fluent in several languages, and the entire event had a distinctly cosmopolitan tone.

In a sense the reception epitomized globalization, by revealing the effects of cultural accumulation in an area where not one but many sets of competing cultural criteria carry high symbolic value. For the capitalist families operating both within and outside of Thailand, symbolic values are set not only by Bangkok, but also by Tokyo, New York, and Paris. These metropolitan symbols of status and power are central to elite thansamai identity.

The honored speaker for the reception was Prem Tinsulanonda. Before his wedding toast, Prem led everyone in saluting the king, after which the king's anthem was played, actions solemnly weaving the king and the nation-state into the wedding rite. Then the privy counselor placed a flower garland on the bride and another on the groom and gave a congratulatory speech. The scene echoes Pierre Bourdieu: "It is practical kin who make marriages; it is official kin who celebrate them" (1977:34). By virtue of his presence and his role in celebrating their marriage, Prem provided the newlyweds and their respective families with enormous prestige and socioeconomic capital. The seniors' high social standing and economic power were redistributed to the young couple through the wedding. Prestige bred prestige.

Many guests had no personal connection to the bride or groom, but rather had relationships with their parents. Guests had many different motivations for attending the reception. Some came to congratulate the young couple; some came to strengthen ties with the families of the bride and groom; others came solely out of social obligation. Some just quickly signed the guest book and then left. I happened to run into a newspaper publisher whom I knew. He said, "I have to come to the reception because I need a loan from the big boss" (*da laoban* [M]), the president of Bangkok Bank. Like this publisher, some felt obliged to attend because they understood the power that the "big boss" wielded in relation to their careers. Of course, others were happy to come, being friends of the couple or seeing their participation as an act of being thansamai and perhaps hoping to make new connections. Thansamai is a concept shared across class. It is also constructed by and through class: the elite class mobilizes the middle class to perpetuate their elite thansamai identity.

As the reception continued, the couple lit two candles; then together they clasped a long sword and raised it to cut the wedding cake. They gave the first slice to Prem and then served senior family members and high-ranking officials. The young couple seemed quite comfortable interacting with persons from many different political and economic backgrounds, smiling and posing for pictures with prominent guests.

Weddings are often both a private and public affair, but this wedding was also a significant social, and even national, event. Photographs and news stories about the engagement and the wedding ran for weeks, and Chinese newspapers published dozens of congratulatory messages from entrepreneurs, businesses, and family friends. The *World News Daily*, for example, covered the story from January through March 1992. Local Chinese newspapers played an important role in emphasizing the Chinese-ness of these two powerful capitalist families. These newspaper stories highlighted the bride's and groom's Chinese names and never mentioned their Thai names.[13] Gender differences were also articulated through the press: the president of Bangkok Bank and the president of Taixin were referred to as "doctor" (*boshi* [M]), even though neither had ever earned such a degree; their wives, however, were not given such an honorable title. Family hierarchical order was expressed typographically in the congratulatory wedding announcements: the names and social positions of the bride's parents and of the groom's brother and sister-in-law (who stood in for the groom's deceased parents) were printed in boldface in the newspaper, two font sizes larger than the names of the bride and groom.[14]

Unlike the two previous weddings I've described, this bride and groom were at the periphery rather than the center of the celebration; although they were obviously key participants, the focus of the celebration was on their families. The couple faced political rather than economic constraints: how to choose an "appropriate" honored guest to give the toast without offending the other powerful figures present, how to arrange the seating for all these elite guests, and how to manage their relationships with guests from a wide range of ethnic, political, and class backgrounds. It is important to note that even though a super wedding is a rare example—extreme in its publicity, its scope, and its wealth—such political calculations are to some degree part of almost every wedding. Wedding rituals are performances acted out by the bride and groom and their families, but also by their guests, and even by strangers like Bangkok's traffic police.

What struck me most about this wedding—besides the use of hybrid cosmopolitan symbols in the Catholic mass and at the reception—was the way in which Thai leaders, Chinese diplomats, the Catholic archbishop, police, journalists, photographers, the entrepreneurs, Chinese community leaders, and thousands of guests were mobilized to participate. Somehow, through their manners, taste, connections, and dress, the capitalist families and the guests together represented an irresistible version of elite thansamai. If the first two weddings show how the bride and groom and their families made use of material goods to demonstrate their middle-class thansamai, the super wedding goes beyond this by using real people as *living* symbols of elite thansamai.

The newlyweds, their families, and the guests competed in displaying their sophistication and glamour. They sought the kinds of symbolic capital that have international recognition and value, in a space where bankers, politicians, businessmen, and professionals intersect with foreign and Euro-American symbols. What set this wedding apart from the previous two was as an expression of elite thansamai, which differs from middle-class thansamai, though the two clearly overlap.

While class is important for understanding the nature of thansamai in the capitalist super wedding, class by itself does not explain everything. Elite thansamai intersects with other elements of identity, including gender. The daughter of the president of Bangkok Bank possesses much more socioeconomic capital than the son of a Chinese immigrant couple or the daughter of a Thai cook. But within the kinship structure, the banker's daughter is not equal to her husband. In accounts of the wedding, the names of the bride and her family were listed *beneath* the names of the groom and his family. The bride was richer than her husband, but she was female—a married-out daughter.

Classed Thansamai

In 1941, according to Kenneth Landon, "while a Chinese bride in white is still a rare sight, the traditional red is losing in popularity to pink. A pink silk dress with a handpainted and diaphanous veil fastened to the head by a wreath of dainty paper flowers is considered very desirable. Paper flowers are thought to be more appropriate for weddings than real ones, which are, perhaps, in the minds of many associated with funerals" (1941:61). A half-century ago a modern Chinese bride wore a pink wedding dress as opposed to a "traditional red" one. Today in Bangkok a thansamai bride wears white instead of red and carries real flowers instead of paper ones. What was thansamai in the 1940s had become "traditional" by the end of the twentieth century. In all areas, not just fashion, "modern" and "traditional" are constantly shifting, being transformed and reproduced through practice.

The three weddings discussed in this chapter demonstrate how Chinese "traditions" have been transformed in Thai society, and how Thai "traditions" have become hybridized. Different traditions shape people's practices, and people's practices also reproduce and hybridize these traditions. Culture is a process "always emergent, always relational, permeated with power, existing through subtle and overt contests over meanings both practical and imaginary, shaping the desires that infuse modernity" (Rofel 1999:13). Rituals and symbols demonstrate the fluidity of cultural practices and the complexity of classed thansamai urban life. Instead of simply displaying sociological certainties in a continuum from traditional to modern, weddings can also tell us about the past and the future, about identity, and about the lives of women and men (Kendall 1996:3). Going beyond the modern versus traditional dichotomy enables us to better understand how people's cross-cultural pasts meet in the present at the intersections of different structures and symbols. Weddings are sites where local, transnational, ethnic, and national cultures come together in their most minute but vital aspects.

The events I have described here—a hybrid wedding, an interethnic wedding, and a capitalist super wedding—are not intended to characterize Bangkok weddings in general. Rather, they are offered as examples of an ongoing process by which Chinese Thai communities create hybrid cultural symbols to articulate their possession of a multiple consciousness, their combined sense of Chinese-ness and Thai-ness and thansamai.

In *Thai Women in the Global Labor Force*, Mary Beth Mills presents a well-grounded ethnography of "Thai modernity," suggesting that we have to understand modernity as being multiple rather than singular (1999:14). She analyzes the ways in which young female factory workers who migrated from rural northeastern Thailand to Bangkok experience Thai concepts of modernity. For these workers, to be modern means having social and geographic mobility, having access to urban life, being able to send remittances back home to fulfill the expectation of being a "good daughter," and owning various material goods such as television sets and blue jeans. In addition, becoming a "modern woman" (*phuying thansamai*) means having light skin, and wearing cosmetics and fashionable clothing. Mills suggests that thansamai for these women means not only having access to jobs and living in the city, but is also part of the cultural struggle to express consumer desires and individual identities.

These workers' desires and acts, it seems to me, are very much informed by their working-class status and their ethnic Lao background. Within the national discourse, ethnic Lao are often thought of as "poor" or "backward" *chaobannok* (rural villagers), because they come from the poorest region in Thailand. Collectively, the Lao have experienced a different kind of ethnicizing process. They are rarely treated as an economic threat to the Thai nation, as Chinese Thai have been. Instead, they are marginalized for being backward.

In Thai society, then, a sense of thansamai is class-specific, for it reflects class taste, socioeconomic status, and access to resources. The elaborate tropical flowers, large ice sculptures, tranquil classical music, and giant video monitors that we observed at the capitalist super wedding speaks of transnational elite class taste. Elite modernity, to a large extent, is expressed through access to socioeconomic resources and Euro-American symbols. In contrast, the working class is visibly constrained by limited resources. Nok, her mother, and her sister tried hard to appear middle class by renting jewelry and buying new clothes. They took pride in their Thai identity, but not in their working-class status. Throughout the wedding, they wanted to be perceived as middle class, even though Nok could not afford a beautician to make her up at home, just as her mother could not afford to hire someone to take care of her disabled son. Although Cao Mama could afford a comfortable home, a domestic worker, and a wedding photographer, she could not afford to have Daeng's wedding reception at a five-star hotel. Daeng and Nawarat did not need to rent a wedding gown or jewelry, but they could never have afforded the designer outfits on display at the capitalist super wedding. Most important, neither these two couples nor their families had access to the rich and powerful individuals who in themselves symbolize privilege, wealth, and membership in the political, social, and economic networks that elite families can call upon. Thus, seemingly simple choices or the carrying out of certain rituals are more than expressions of cultural identity; as an articulation of class status, ethnic consciousness, and gender difference, they express an angle of vision.

8

Naturalized Sexuality and
Middle-Class Respectability

Because sexuality is a nexus of the relationships between genders, much of
the oppression of women is borne by, mediated through, and constituted within,
sexuality.

—GAYLE RUBIN, "Thinking sex"

POLYGYNY, ONCE PREDOMINATELY a rich man's practice, is now quite
common among men of different classes in Thailand.[1] As Sanitsuda
Ekachai points out, polygyny "is not only alive and well in modern
Thailand, it has filtered from the elite down to the bottom through the
breakdown of social controls in farm communities, which used to be largely
monogamous" (2003). In 1996 one of the most popular songs in Bangkok
was entitled "I have no time to visit my minor wife" (*maimi Wela paiha
mianoi*). Listening to the song at Yan Mama's home prompted Jiap, Yan
Mama's live-in maid, to tell me about her father. A farmer, then a monk, and
now a taxi driver in Bangkok, he had recently married a third wife and
stopped supporting both his first wife (Jiap's mother) and his second wife
and their young son. Jiap said: "My heart was full of sorrow (*nu siachai mak-
mak*). I told my father, 'You should just make up your mind and stay with
one wife. Why do you go back and forth? When you became a monk, we
survived. We can live without you.' Sometimes I think it is a sin (*bap*) to talk
to my father this way. He is fifty now. His vision is getting poorer. It is not
easy to drive a taxi in Bangkok." Jiap accepted the hierarchy between father
and daughter and acknowledged his sexual privilege, but she still questioned
his behavior. For more than two years Jiap had been supporting her mother,
who had lost her job in a laundry. With no income and no network of kin

in Bangkok, Jiap's mother had much less power to bargain with her husband than she did when the family lived in a village.

Like their fathers, many lukchin men would describe Jiap's father as the stereotypical irresponsible Thai man who marries several women and sires numerous children but fails to support them. What these Chinese Thai men object to is not polygyny itself, but the polygynist's inability to provide for his family. Unlike their chinkao fathers, who often associated sexual intercourse with the cosmological order of yin and yang, lukchin refer to it using metaphors such as a bee gathering the nectar from a blooming flower or a fish swimming through an underwater cave—culturally specific symbols that obscure fundamental differences between socialized human behavior and biological animal behavior. Although generational differences are articulated in the different cultural symbols they use, both chinkao and lukchin associate sex with "nature."

This notion of nature permeates Thai society. Government officials encourage men to participate in sports as a substitute for visiting brothels, thereby perpetuating the notion that men's sexual behavior is biologically determined and obscuring the social fact of male sexual privilege. They overlook the structural inequalities of gender and class asymmetry hidden in men's sexual practices.

In fact, participatory sports are an arena where middle- and upper-class men demonstrate their wealth and masculinity. Since 1981 the number of amateur golfers in Thailand has been increasing by 10,000 or so every year. Some male golfers hire three or even four young female caddies at a time. One caddie will hold the man's umbrella to shield him from the sun, while another carries his golf bag. As the golfer waits to play his next shot, a third caddie may open up his folding chair, hand him a towel, wipe the sweat off his face, or light his cigarette. I knew a few upper-class wives who went golfing with their husbands just to keep an eye on them. One friend's husband even asked me if I knew of any Western psychological approaches that he could use to stop his wife from "tailing" him.

Like their mothers, lukchin women have ambivalent feelings about chaochu masculinity. Although many believe it is a man's nature to be a womanizer, they often try to limit their own husband's extramarital sex because it can profoundly affect the family's finances, health, and stability. In addition, the sheer existence of a minor wife can undermine the major wife's middle-class respectability by implying that it is somehow the major wife's fault that her husband has turned to another woman. Torn by such feelings, some women spy on their husbands in an effort to manage their delicate conjugal relationship. A well-connected female Chinese newspaper editor told me: "Whenever my good friends ask me to help find out whether their husbands are having an affair, I always say, 'If I discover he does have a minor wife, can you afford to divorce him?'" Considerations of being able to afford the divorce conjure up both emotional and economic concerns. Like their mothers, lukchin women weigh the costs and benefits along fairly conventional lines, often focusing on the well-being of their children. Some women prefer not to know whether their husbands have minor wives. But for many, the price of not knowing is too high; an innocent phone call from an unfamiliar woman can trigger great emotional distress.

Some women think that if they please and serve their husbands, they may change or at least moderate their husbands' extramarital sexual behavior. As one woman put it: "Don't complain when they [husbands] are home and treat them well. . . . If we talk to them nicely, they may do it less . . . if we don't complain when he is back home, he won't go out. We have to be nice to him and talk to him gently. . . . In bed, we must let them have it their way. Do whatever he wants" (VanLandingham et al. 1995:31). Because wives internalize the sexism that prevails in society at large, they regard the exercise of a husband's sexual privilege as an individual problem, and structural inequality remains intact.

A few lukchin women do cross sexual boundaries to seek companionship or sexual pleasure, but they rarely talk about it. The consequences of revealing one's extramarital experiences are very different for women than for men. A woman risks public humiliation and even the possibility of being divorced for adultery, because her extramarital behavior not only challenges the cultural construction of femininity but also her husband's masculinity and their middle-class respectability.

The different stories that the men and women told me about marriage and sex illustrate how naturalization is intertwined with social and economic forces and with Chinese Thai middle-class respectability in Bangkok. To understand how family gender politics and identity formation work for the lukchin generation, we have to discover "how culturally-specific domains have been dialectically formed and transformed . . . and how meanings have migrated across domain boundaries" (Yanagisako and Delaney 1995:11).

From Open to Hidden Polygyny

Pei Jie, the woman who loved ballroom dancing, considered herself lucky because as "the apple of her father's eye" she had been allowed to attend college in Australia in the early 1960s, a time when few women in Thailand studied abroad. After graduating, she asked her parents if she could marry a Thai schoolmate. They answered that a Thai husband was unacceptable. Pei Jie recalled: "My mother had told me not to marry a white man. I had not known they were also against me marrying a Thai." Her father quickly attempted to marry her off to a lukchin, the son of a wealthy automobile dealer, but Pei Jie refused, unable to see how such a match would make her happy. She turned to her grandfather, the founder of the family business, for help. Her grandfather had his own agenda: he wanted to see a great-grandchild before he died. By enlisting his support, Pei Jie managed to marry her schoolmate. She described her marriage as mostly harmonious but complicated by her husband's womanizing: "We never quarreled while we were married. He never raised his voice. He also addressed me as Khun Pei [Khun is a prefix conveying respect]. He respected me and I trusted him. I told him that he could visit prostitutes but should not focus on any individual one (*pai thieodai, tae maibentua benton*). I had to please (*aochai*) him, since other men were all doing the same thing."

By asking her husband not to become involved with a particular sex worker, Pei Jie hoped he would not turn a sexual encounter into a permanent relationship. But, as we saw in chapter 6, her husband did secretly take a minor wife—a woman Pei Jie first encountered while visiting her injured husband in the hospital. As husbands became aware of their wives' and adult children's resistance to polygyny, it became more common to hide it. But the discovery of a hidden polygyny often traumatized the conjugal relationship.

In 1982 Phi Tatsani, at age thirty-two, married Thaokae Ding, a lukchin. They worked together along with a few seasonal employees in a family-owned cement business that Thaokae Ding had inherited from his father. In the summer of 1990 Phi Tatsani suspected that her husband was having an affair, so she asked her younger sister, a lawyer, to help her investigate. At the same time, she approached Thaokae Ding and asked if he would hand over the family ATM card for two months to prove that nothing unusual was going on. When he refused, Phi Tatsani suggested that for the next two months she accompany him everywhere he went. He agreed to this.

Two months passed and nothing happened. Phi Tatsani was so relieved that she gathered the entire family in a park to celebrate. After returning home, a Thai woman with three children in tow appeared and knocked on the front door. She was Thaokae Ding's major wife. Without saying a word, she deposited her children on the doorstep and left.

Phi Tatsani was overwhelmed with anger and grief: after eight years of marriage she suddenly discovered that her husband was a secret polygynist, and that in fact she was his minor wife. Enraged by his betrayal, she grabbed a kitchen knife and stabbed him in the arm. She recalled, "Seeing his blood made me feel better. Many men would have fought back if their wives did this. He did not. After that, I was able to control my heart (*thamchai*)." She believed that her husband did not fight back because he still cared about their relationship. Even though prompted by her husband's betrayal, her violent act was seen as an aberrant individual action whereas her husband's transgression was seen as natural. Phi Tatsani saw herself as the transgressor.

Mei Nainai, the woman who brought her adopted son with her to Thailand and left her biological daughter back in China, was Phi Tatsani's mother. She blamed her daughter for marrying Thaokae Ding in the first place, instead of accepting a marriage that Mei Nainai had arranged for her. Mei Nainai believed that arranged marriages were better because "parents know what is best for their children."

Phi Tatsani's natal family was outraged by her husband's duplicity. One of her brothers wanted to beat him up, but Phi Tatsani intervened. Her mediation, however, created tension between herself and her siblings. Her brothers and sisters accused her of "spoiling" Thaokae Ding. Phi Tatsani explained, "My husband is the first and only man that I have ever lived with. Single people do not know the feelings that exist between a husband and a wife." (Three of her sisters were unmarried.) Her contradictory behavior— stabbing Thaokae Ding but preventing her brother from beating him up— indicated a profound ambivalence.

Within the Thai and the Chinese kinship systems, a major wife's position was considered far superior to that of a minor wife. A Thai proverb depicts a minor wife as "A woman who has to be content to drink water beneath the elbow of another woman." That is, no matter how thirsty the minor wife may be, she must wait for the few drops of water that may leak to her mouth from the cupped hands of the major wife (Sumalee 1995:107). Chronologically, Phi Tatsani was Thaokae Ding's minor wife, but she refused to acknowledge this hierarchical order. As a *Bangkok Post* article pointed out, "*Mia noi* [minor wives] in the old days were generally people of inferior status seeking to step up the social ladder. Not anymore. Nowadays, they are well educated and even rich themselves. And they don't consider themselves *mia noi*. They are only the ones who incidentally come later" (Sanitsuda 1991). Presenting herself as the Number One wife was Phi

Tatsani's tactic to reassert her status within the family and to maintain her class respectability.

I never heard Phi Tatsani address Thaokae Ding's major wife by name; instead she simply called her "*i nan*" (that woman). Her respectability was expressed by denouncing the other wife. In this context, the prefix i was derogatory. Phi Tatsani told me that i nan was a Thai bar girl who lived off of Thaokae Ding and knew nothing about running a business. By linking this Thai woman with the sex entertainment industry, she implied a connection between her own Chinese-ness and the family business. These occupational, ethnic, and class differences established the distinctions between a Thai woman who worked in a bar and a Chinese woman devoted to her family business. Thus Phi Tatsani turned her economic capital into ethnicized capital: positive Chinese-ness was expressed at the expense of negative Thai-ness. Phi Tatsani sought to maintain her own class status and self-respect by attacking her rival's morality and respectability.

Although Thaokae Ding had not registered either marriage, according to Phi Tatsani i nan initiated divorce proceedings. This seemingly illogical practice—legally registering the divorce without ever having registered the marriage—is not unusual in Thailand (Napaporn 1989:206). By recording the divorce, a wife can sometimes gain access to a financial settlement from her husband or, if she is the one who has the money, cut him off completely through judicial decision. Again marginalizing the other woman's Thai-ness, Phi Tatsani commented: "Thai women like to live an easy life." In practice, she knew that a divorced mother with three children to raise would not have an easy life; indeed, this was partly why she herself endured her marriage. Later Phi Tatsani told me that she had convinced i nan not to divorce Thaokae Ding for the sake of her children. She said: "I pity the children. They are quite lovely. Last year I sent them some gifts. It's like worshiping Buddha—I make merit." She stayed emotionally detached because she could not afford to become too fond of these lovely children, who might one day compete with her own. Since she now effectively ran the family business and controlled the purse strings, the other wife received very little money from Thaokae Ding. Eventually the major wife was forced to go to work full time and leave her children with her parents in the countryside.

Caught between male sexual privilege and her socially marginalized marital status, Phi Tatsani had to compete with i nan for limited economic and social capital. Even though the other woman suffered as much, if not more, from the difficult circumstances created by Thaokae Ding's polygyny, she received no sympathy or help from Phi Tatsani. Thus, class and family interests divided two wives who shared identical gender interests. The prevailing notion that a minor wife always fights against the major wife is a misreading of social inequality.[2] It is the patriarchal family and society at large that mobilize one wife to fight against another; the marital conflicts, tensions, and contradictions that individual women experience acutely are created by state regimes and family gender politics.

A Respectable Womanizer: "Romantic, not Vulgar"

Lan Jizhe was born in Bangkok in 1940. When I met him, he was a journalist (*jizhe* [M]) and the editor for a local Chinese newspaper. Even before interviewing him, I knew of his reputation as a chaochu. For my first interview, I asked one of his female friends to join us at the restaurant. He was delighted to have two women as an audience, and this may have set the tone for his boasting in the interviews that followed. Lan Jizhe was the only man I interviewed who mentioned "respecting" and giving pleasure to the women he had sex with. To some degree, his narrative was a kind of seduction:

> I think I have enjoyed my life more than some millionaires. . . . My boss's son asked me how I attract so many girls. I have no tricks. I just respect them and say good things about them.
>
> Dance girls, bar girls, masseuses, and prostitutes all have an inferiority complex. Men pay for the service and some men manipulate them. I never do that. I please women. Some women tell me they have never had an orgasm with other men. But with me, they can have two or three orgasms. I care about them. They like me. We become good friends. Some give me special services.

Lan Jizhe repeatedly emphasized that he was "romantic, not vulgar" (*fengliu bu xialiu* [M]). I asked him to explain what he meant:

> I can give you many examples. For instance, some men would point out a woman to his friends and say, "I have slept with her." I never do that. You would never suspect we were involved, even if the woman were standing right here next to us. I disguise my feelings very well.
>
> Once a girl showed me her marriage license. I asked her why she still wanted to sleep with me. She said, "That is my business. I am not married yet." I told her that I could no longer have a relationship with her because she was "a flower with an owner" (*minghua youzhu* [M]). I did not want to

have her husband wear a "green hat" (*lu maozi* [M]) [to cuckold a husband]. Most men would not care and would sleep with her anyway. I cared, so I did not sleep with her.

His narrative demonstrated what he thought would seem romantic but not disreputable. But he might display his middle-class chaochu masculinity quite differently when out with a group of male friends. Also, the term *xialiu* (vulgar) contains a class element, for it is often used to refer to lower-class behavior. In contrast, *fengliu* (romantic) indicates a distinguished and admirable person who may have an unconventional lifestyle. More important, by not identifying the women he slept with to others, Lan Jizhe increased his chances for future sexual encounters with them. Another aspect of being romantic, not vulgar, was not to have sex with a married woman. Although male sexual privilege is naturalized, having sex with a married woman is regarded as disruptive to social and familial order because it challenges another man's right to his wife's sexuality.

Lan Jizhe then spoke of an encounter with a university student: "I told the girl that I would give her something for her companionship. She was very surprised. Other men would just take advantage of her. But, you know, this is just my personality." In this context, his romance centered upon an "equal" exchange of money for sex. And boasting about how a young university student wanted to have sex with him for nothing again magnified his chaochu masculinity. He continued his bragging:

> I also knew a famous dancer. A newspaper owner made her pregnant. He refused to take responsibility for his actions. Finally, the dancer had an abortion. Later, I met her at a party. All the others had left. Only the two of us were there. She said I could take her wherever I liked. I took her to a hotel. In the middle of making love, I suddenly remembered that she had gotten pregnant before. I asked her if she had a condom.
>
> Not long after this, I went to a business party. This same woman was there. At first we were both very surprised. But I calmed down and, when I was formally introduced to her as the wife of a film director, I just acted like we had never met before. This helped her compose herself. I am adept at controlling myself.

Requesting a condom was presented as proof of Lan Jizhe's sense of responsibility. However, I later discovered that Lan Jizhe was infertile; asking for a condom was a performance. Apparently he felt that revealing his infertility would make him appear less manly. Throughout our interviews,

Lan Jizhe carefully selected information to play up his chaochu identity—always, it seemed, keeping his female audience in mind.

Since he had many sexual partners, I asked if he was concerned about contracting HIV or other sexually transmitted diseases. He said: "I am quite healthy. I have only had syphilis twice. After recovering, I go do it again. Now I only sleep with special women. I meet them through my social contacts so I can tell that they do not have these problems." He was convinced that these women were free of the diseases that commonly plague the sex industry. One of his special women was a "mainland little sister" (*dalumei* [M]), the nickname given undocumented Chinese immigrant women who began entering Thailand in the late 1980s. Many of these women were funneled into bar girl jobs in nightclubs where most of the customers are Mandarin-speaking lukchin men or Chinese tourists from Taiwan, Hong Kong, Malaysia, and Singapore. Lan Jizhe described his mainland little sister as follows:

> She was a singer. She did not ask me for anything. After I conquered her, I bought her new clothes. When my wife ran a retail clothing business in the Mabunkhong Department Store, I took clothing from her shop to give to my *biaomei* [M] (female cousin on the mother's side). The biaomei was crazy about sex. But after having sex, she felt remorseful and told me she was "out of balance." She often confused me because she was so different from the Thai women I slept with.

To highlight his close relationship with this special woman, he switched from the negative term dalumei to the positive kin term biaomei. Nevertheless, the meaning of *mei*, "little sister," which implies being a lover, remained unchanged. He continued, "It is *yuan* [M] (a predestined relationship). I would never have imagined that I would have a biaomei. She was born in China and I was born in Thailand."[3] He made use of the term yuan to explain his sexual encounter. He also attributed his biaomei's contradictory behavior—enjoying the sex but feeling out of balance afterwards—to being Chinese. At this moment, he firmly positioned himself as Thai, although he frequently referred to himself as Teochiu Chinese.

I asked Lan Jizhe if his middle-aged wife could have a *biaoge* [M] or "male cousin on the mother's side" as her lover, since he had a biaomei. His answer was this: "I would divorce her. A woman should not have a 'second spring' (*dier chun* [M])." He took male sexual privilege so much for granted that he could not see my point about gender inequality. I commented, "Both men and women are human beings. Why should only men be allowed to do it?" He responded emotionally: "Nonsense. Can my wife support me? I give her everything, land, a house, money. . . . If my wife did this she would be 'stealing a man' (*touhan* [M]). She would be finished. This is a man's world. You see, only men visit massage parlors and brothels. No woman would dare to do it."

He apparently thought that his economic success entitled him to a "second spring." His comment—"This is a man's world"—also indicates his awareness of the existence of the patriarchal power structure. If a woman had an affair, she would be accused of stealing a man, whereas no man could ever be accused of "stealing a woman"—no such phrase exists. The Chinese term "stealing a man" echoes gendered Thai linguistic practices: adultery applies only to married women. Nevertheless, the fact that Lan Jizhe talked about it this way shows that naturalization is never complete and that there is always some latent resistance in it. If it really was a woman's nature to be a chaste mother, then why was so much energy being expended to discipline and constrain a woman's sexuality?

Later, Lan Jizhe implied that only men who can afford to pay for it are entitled to a "second spring":

> I make good money. My salary is 18,000 baht [US $720] a month, but I have extra income. Last month I made 170,000 baht [US $6,800]. I got 20,000 baht [US $800] just for one advertisement [his commission for selling advertising space in the newspaper]. I also take very good care of my wife. I registered our house, worth nearly 1,000,000 baht [US $40,000], and a piece of land in Chiang Mai, under her name. My friends register their houses or land under their own names, or under both names. I am responsible to my wife. She does not need to worry about her life. I have arranged everything for her.

I gradually came to realize that Lan Jizhe talked no differently about his conjugal relationship than he spoke about giving gifts to his special women or paying the university student for sex. All his relationships with women were characterized by an exchange of money for sex.

My interviews with this proud womanizer were especially challenging. I saw them as good opportunities to better comprehend his experiences and his logic, but his chauvinistic boasting and his presumption that I was gullible and exploitable made me uneasy. Sometimes I posed moralistic questions just to provoke a response, as when I asked if he ever felt guilty about going back and forth between his wife and his mistress: "Guilty? Only you Chinese would have that kind of feeling. It is common in Thailand.

Sometimes I get home at 1 A.M. I say, 'I am hungry.' My wife says, 'How could you be hungry? Didn't you just come back from a party?' She knows where I've really been, but she pretends not to know." He attributed feeling guilty to being Chinese, just as he earlier attributed being unbalanced to being Chinese.

In addition to distinguishing married from unmarried women, he talked about how a wife and a mistress have different duties and provide him with different kinds of pleasure:

> A wife is a wife, and a mistress is a mistress. But this is hard to describe. My wife is my friend. We do not have much to talk about. When I get home she helps take off my clothes and gives me a cup of tea and cooks for me. Sometimes she sees that I am so tired that she goes out and rents pornographic videotapes for me to watch. But she doesn't watch them with me.
>
> My mistresses do not have such duties. My wife usually does not wear makeup or try to please me as a lover. The mistresses are often dressed up and talk to me. They please me and give me emotional comfort. I sometimes think that men are very strange. Men like for women to talk sweetly to them and to please them.

Although our interviews were conducted in Mandarin, he occasionally used Thai words such as *pronibat* when he talked about how his wife took care of him. Pronibat is generally used to describe how a person in a lower social position pleases and serves someone in a higher position. For example, a boy would pronibat a monk, a child would pronibat her parents, a wife would pronibat her husband, or a sex worker would pronibat her customer. The opposite would only occur in exceptional cases, such as a mother who might pronibat her sick child.

Lan Jizhe continued: "I don't want a minor wife. I just need a mistress. If I had a minor wife I would wonder what she was doing when I was with my major wife. I would never feel at peace. I am responsible to my mistress, and I treat her like my minor wife, but we can break up any time we like." He carefully differentiated a mistress from a minor wife. In his view, having short-term affairs is more expensive than visiting brothels because affairs require gifts: help with the rent, money to eat out, and so on. Nevertheless, having a mistress is still cheaper than taking a minor wife, because a man no longer needs to fulfill the financial obligations that conventional kinship imposes on a polygynist. In addition, it is easier to discard a mistress than a minor wife.

Over time I learned that what Lan Jizhe had said about not wanting to be a polygynist turned out to only be partly true. His colleague told me that Lan Jizhe had asked his wife to propose marriage to the biaomei on his behalf. But this time his wife, who had long pretended to know nothing about her husband's extramarital affairs, refused.[4] Her marital acts—both pleasing her husband and refusing his request to marry a minor wife—reveal her flexible negotiating tactics. She could put up with a chaochu husband traveling between different women, but not with him marrying a minor wife. She was hardly the docile and obedient wife that Lan Jizhe portrayed her as being.

Visiting a Brothel for Women

Driving back from the ballroom dance held in the restaurant, Pei Jie told me that she had once visited a "women's club," a brothel for women. After commenting on how attractive she found a tall and handsome male sex worker, Pei Jie smiled. "I couldn't do it," she said. "He was so young, even younger than my children." What struck me was not the fact that Pei Jie visited a brothel, but rather how the notion of motherhood subverted her desire for sex. I never heard a man associate the age of a female sex worker with the age of his children. That a woman should link the youth of a male sex worker to the mother-child relationship, and that a man should see contact with virgin girls as proof of his own vigor, are effects of the cultural construction of femininity and masculinity.

Pei Jie saw herself as an active sexual agent who could afford to purchase sex services, even though visiting a male brothel is considered rebelling against a woman's nature, something that a "respectable" woman would not do. But the impact of regulated motherhood was so profound that she could feel it even in a brothel. The fact that she had been divorced for twenty years may have been the reason she felt comfortable enough to tell her amusing sex tale to a trusted outsider. Furthermore, she did not sleep with the young sex worker, so her middle-class respectability remained intact.

"If a Hen Crows, She Is Killed"

Born in Thailand in 1915, Xing Mama was forced into an arranged marriage at age sixteen. A few months later when she was already pregnant, she made local news as "a rebellious daughter" by running away from her husband. Hu Xiansheng, a Chinese immigrant who worked as a newspaper reporter, interviewed her, became her admirer, and asked her to marry him. At first Xing Mama was happy with her new husband, but over time she came to realize that he was an inveterate womanizer:

> No one knew that he lived a double life. His friends loved and respected him because he was generous to others even when we did not have much money. He often quarreled with me. I sometimes had to be ferocious with him so that he would be afraid of me. He had relations with many women but he would not allow me to go out and find a job. If he had not been so poorly paid he would have had dozens of wives. This is a man's society. If a hen crows, she is killed. But it is fine when a cock crows because crowing is part of the cock's nature.

Hu Xiansheng had died less than two months before I interviewed Xing Mama. Far from mourning him, she poured out a lifetime's accumulated resentment. She acknowledged gender inequality but naturalized it by associating cocks with men and hens with women. Her contradictory statements, it seemed to me, embodied the profound ambivalence that many lukchin women share with regard to chaochu masculinity. In a bitter reflection on more than fifty years of marriage, Xing Mama said: "Marriage is unpredictable. A married woman is just like a blind person crossing the street. If she is lucky, she makes it safely to the other side. If she is unlucky, she gets run over and killed by a car."

Xing Mama's daughter, Phi Pasuk, was a multilingual intellectual who talked to me extensively about herself and her parents. Her lukchin mother and chinkao father tried to raise their children to be Chinese, and they were not allowed to speak Thai at home. By the time she was in high school, she openly rebelled against her parents' discipline. She longed to fit in with the other students, but this desire was often thwarted by her inability to pass as Thai. She remembered a bitter quarrel she had with her father after she refused to attend his lecture on Chinese culture at a Chinese association meeting: "My father cursed me. He said, 'You are Chinese, but you dare to insult Chinese culture! May your liver and heart turn all black' (*nide xingan doushi heide* [M]). I asked him, 'Is a Thai worse than a Chinese?' He said 'You know nothing. Chinese culture is the greatest culture in the world.' 'Bullshit,' I said. He slapped me. It was the only time in his life he ever hit me." In this fight, the cultural pride of an immigrant man collided with the shame his daughter felt at being singled out as Chinese in a Thai school. Phi Pasuk eventually changed her Chinese name to a Thai name without telling her parents.

In addition to her identity struggle, Phi Pasuk was acutely aware of her parents' marital problems:

> My mother was so burdened by being a woman. She had more education than my father. Being the wife of a devoted professional, she had no chance to be herself. Once she said to me, "I am like a bird. I have lived with my eight children in a cage for so long that my wings are broken and I cannot fly anymore."
>
> My father was brought up by a widow and lived among women from the time he was six years old. He told me that he could never forget how the feudalist marital system drove one of his playmates, a female cousin, to commit suicide. He considered himself a revolutionary because he hated feudalism, which was one reason why he married my mother; he really admired my mother's courage for escaping from her arranged marriage. He respected women, but he was also a womanizer. He was weird even when he was in his sixties. Once he told my mother, "I cannot divorce you. If I do, I will lose face. Why don't you commit suicide and give me my liberty?" I was on my mother's side and fought with my father.

Hu Xiansheng was an enigma. He believed that women were being oppressed by the patriarchal system, but he would not let his wife work outside the home. He fought against feudalism by marrying a woman who escaped from an arranged marriage and who had a child with another man, but he was also a womanizer. Although Hu Xiansheng had completed only three years of school, he became a well-known figure in his field. Xing Mama had completed middle school, but her education never led to a good job. In addition, in the 1950s Hu Xiangsheng was imprisoned and served five years for being a "Chinese communist." Friends and neighbors were reluctant to visit Xing Mama, fearing they might also be accused of being part of a communist network. She struggled to raise her children, most of whom were teenagers during this period. Saying that she felt like an imprisoned bird with broken wings vividly captured her isolation, her yearning, and her frustration.

Phi Pasuk admired her father as a self-made man, but was angered by his womanizing: "He was like a Japanese man who led two lives. Between 9 A.M. to 6 P.M. he was a working man, but from 9 P.M. to 2 A.M. he was a sexual freak. In this way he balanced his life. . . . He loved his job and did it well. But his sexual desire made him vulnerable." Hu Xiansheng regarded his sexual "appetite" as part of his nature; Phi Pasuk did too. She pitied him for it, because, as she saw it, his inability to control his "animal nature" made him vulnerable to the excesses of his desire.

Instead of pretending she knew nothing about her husband's extramarital affairs, Xing Mama found out the details and sometimes even directly confronted the other woman: "Once a girl drove him crazy. She was in her early twenties, almost forty years younger than he was. She came from a very poor family; she enjoyed his money and appreciated his wit. I went to see her and knelt down to her. I begged her not to see my husband anymore. She was shocked and denied having a relationship with him." Xing Mama used any strategy she could think of: being "ferocious" to confront her husband or "kneeling down" to a much younger woman. Her negotiating stance stood in stark contrast to the strategy of "pleasing and serving" or "spoiling" a husband.

Regarding her father's womanizing, Phi Pasuk said:

> My father never felt bad about his womanizing because he gave my mother his entire salary. My father worked additional hours for extra money, which he kept for himself. He tried to hide this money. Sometimes he forgot to lock his drawer [where he hid the money], so he would phone us to lock it up for him.
>
> When he got older, he would go play mahjong at Tou Xian She, a club run by a Hakka Chinese. While a man played mahjong, a girl came around and rubbed his shoulders. If he was turned on, they went into another room and he paid her for sex. My father did not have much money. That place was cheap. But he had rich friends, and sometimes they invited him to go out with them.

Hu Xiansheng was hospitalized six times the year he died, and Phi Pasuk described him as a very demanding patient:

> He knew he was going to die and he wanted us to visit him every day. We had our jobs to think about and also the traffic killed us. My mother never went once to visit him. She said that her feet hurt, but that was not the real reason. She could not forgive my father. One day I could not help myself and confronted him: "Dad, why are you so mean to mom? If you were nice to her, she would come and take care of you." You know what he said? "Did you know your mother slept with another man?" I was startled. I suddenly recalled one night when my mother was away. At that time I think I was about eight years old and my father was still in prison. She was

gone for several hours, which seemed like a long absence to a child. When she came back, she gave me a doll.

My memory confirmed what my father told me. My heart thanked him for telling me his secret. He shattered the high esteem I held my mother in. Now I see my parents as human beings and not as monuments. My mother is not a bad woman. She has gone through things that most women do not have to deal with. She is a human being. If my father had not told me this heartbreaking truth, I would never be free of my family.

After the shock of hearing her parents' great secret, Phi Pasuk felt liberated. Ironically, she saw her mother's single transgression as equivalent to her father's lifelong womanizing—another example of "natural" sexual desire disguising structural gender inequality.

Hu Xiansheng maintained silence about his wife's extramarital affair for nearly a lifetime. But if he had admitted knowledge of it, his reputation would have suffered; he would have been known as a man who could not protect or satisfy his wife. Naturalized male sexual privilege kept him from seeing how his chaochu masculinity was part of the patriarchal system he had fought against for years, and it also made him ashamed to talk about his wife's affair. It may have never occurred to him that his wife could also seek sexual expression. For her part, Xing Mama knew that keeping silent yielded a better payoff than defending her behavior; better to be seen as a sacrificing mother than a crowing hen.

"Finding Happiness in the Bitterness"

Born in 1937, Aying Jie was well known in her community for her beauty. Her widowed mother had arranged her marriage to a rich man's son when she turned twenty-one. Her marriage was seen by outsiders as "a capable husband paired with a beautiful wife" (*nancai nümao* [M]), and such couples were said to "fit together like a golden branch and a jade leaf" (*jinzhi yuye* [M]). Nevertheless, Aying Jie disliked her husband. She married him as an act of filial piety: "My mother needed milk money to pay off her debts and to raise my younger brothers." Before she married, Aying Jie had worked at a radio station and loved playing basketball. After her marriage she had to quit her job, leave the basketball team, and work in the family business. She was not allowed to interact with customers or to go out by herself because her husband and her chinkao in-laws were afraid that her beauty would attract unwanted attention. She grew disheartened and was even hospitalized for depression. Aying Jie recalled her mother's regret, "I knew you did not like this marriage, but I did not know you would be so unhappy."

In 1975, after both her in-laws, the founders of the family business, had passed away, Aying Jie became a key player in the company because she was the only one who could speak and write Chinese. Her career shifted into high gear. She conducted market surveys, and the company began offering boating equipment comparable to the products manufactured in the United States, West Germany, and Japan. Aying Jie traveled throughout Thailand, visited China, and directly contacted factories to negotiate better prices. By the time I interviewed her, she held several business titles, including vice president of the family firm.

Despite her frenetic schedule, she devoted herself to creative writing in the evening: "Writing makes me happy. I write for myself and use my heart, blood, and tears for inspiration." In Bangkok, the author pays the costs of publishing a novel or book of essays written in Chinese, and Aying Jie had the money to publish her stories. But she had to confront a resentful husband: "My husband doesn't like to see me write. When he sees me writing, he will shout and lose his temper. I don't know why. It might be jealousy. He is Chinese but he does not read Chinese. I often get up at 2 A.M. or 3 A.M. to write secretly."

Aying Jie described her marriage as "cooked rice," meaning that it was finished, "over with." She had detached herself from her husband: "I do not feel jealous when he spends the night with another woman. I do not wear makeup. I don't care anymore." She handled her unhappy marriage by keeping busy: conducting family business during the day and writing fiction at night. Aying Jie saw herself as a fast-paced modern woman who shifted between two different worlds. This was her way to "find happiness in the bitterness" (*kuzhong zuole* [M]). In her writing she focused on emotional subjects such as loneliness, romance, or star-crossed lovers forced to live separately. Here is a typical example: "After you left me, I have not given myself a moment even to catch my breath. . . . I am avoiding an attack of loneliness; I am attempting to forget the pain of our separation. When evening comes, the pain increases. I keep imagining I hear your voice." This theme repeated itself in another story:

> The heavy mood of separation again occupies my entire heart. It means the end of a sweet happy life, and begins a new longing, and long wait until our next meeting. Time is so cruel and merciless. It forces those of us who do not want to be apart to go back to places each of us is unwilling to go!

I am no longer struggling under the pressure; I no longer hesitate out of weariness. The loss of my first love was already sad enough. Not a second time. I pray, Heaven, please pity us! Grant us the strength to overcome all the obstacles on the road which is full of thistles and thorns.

Slowly, bit by bit, I came to realize from her friends, her publications, and a review article that some of Aying Jie's stories were based on her own experiences with her lover, who was a businessman and a writer himself. Constrained by the notion of chaste femininity, she never mentioned him in our interviews. Yet in a very muted way she expressed her emotions in her writing, overcoming the constraints she labored under as a wife and mother.

———

The different social categories mentioned in this chapter—wife, minor wife, mistress, biaomei, mainland little sister, and prostitute—reveal how women are categorized according to their relations with men; these social categories and the patriarchal system overlap and intersect at many points. A reverence for motherhood, for example, is central to the existence of the patriarchal system, which is why such overwhelming social importance is invested in a girl's virginity and a married woman's chastity.

Chaochu masculinity and chaste femininity simultaneously empower and constrain men and women. Lukchin men are not supposed to have extramarital sex with married women; some feel pressured to visit brothels with their friends; others consider it fashionable to have affairs with unmarried women because that confirms their sense of masculinity and class status. While they are constrained to not divorce their wives, some secretly take a second wife; others ask their wives for "permission" to marry a minor wife. The cultural construction of womanizing masculinity compels a man to conceal his infertility or to remain silent about his wife's extramarital affair. In contrast, lukchin women struggle between accepting and contesting naturalized male sexual privilege; the dominant notions of motherhood and chastity have made them experience their own sexual passion and desire as dangerous. A woman who loses her virginity to a legitimate husband enhances her femininity, but a woman who loses it in any other way is condemned as a "bad" woman. Middle-class sexuality becomes the nexus in which the cultural identities of lukchin men and women are reshaped. And yet, despite all this, the naturalization of sex is always partial, for it is being challenged in various forms even as it is being reinforced.

One of the most far-reaching effects of this naturalization is that it compels men and women to perceive their marital conflicts not as expressions of a larger social problem but as individual problems to be handled within the family. Thus an angry wife may turn violent, directly attacking her husband's penis: around a hundred such incidents occurred in Thailand between 1973 and 1980 (*San Francisco Chronicle*, 9 October 1993). In 1997, when one woman discovered her husband's secret polygyny, she drugged him unconscious and cut off his penis; she then fastened his severed organ to a bunch of balloons and released the balloons into the sky to prevent his penis from being surgically reattached (*Bangkok Post*, 18 March 1997). Since men's sexual privilege is believed to be rooted in biological need, cutting off the offending sexual organ is certainly connected with the wish to end this need. By treating the incident as a sensational individual event, the media helps to further disguise the structural basis of sexual and gender inequality.

Today an increasing number of white-collar and professional lukchin women are rejecting the key symbol of feminine accomplishment—a husband. For them, marriage is no longer the sign of having become a "complete" person. Nevertheless, even if these single women can afford to buy a house, they are still expected to live with their natal families. So when these women with no commitment to marriage have sexual relations with men, they must be superb actors.

Phi Pasuk told me that she could do anything a man could do and that sexuality is the only thing that can make her vulnerable. This vulnerability—her father's vulnerability in relation to his extramarital sex, and hers in relation to being a single woman—again illustrates the effects of naturalizing chaochu masculinity and chaste femininity. Nearly two decades ago Phi Pasuk married a graduate student from Cornell University, which made her Thai and Chinese cultural identities even more complicated. She described her life in the United States as that of "a tropical fish in the wrong water," and her marriage soon collapsed. Now Phi Pasuk has turned to Buddhist teachings and has cultivated sexual detachment. She practices meditation and follows the Four Noble Truths: human existence is suffering; the cause of human suffering is desire; if there is no desire, there is no suffering; the way to avoid suffering is the middle path. Her new way of dealing with her sexuality is through Buddhism.

9

Shang Jia:
"Family Business"

There is no conflict between my career and doing the housework. Both are my work.

—LU LAOSHI, a lukchin woman

THE MANDARIN PHRASE *shang jia* literally means "family business"; it encompasses all the relations between a family and that family's economic enterprise. Questions about the division of labor, whom to marry, how and where the family should live, or which college majors or careers children should choose are often decided not according to individual preferences but with the collective interests of the family and the business in mind. In this chapter I suggest that a family-oriented business is a conflation of production, reproduction, money, and conjugal sex, and hence I am challenging the presumed binary opposition between production and reproduction and between the family and the business.

The history of Chinese entrepreneurship in Southeast Asia is often rendered as the history of "great men"; women are rarely mentioned (e.g., Cushman 1991; Freedman 1979; M. Lim 1981; Mackie 1992a, 1992b). Female entrepreneurs, and especially the wives of businessmen, have been overshadowed by their husbands. More recent research on family businesses conducted in Taiwan has found that wives play an important role because of their cheap or unpaid labor (Greenhalgh 1994; Hsiung 1996). I would argue, however, that a wife is considered *the* most desirable laborer not only because her labor is so cheap but even more because it is so reliable: a wife is bound to a family business by her sexual commitment to her husband and by her obligations to the family. Most important, family gender politics conceal the fact that many women are powerful economic players and skill-

144

ful money managers. The cultural construction of masculinity prevents a Chinese Thai husband from seeing his wife as an equal player; instead, he sees her as his "assistant" (*phuchuai*). Although the Thai word phuchuai does not make a locational distinction, it echoes the Chinese term *neizhu*, inside assistant. Nonetheless, a lukchin businesswoman is endowed with a certain autonomy; her power extends far beyond the confines of the household and subsistence activities. But because business leadership has been masculinized, and assistantship feminized, a businesswoman understands that she can better serve her interests by downplaying her economic accomplishments and disguising her leadership, skills, and sexual desire. No woman wants to be perceived as a "crowing hen" in the realms of sex or business.

Indeed, a businesswoman encounters problems that a man never faces: how to display her achievements and financial sophistication while identifying herself as her husband's assistant and her children's mother. She has to accomplish her goals but also appear as a subordinate within the hierarchical business and kinship structures. In many cases the women's emotional management of this dilemma is crucial to the stability of the family and the survival of the family business. By paying special attention to the *connections* between production, reproduction, nei/wai sex, and emotional conflicts in family businesses—which are the most prevalent socioeconomic institutions among the ethnic Chinese in Thailand and in Southeast Asia—we can gain a clearer view of women's work, dilemmas, and accomplishments.

New Types of *"Mother of the House"* (Maeban)

In the 1990s the boundaries between mother of the house and breadwinner became even more ambiguous for middle-class lukchin women. Of the twenty-three lukchin I interviewed for this project, all the men and all but three of the women had regular income-producing jobs; no one engaged in piecework. One maeban earned "fast and easy money" playing the stock market and another sold real estate.

Chuchu Jie, born in 1941, never had a chance to attend school. Instead, she took care of five younger siblings, starting when she was seven years old. She vividly recalled once being whipped by her mother for going off to play and leaving her baby brother on the ground where he was terribly bitten by insects. She taught herself to read and write by studying her brothers' textbooks. After she got married and had two children of her own, she elected to be a maeban, claiming that her lack of education prevented her from earning enough money to justify the time spent away from her children. Nevertheless, over the prior fifteen years she had closed several real estate deals and used the profits to buy two houses as investments:

> If I worked like my husband does, we would never have been able to buy our own house. My husband [the manager of a Coca-Cola plant] sells himself to his company. He doesn't know how to make money. I've used his money to make money. I have a man's mind; I like to read about politics and economic news, not love stories.

By demonstrating her skill at handling money, Chuchu Jie justified crossing the boundaries between housework and moneymaking. But she attributed her success to having a "man's mind." Although her actions challenged the stereotype that men are naturally more adept at doing business, she saw her ability as a masculine attribute, just as she assumed that women are naturally more interested in romantic stories than in politics or economics. Family gender politics also informed her handling of money: she used her real estate profits to purchase a dental clinic for her son without making a similar investment in her daughter's career. She followed the rule that she learned from her parents: invest in sons, not in daughters.

For middle-class lukchin, the wherewithal to employ a domestic worker has become an index of class status. Domestic workers are expected to rise at dawn, water the plants, mop the floor, clean the house, do the laundry, iron the clothes, prepare food, eat the leftovers after the family has finished their meal, do the dishes, look after the children, run errands, and sleep only after everyone else has gone to bed. A few even perform Chinese ancestor worship on their employer's behalf. The chinkao in this project regarded ancestor worship as a genuine expression of respect, but one lukchin woman who regarded it as a chore told me that she was simply "too busy to remember the worship days" (four days each lunar month). Her main concern was to have the rituals routinely conducted so that her ancestors would continue protecting her family. Who actually performed the ancestor worship, except on Chinese New Year and Qingming, was irrelevant to her. The fact that some lukchin women used their economic capital to avoid performing housework challenges one of our most stubborn stereotypes: "woman equals reproduction" (Lock and Kaufert 1998:3).

The following lukchin entrepreneurs operated three different types of family businesses. The first is a family business cofounded by a husband and wife. Each spouse brings to the enterprise all available resources, skills, and social connections—anything that can be used to strengthen the business. The second is a family business that a husband inherits from his parents. In these businesses, generational conflicts add another level of complexity because a lukchin wife must negotiate with her in-laws as well as her husband. The third type is a business established and controlled by a female entrepreneur who does *not* gain the advantage of having her husband act as her assistant. Certain types of businesses overlap with certain types of kinship structures. By situating a family business within a broader framework informed by ideological, judicial, and socioeconomic forces, we will see how women transgress various boundaries while conducting business, raising a family, and managing conjugal conflicts.

Family Businesses Founded by Husband and Wife

Wong Laoban, a typewriter repairman, and his wife, twenty-seven-year-old Feng Ayi, purchased a bankrupt repair shop in 1966. Feng Ayi, the fourth child among ten siblings, came from a very poor family: "I started working when I was six. I was the baby sitter for a noodle vendor's daughter. She gave me free noodles as my pay. When I was about thirteen, I worked making paper bags. I earned about six baht a day. I went to school at night to study Chinese." By the time she married, she was no longer impoverished, but when she and her husband opened the shop, they could not afford to hire an employee, so Feng Ayi resigned her bookkeeping job to assist her husband by waiting on customers out front while he repaired typewriters in the back. Thanks to demand from the U.S. military during the Vietnam War, their business rapidly expanded. Then, in part because of its location on one of Bangkok's busiest commercial streets, their shop became an IBM affiliate. Feng Ayi reinvested their profits in real estate that, over time, made them rich: "Our business appears to others as a beautiful, stupendous mansion. But no one knows the hardship and hard work we have been through."

Feng Ayi gained expertise and became the chief decision maker, even though her husband was officially in charge. She used to wish that her husband would "be the leader" (*pen phunam*) so that she would not have to take on so much responsibility:

> My husband and I are very different. He is passive. He does not try to improve himself. In the shop he would make excuses and not have work completed at the time he promised. I used to push him, but now I've stopped. He is the way he is. It is difficult to live with a passive husband.

The good thing about him is that he's an honest man. He is not like other men who constantly have affairs with other women.

Being the key decision maker in the family business is apparently considered in some sense "unwomanly." While Chuchu Jie attributed her success in real estate to having a "man's mind," Feng Ayi did not want to do a "man's job," although she did it well. Being a shrewd businesswoman who outshines her husband would tarnish her image as a dutiful assistant and maeban. She was frustrated by her husband's passivity, but she valued his fidelity so she put up with him.

In the second case in this category, Phi Salapi and her husband had also worked separately at different endeavors before launching their own business—a souvenir shop that specialized in selling silk to foreign tourists. Previously, Phi Salapi had worked in a silk factory and her husband had been a loan officer in a bank. They opened their shop in 1965 (three years after they married), and by 1985 they were rich enough to build a fully furnished fifty-room guesthouse in downtown Bangkok. Most of their customers were Japanese businessmen. Recalling the rapid growth of the family business, Phi Salapi said:

> For the first fifteen years I worked especially hard. I had six children. During the day my maid looked after my children, but I fed them and kept an eye on them. The shop was open from 8 A.M. to 8 P.M. year round. We only closed for three days to celebrate Chinese New Year. My husband does not like to deal with customers, so I do it. He is in charge of exporting and financial matters.
>
> Sometimes a husband is afraid that his wife will interfere in his business, so he asks her to take care of the children and family. Then a husband and a wife live in different worlds. A wife has to teach her husband to understand that she would like to assist him and that he cannot live without her. A wife does not create problems. A good couple should be like "a dustpan and a broom."

By emphasizing an interdependent relationship, Phi Salapi convinced her husband that her participation would benefit both their business and the family. Her husband worked in a small but comfortable and brightly lit office. When he traveled abroad to purchase supplies, he stayed at nice hotels. Phi Salapi dealt with customers in the store twelve hours a day, 362 days a year, and raised six children with the help of a maid. Because she was acutely aware of family gender politics, she acted as her husband's indispensable "assistant," but she also thought carefully about how to guide him so that he couldn't "live without her." Phi Salapi deliberately cultivated a collaborative and mutually dependent relationship to disguise the asymmetrical relationship she so keenly experienced. She was never a passive assistant but rather an ingenious negotiator, decision maker, planner, and breadwinner, who purposely made her leadership invisible to her husband.

The third case in this category began in 1970, when Lili Jie, a thirty-two-year-old jewelry retailer, married a thirty-seven-year-old attorney, Chen Laoban. At the time Lili Jie was richer than her husband, whose career had been interrupted in the mid-1960s when he served four years in prison for "communist activities." Soon after they wed, they used their savings, Chen Laoban's legal knowledge, and Lili Jie's business acumen to establish a law and accounting firm.

When I first met them in 1991, Chen Laoban was introduced as the firm's head lawyer and Lili Jie as the chief administrator in charge of more than forty employees. A four-story building served both as business office and family home: the two bottom floors were administrative offices; the two top floors, the family's residence. In describing how they divided the work, Lili Jie referred to herself as the "minister of foreign affairs" and to Chen Laoban as the "minister of internal affairs"—a reversal of conventional gender roles. Meanwhile, Lili Jie also self-identified as her husband's assistant, taking part in time-consuming public functions such as funerals, weddings, and parties on his behalf. She explained that her assistance enabled her husband to spend more time on the "important matters." She performed both "men's work" (being the chief administrator, purchasing cars, giving bonuses to employees) and "women's work" (taking care of her husband and children, supervising two drivers, a cook, and three other live-in domestic workers). Lili Jie acted in several different roles assigned to women only: assistant, wife, and mother of the house. Because she understood that a family business encompassed both economic and family activities, she rarely complained about having to work a double shift.

When I visited the family again in 1996, however, things had changed. Chen Laoban had divorced Lili Jie and married Guihua, Lili Jie's best friend.[1] Lili Jie recalled:

> After Guihua had worked in our company for a year, my husband asked me if he could marry her. I was shocked, but he was serious. Yes, he had worked very hard for the family. He said he wanted to marry her and enjoy his life a little bit. You know, if I had said no, he might have married someone else.

Guihua cannot bear children. She can help the firm. And, if my husband married her, we would not need to spend a lot of money getting her Thai citizenship. I thought we would only be adding one more mouth to feed. I put forward two preconditions before consenting to the marriage: first, we all have to endure. When two people quarrel, the third party should not be involved. Second, we all have to live together because he is afraid of being lonely.

Unlike Lan Jizhe's wife, who had refused to let her husband marry his biaomei, Lili Jie feared that if she rebuffed her husband, he might marry a younger woman, which could pose an even greater threat to her interests. Guihua was too old to produce any rival heirs who might compete to inherit family property, and her language ability (she was fluent in Thai, Teochiu, and Mandarin) would benefit the family enterprise. After carefully calculating the possible gains and losses—the interests of her husband, her children, and the business, Lili Jie chose the middle way: neither passive acceptance, outright agreement, or rejection, but a conditional yes. This middle way, profoundly related to Thai Buddhist beliefs, embraced acts of both accommodation and resistance, mirroring Lili Jie's precarious position.

I later discovered that Lili Jie had agreed to the divorce only after the house, main bank account, and ownership of the family business had been transferred into her name. With these property transfers and Chen Laoban's acceptance of her two conditions, Lili Jie believed that she had made the best decision available to her. She and Chen Laoban registered their divorce, and Chen Laoban and Guihua registered their marriage on the same day. The divorce agreement was dated one day before the marriage license, to make the sequence of events appear proper, but the registry officer who processed both documents showed no concern over the doctored dates.

Legally, Lili Jie became a divorcée; Chen Laoban and Guihua, a married couple. But in practice Chen Laoban now had a major wife and a minor wife. All three parties understood the nature of the polygyny; all their neighbors and friends understood—this was nothing new or unusual for cosmopolitans in Bangkok. Marriage, divorce, property, business ownership, and sex were all integrated at the site where the family and the family business converged.

This overt manipulation of marriage regulations exists side by side with the more prevalent practice of hidden polygyny in Bangkok. What was unusual was that Lili Jie organized and hosted Chen Laoban and Guihua's wedding:

> I invited several of my good friends to the wedding, held at a hotel. My husband and I sat on a sofa, and my husband said to Guihua, "Lili nodded her head for this marriage [gave her permission]. You have to kneel and kowtow to her." Guihua smiled and said, "It is too embarrassing. Please let me escape with this." She gave me a kiss.

By asking Guihua to kowtow to Lili Jie, Chen Laoban publicly acknowledged that Lili Jie, his major wife, was superior to Guihua, his minor wife. However, Guihua did not want to acquiesce so readily. Rather than kowtow, she found her own middle way by giving Lili Jie a less hierarchical kiss instead. Chen Laoban was delighted when Lili Jie then presented Guihua with a Rolex watch as a wedding gift, an extravagance she never would have bought for herself. "I did not want people to think that my husband married a minor wife because I was a bad wife," Lili Jie explained. The expensive gift was her attempt to control the situation by reinforcing her authority over Guihua and making it clear to others—including Chen Laoban—that she was a "good wife."

According to Lili Jie, Chen Laoban felt embarrassed about joining Guihua in her bedroom on their wedding night, fearing that this would make his children uncomfortable.[2] But Lili Jie made him go. She apparently wanted to convey the impression that she was an enduring wife rather than a jealous one. Chen Laoban was caught up in the tension between the contradictory expectations that he act as both virile husband and good father. He was genuinely concerned about hurting his children's feelings by openly sleeping with Guihua, who was his legal wife in the eyes of the law but his minor wife in the eyes of his children.

From that day forward, everything changed. Lili Jie soon concluded that she had "made a big mistake" in consenting to the marriage. Less than two weeks after the wedding Lili Jie and Guihua got into an argument, and Guihua pointed out that she was the *legal* wife and Lili the *ex-wife*. Lili Jie was furious: "Let we three go out together and see who is a *REAL* wife [in the public's eye]." To punish Guihua, Lili Jie had a family portrait taken—excluding Guihua. She then had the portrait enlarged, framed, and hung at the focal point of the living room. The photo was used to remind Guihua of her subordinate position in the family and to show who was the real "mother of the house." Lili Jie gave me a copy of the picture as a keepsake: "My friends were surprised that my husband was willing to be in this picture without Guihua," she said with a smile. But on another occasion, one of Lili Jie's daughters told me that she "hated" this picture because she had experienced the tension, conflict, and bitterness that were present behind the phony smiles. Lili Jie could erase Guihua from the family portrait, but she could not eliminate the negative impact that Chen Laoban's polygyny had on her children and on her life.

One day Chen Laoban talked to me at length about why he had married Guihua:

> I am very tired. I am old [sixty-three]. I will leave this world very soon. Can't I enjoy my life a little bit? What is life for? I asked Lili to let me marry Guihua and also asked Guihua to convince Lili to let us marry. Lili did not have much choice.
>
> I married Guihua for my family. She has no children, no family, no burdens (*mei fudan* [M]). Outside workers are not reliable. A wife is reliable. My children are still too young to take over my business. I need an assistant. I did not marry her for sex. She's fifty years old! It would be funny for me to do that.
>
> I first realized that Lili did not like the idea of our marriage when we were searching for a lucky wedding day. I thought she only had a temporary problem with it (*yishi xiangbukai* [M]). I thought things would get better as time went on. Ten days after our wedding I found that she and my children could not accept the fact that I have another wife. So I thought it might be good for Guihua to go to Australia for a year to give my wife and children time to accept her, but they thought I would move to Australia with her. Lili does not understand me. How could I leave my children and my employees behind? I would never do that. Maybe after all my children have MA degrees, then I will leave for Australia, or maybe I will become a monk.

Chen Laoban sincerely believed that marrying Guihua would strengthen the family business, which reveals how enmeshed kinship, work, and conjugal sex really are, and the extent to which male sexual privilege has become naturalized. He began with rhetorical questions like "Can't I enjoy my life a little bit?" and "What is life for?" Enjoying life, from his perspective, meant becoming a polygynist. He regarded it as reasonable and normal to ask Lili Jie to "let" him marry Guihua. Then, however, he emphasized that he married Guihua for the "family"—not for "sex." On the one hand, he clearly perceived adding another wife as a crucial means for improving the business. He believed Guihua to be more reliable, trustworthy, and devoted than any outside worker. On the other hand, talking about feeling desire or affection for a fifty-year-old woman might not be considered manly in Bangkok, so he desexualized older women by linking sexual pleasure only with young women and connecting older women with family and work. Thus, naturalized male sexual privilege is constrained not only through the distinction between married and unmarried women, but also between young and old women within the unmarried category.

Chen Laoban and Lili Jie, despite having very different agendas, held two opinions in common—at least initially: polygyny was Chen Laoban's reward for years of hard work on the family's behalf; and Guihua could provide reliable and inexpensive labor for the family firm. As Lili Jie put it at first, "We would only be adding one more mouth to feed." Both she and Chen Laoban saw polygyny as deeply connected to work and money. Neither of them imagined that polygyny would so completely disrupt the family and the family business.

Chen Laoban regarded himself as a responsible man who would never leave his children and employees behind. Nonetheless, his polygyny severely weakened the family business; it turned Lili Jie and Guihua, once best friends, into bitter enemies. Lili Jie refused to continue doing what she now called "secretarial work" and demanded a bigger salary. Two of the daughters changed their majors in school from the ones their parents had picked out because they no longer wanted to work for the family business. Guihua demanded a house of her own. Instead of having two women to please him, Chen Laoban became endlessly occupied with one business or family crisis after another.

Polygyny causes women to suffer a great deal, but it does not necessarily provide the happiness or pleasure for the husband that "Western fantasies about harems suggest" (Abu-Lughod 1993:19).

Family Businesses Inherited by the Husband

In a family business that a lukchin man has inherited from his chinkao parents, the conjugal division of labor is often complicated by the relationship between the lukchin daughter-in-law and her chinkao in-laws, and between the son and his parents. Generational, cultural, and gender differences coexist at the site of the business.

In the first case of this type, Phi Ponchai, who inherited a barbershop from his Chinese immigrant parents, had upset them by "allowing" his wife to attend beautician's school: "My parents thought my wife should help me at home [in the barbershop] and learn from me. I did not agree with them. I believe a wife has to learn new skills so that she can help the family. I can find someone else to do the housework. I tutor my wife. I have been re-educating her for thirty years. I am 60 percent successful." Phi Ponchai, who described himself as liberal, conceived of himself as superior to his wife and more farsighted than his parents. However, his wife disagreed: "I am an adult now. I am capable too. I do not need to ask for his opinions anymore." By connecting capability with maturity, she presented herself as an independent woman who did not need to seek her husband's approval. Interestingly, she raised only the gender issue, leaving generational conflicts aside.

In the second case Guoling and his wife both worked in a family-run shoe store. But because of conflict with her in-laws, Guoling's wife went back to work for her natal family, directly challenging the authority of her husband and her in-laws. This rarely happened. A wife is expected to work for her husband's family, contributing labor to her natal family only on special occasions. Her absence put Guoling in a very difficult situation. To prove that he was "a man of social standing," he separated from his wife. The following year his father died and Guoling's wife refused to attend the funeral—an unforgivable insult. Family pressure then compelled Guoling to divorce her. He bitterly commented: "I have videotapes of our wedding and of the registry officer signing our divorce papers."

In contrast to the lukchin woman who cofounded a family business with her husband, neither Phi Ponchai's wife nor Guoling's had anything to gain by being identified as her husband's assistant. Because the patriarchal kinship system already diminishes a daughter-in-law's status, the role of assistant simply reinforces her subordinate position within the extended family. To be a good assistant in this type of family business requires even greater skill in juggling the roles of daughter-in-law, business employee, wife, and mother of the house.

Not all in-laws had such a firm grip on their sons and daughters-in-law. Compared to the wives in the two previous cases, Phi Tatsani, the woman in chapter 8 who stabbed her husband in the arm, had more autonomy, perhaps because her widowed father-in-law was already in his late seventies and no longer active in the daily operation of the business and also because her sister-in-law lived with them but worked for a different company.

According to Thai family law, all assets a couple accumulates after registering their marriage are community property and belong equally to husband and wife. When Phi Tatsani discovered that her husband had not registered his marriage with his Thai wife, she still chose not to register hers: "It is better not to register. If I die suddenly, my children will inherit my money. If we register, the money would be managed by my husband. I bought gold and put it in the bank for my children. I have a will. My little sister, a lawyer, will protect my children." Even though she considered herself to be the wife, what mattered most to her in this context was how to best protect her children's interests.

Although Phi Tatsani did not register her marriage, she did try to gain control of the family business by putting it into her name. When Thaokae Ding and his father refused to accept this, she devised a plan to put it in the name of Suriya, Thaokae Ding's sister. Suriya understood that this strengthened her position in the family and would prevent her brother from ever selling the business to someone outside the family. The two women— who were both distressed and threatened by Thaokae Ding's polygyny— established a new type of reciprocal relationship to protect their common interests. Suriya would pass on ownership of the business to her nephew, the son of Thaokae Ding and Phi Tatsani. In return, the nephew would assume the duty of caring for Suriya, who preferred to remain single, when she grew old.

The high level of conjugal tension, uncertainty, and conflict between Phi Tatsani and Thaokae Ding spilled over into their work relationship. Phi Tatsani stopped functioning as her husband's assistant and cut her own business deals; she took command of the family income and began paying her husband a monthly salary, treating him like any other employee. The power she had gained, however, did not ease her emotional pain; she repeatedly stated that her most difficult daily task was not running the business but managing her emotions:

> The first year [after discovering the polygyny] was extremely difficult. Each day seemed to pass as slowly as a year. I lost weight. I brooded a lot. Even when I knew he was out on business, I imagined that he had gone to meet with that woman again. I told myself, "I should not care about him!" Do you know the Thai proverb "when a husband steps down three steps, he is no longer your husband" (*phuarao long kadai samchan ko maichai phuarao*)? Men are untrustworthy (*phuchai chuachai maidai*).
>
> I have one heart for him. He divides his heart into two and gives me half and gives her half. I try to feel indifferent (*choeichoei*). But my heart is

still very much in pain (*chepchai mak*). I have to control my heart (*thamchai*). If I cannot? I have no alternative. I have to swallow it, even when I feel I cannot swallow any more.

These highly charged emotional terms—feeling "indifferent," "controlling" her heart, and "swallowing" her pain—reveal how much she suffered by remaining in the marriage. She was caught between attempting to remain detached from this untrustworthy husband and feeling deeply hurt by his betrayal. In talking about her marriage and the business, she often wore a forced smile while tears streamed down her face—an expression of the mixed emotions she was experiencing. Or, as she put it, her life was being filled with various flavors: "some sweet, some bitter, and some sour" (*mi pieo, wan, man, khem*).

The business prospered under Phi Tatsani's guidance. And yet, like the entrepreneurial wives I discussed earlier, she tended to minimize her breadwinner role and to emphasize caring for her children, the "sweet" side of her life. "I do not want my children to be stigmatized (*bumdoi*)," she said. "If I divorce, where will we live? I cannot support the children by myself (*liangluk maiwai*). We stick together out of necessity (*yuduaikan duai khuamchampen*), for the sake of the children (*henkaeluk*). My children are my hope." Although divorce was less stigmatized among lukchin by the 1990s, Phi Tatsani did not see how a divorce would improve her situation. By remaining in her marriage, she could still draw income from the family business—a business increasingly coming under her control—and she and her children could continue to live in their current residence. If she divorced her husband, she would have to move out and find a new job.

Despite her good intentions, her unsettled emotions led her children to take sides in the marital conflict. Her nine-year-old daughter told her, "Mom, don't be angry (*yakhiat*). You don't need to care about (*maitong sonchai*) him [Thaokae Ding]." Like Phi Tatsani's daughter, I also gradually became involved. When I asked if I could interview her husband, she said no and asked me to pretend that I knew nothing about their marital problems. I agreed to do this, and while it cost me the opportunity to interview Thaokae Ding, it did enable me to observe how Phi Tatsani managed her emotions and how she performed in public when interacting with her husband.

Just before I left Thailand, I went out to dinner with Phi Tatsani and Thaokae Ding. In the restaurant she freshened her husband's drink and peeled his shrimp—actions in stunning contrast to the anger she had expressed to me over his betrayal. In her desire to be perceived as a good and caring wife, she tried hard to please Thaokae Ding and stay in his good graces. When dinner was over, as she and I fought for the check, Thaokae Ding looked uncomfortable. Even though—with Phi Tatsani's help—he presented himself in public as a respectable husband, the embarrassment he felt over his diminished economic power was all too clear.

Although he no longer controlled the family business, Thaokae Ding retained his sexual privilege. In the past he had secretly rotated between two homes under the pretense of having two jobs. Now he openly traveled between his two wives. On Mondays, Wednesdays, and Fridays he spent the night with his Thai wife; on Tuesdays, Thursdays, and weekends he stayed with Phi Tatsani. The disjunction between his sexual privilege and Phi Tatsani's economic power created tremendous tension in their business and in their conjugal relationship.

When I called her to say goodbye, Phi Tatsani offered me a final bit of advice: "A woman should not love her husband 100 percent. And she should not give all the money to her husband. Otherwise, she will be hurt twice as much."

Family Businesses Established by Wives

Pa Pipada, a Hakka Chinese woman born in 1924 in northern Thailand, regarded her father as "enlightened" (*kaiming* [M]) because he sent her to Meixian county, China, for five years of education. He also trained her to use an abacus with her left hand and do bookkeeping with her right hand, important skills for conducting business efficiently at that time. However, Pa Pipada believed that if her brother, sixteen years her junior, had been born first, her father would never have raised her "like a son."

In the 1940s, "Chinese marrying Chinese" meant marrying within the same dialect group: Teochiu marrying Teochiu, Hakka marrying Hakka, Hainanese marrying Hainanese, and so on. When Pa Pipada decided to marry a Hainan Chinese man who worked as a clerk in her family's grocery store, their cross-dialect marriage caused a sensation. Many Hakka considered themselves superior to the Hainanese because, collectively, the Hakka men had more education. One man took her marriage to be an insult to the entire Hakka community, asking Pa Pipada to her face, "Is there no Hakka man you can marry?"

A few years after her marriage Pa Pipada and her husband opened a small grocery, and she soon discovered that she was the one with the knack for operating a business:

My husband had a very kind heart, too kind to do business well. For example, he trusted the customers and let them use our sacks to carry goods home in. I suggested he charge those who might not return the sacks, or give a discount to those who did bring them back. He said, "You always think the worst about people." But the truth was that we never got those sacks back.

The price of local products in Bangkok often fluctuated. Once when the price of peanuts went up, he sent in peanuts that were not yet dry. I had warned him that the peanuts would go bad in transit, but he didn't listen to me. Finally, we lost the business. He never listened to me until after he failed.

I couldn't continue to do business with him; what would we leave behind for our children? Finally, I told him that I would like to have my own business to manage. At that time I was thirty-nine. I took four children with me to Bangkok and started my own business.

Rather than emphasizing her business talents as the reason for this move, Pa Pipada highlighted her motherly concerns: "What would we leave behind for our children?" Motherhood was invoked as a strategy for escaping the very regime that prevented a mother from being the key bread-winner and chief decision maker. When a man started a business, he could expect assistance from his wife, but Pa Pipada could not count on her husband's labor or his assistance. After she moved to Bangkok, her husband started up a leather shop on the border between Thailand and Laos. Living apart soon affected their marriage, and her husband took a minor wife. Of this development Pa Pipada said:

> It was okay. He had no place to visit prostitutes there. I just told him that he had to make sure she was a good woman. Unfortunately, I found out that she was helping her ex-husband [who was in jail] with the money my husband gave to her. I told my husband this, but he didn't believe me. I asked him to check the bank account he had opened for her, and he found out there was only a few thousand baht left. My husband was so angry he drove her out.
>
> My children hated my husband for taking a minor wife. I told them, "You are his children. He is your father. I have the right to question him, but you cannot do that. You still have to show filial piety (*xiaoshun* [M]) to him." I never let my children see my sadness. When I was in a bad mood or I cried, I stayed alone. I was similar to my mother. My father had several minor wives, and my mother treated them all very well. She said that a person came into this world with nothing and left the world with nothing.

My husband came back to live with me when he was really sick. I took good care of him. Before he died, he said that I was his good wife. He died at age fifty-nine. I was forty-nine.

Pa Pipada seemed to accept her husband's polygyny because he had "no place to visit prostitutes." She intended to follow her mother's lead: treat the minor wife well. Before long, however, she surreptitiously investigated the minor wife. She undermined the polygyny not by challenging her husband's privilege, but by showing him that his minor wife played him for a fool by spending the money he gave her on another man. Just as Pa Pipada emphasized her motherhood and her concern for her children's future to justify running her own business, here she used her "good" womanhood to assist her husband in getting rid of a "bad" woman. Her actions reveal both individual agency and the structural constraints imposed on women. She invariably presented herself as a good woman, who understood men's sexual "needs" and followed the patriarchal family's order, even in the absence of an authoritative male figure. By emphasizing how her husband acknowledged her as a good wife on his deathbed, Pa Pipada again used an authoritative male voice to legitimize her actions as an independent businesswoman.

Establishing a new business in Bangkok while raising four children was no easy task. "I often asked myself when I would finally be able to raise the family out of poverty," Pa Pipada said. "Our meals were very simple. My son told my daughters that we ate not for enjoyment, but to stave off hunger. He understood my hard struggle. For a while I also ran a family restaurant. My son passed out flyers to advertise my restaurant. He was not afraid that he would be laughed at."

With a loan from a *yuehui* [M], a private mutual credit society, Pa Pipada opened a small lingerie shop. She eventually made her fortune not through the shop but in real estate. By helping the chairman of her surname association to buy 400 rai (640 hectares) of land, she made a 5 percent commission, which enabled her to start her own business in partnership with another woman. They would buy a large parcel of land and then divide it into small lots for resale. It was harder and more time-consuming to sell many small parcels instead of one large one, but by doing so, Pa Pipada found customers who could not otherwise have afforded to purchase land. By continually buying and selling land she eventually grew rich: "I often tell my employees and friends that I started out much poorer than they are now." She continued, "When I started my business, I never spent money for soft drinks. I usually carried a basket with a bottle of boiled water, bananas, and some medicine. The water and bananas were for myself. I prepared the medicine for the villagers."

Even as her real estate business flourished, she continued to run her lingerie shop. Her children had to pitch in to keep the family business going:

> Weekdays I took care of my lingerie shop and my family. I could not afford a maid at that time. My daughters washed clothes and I ironed. On weekends my children ran the shop while I went out to survey and buy land. Once I used a boat to survey some land. At that time Bangkok had much more water than now. The boat overturned, and I didn't know how to swim. Fortunately the water was not very deep, but it was very dirty. I looked like a little wet dog. It was not an easy life.

In the mid-1970s political instability threatened her business. Urban-based students made an alliance with Thailand's rural-based Communist Party. After the United States withdrew from Vietnam in 1975, some wealthy people sold their property and fled to the United States or Europe. Her partner panicked and quit the business, but Pa Pipada boldly resisted the trend and bought more land, at better prices. These purchases became the foundation for her future wealth, which grew exponentially from the 1980s through the mid-1990s coincident with Thailand's economic expansion. Compared with the other lukchin in this project, Pa Pipada was especially successful.

After her son, Sawang, graduated from college, he convinced his mother to expand her business by building golf courses on some of her property; Pa Pipada took his suggestion and hired one of the world's leading golf course designers for the project. As golf's popularity continued to grow, Pa Pipada developed more courses throughout Thailand. In addition, her company built and sold custom homes along these golf courses.

In 1992 I attended the grand opening sale at one of the homes. Two new cars and several other prizes were offered in a lottery to encourage customers to buy. In the main hall, company employees used video monitors, magazine-quality sales brochures, and construction models to tempt investors. At the reception, customers and invited guests were served a complimentary gourmet meal. That evening Pa Pipada, the company's president, wearing an elegant designer dress with matching jewelry, walked up to the stage holding hands with her little grandson and delivered a rousing speech to the crowd—which included her American son-in-law (a Caucasian). Following her speech, a documentary film describing the company's success was shown, followed by a modern dance performance. The affair ended with a water ballet in the mansion's Olympic-size swimming pool.

Unlike Phi Salapi, the co-owner of the souvenir shop, Pa Pipada did not disguise her leadership. As a "virtuous" widow and self-made business-woman, she felt comfortable enough to talk about her work ethic, frugal life-style, cooperation among family members, and her courageous risk-taking in conducting business. However, she rarely talked about her business empire without mentioning her family. Even at the grand opening sale, she brought along her entire extended family: children, in-laws, and grand-children. The family business was part of the family's identity.

In preparing for her retirement, Pa Pipada divided the business assets among her four children. She granted her three daughters the right to inherit property, but gave a controlling interest in the business to Sawang, her son. Even in the 1990s, it was still considered radical among the Chinese Thai to give shares of the family business to married-out daugh-ters. Wealthy lukchin often supported education for all their children regardless of gender, but when it came to inheritance, they usually gave the family business to a son. Pa Pipada was keenly aware of the constraints that a woman encountered in the family and in larger society. She wanted her daughters to be independent, and so she assisted them with capital and busi-ness opportunities. Still, she could not completely escape the influence of conventional family gender politics: with a controlling interest in the business, her son would be the company's future president and carry the family's name into the next generation.

Pa Pipada once told me that "marriage is marriage and business is busi-ness," but in practice she never separated the two. In the late 1980s Sawang, who had once opposed his father's polygyny, wanted to marry a minor wife on the grounds that his wife, Sani, had a "bad temper" and had confronted him both publicly and privately. Although Pa Pipada was fond of Sani and considered her "an excellent businesswoman, better than I am," she did not undermine her son's polygyny as she had her husband's. The stability of Sawang's marriage would be an important factor in maintaining the family business empire. Therefore, Sawang's minor wife was asked to have a tubal ligation as a precondition for becoming a family member. This stipulation recalls Lili Jie's demands before agreeing to let Chen Laoban marry a minor wife. Pa Pipada wanted to ensure that her current grandchildren would inherit the family business. Sani was given an independent business to run as compensation for accepting the polygyny; Sawang was allowed to marry a minor wife, but one who could not bear children. To prevent the possibility of splitting up the family or the family business, Pa Pipada used one to counterbalance the other, forming an inseparable nexus.

Pa Pipada acted the part of a kind and gentle grandmother, but she was an exceptionally tough and flexible negotiator who constantly shifted positions, resolving conflicts and dissolving tensions within the business and the family. Her complicated emotional and financial maneuvering in dealing with her son's polygyny revealed the interlocking nature of marriage and business: marriage carried economic consequences, and business enhanced the kinship network and the division of labor. The interactions between production, reproduction, and sexuality profoundly affect how labor is organized, how family economic resources are redistributed, and how nei/wai sex is managed.

A widow at forty-nine, Pa Pipada never remarried. If she were to do so again, she would be expected to marry a man of comparable social status. But a rich and powerful man would be more likely to want a much younger wife. And what would Pa Pipada gain from such a union? She already had her children, whom she described as the "best thing" from her previous marriage. Now she was her own boss. She was free to devote herself to her family and finish the projects she had begun: developing her company's subsidiary in Hong Kong, making improvements to the primary school in northern Thailand built from her donations, and helping the village near that school establish small handicraft businesses.

To succeed as an independent businesswoman, Pa Pipada had to climb every rung on the ladder that an entrepreneurial man has to climb, but she also had to overcome a barrier that no man has to contend with: confronting a business world that does not welcome an entrepreneurial woman. Her decades of effort—running a restaurant, operating a lingerie shop, becoming a real estate agent, and finally developing and building golf courses and luxury homes—represent both a class and a gender struggle. That is why her narrative was so full of stops and starts, as she maneuvered both within and around the patriarchal system.

———

Indeed, *khuam pen chin*, "Chinese-ness," takes on gendered meanings in the context of the family business, for a family business is a complex amalgam of production and reproduction, involving kinship, money, and sex, among other things. Behind a husband there often stands an equally capable middle-class businesswoman, sharing the work but not the credit. When an entrepreneurial woman presents herself as an "assistant" and a "mother of the house"—crucial emblems of her class respectability—she should not automatically be regarded as her husband's subordinate, nor should we assume that he in fact runs the business. We need to understand a gender-specific practice: a businesswoman maneuvers within and around these hierarchical structures, often transgressing them while she seems to be conforming to them, and vice versa.

A lukchin man's business success—at least as exhibited in this chapter—is tied to his wife's labor; and sexuality is one of the factors that all of this hinges upon. His middle-class respectability allows him to transform his business success into polygyny on behalf of the family and the business; he is not bound by his marriage in the same way that a wife is bound by hers. Therefore, a businessman's structural privileges embedded in kinship and the sexual domain serve to mask an exploitative labor relationship within the family business.

A lukchin businesswoman is often expected to contribute her labor to the family business while continuing to take charge of the housework—but the reverse is not true. With or without the help of a domestic worker, she feeds, clothes, and looks after the family; she reproduces human life; she interacts with customers and often performs the most minute kinds of administrative work. She seems forever in motion, constantly at work, doing several things simultaneously. The economic accomplishments of the Chinese Thai testify to the value of the women's labor. Often neither the family nor a newly established family business would survive without the unremitting and unacknowledged labor these businesswomen provide.

PART IV

THE CHINESE THAI
AMERICAN EXPERIENCE

10

Multiple Belongings

Thai people don't think I'm a Thai because I'm really Chinese, and Chinese people don't think I'm Chinese because I speak Thai and I eat Thai. I'm culturally Thai. But my blood is Chinese because my grandparents are from China. . . . And then I look Korean too. The first day I walked into Thai class, they were all thinking, "What is this Korean girl doing in this class?" Later, when they found out I was Thai, they all just started laughing. . . . But if you are asking me what I identify with, I would probably say "Asian American"—I feel that's different from "American." You are whatever you think you are.

—MARY, a Chinese Thai American

LIKE MOST CHINESE Thai Americans, what Mary expressed in the epigraph above reveals many of the same issues her parents and grandparents had struggled with; at the same time, however, she encountered a wider assortment of identity categories—Thai, Chinese, Korean, Asian American, and American—than they had to deal with. To believe that "you are whatever you think you are" must be empowering. But as our interviews progressed, it became clear that despite her belief, she could not avoid the constraints imposed by American identity politics and family gender politics, a topic I will discuss in more detail below.

For many years, scholars have argued that women in Southeast Asia enjoy "higher status" than women in China and India (Reid 1988:629; Van Esterik 1982a:1). Thai women, for example, have historically been known for controlling family finances, actively participating in small businesses, and inheriting family property. However, the situation is more complex than it might at first appear.[1] The chinkao and lukchin cases demonstrate that the issue is not just who handles the family money, but what the money is used for, and what culturally specific meanings are assigned to women's

economic role. Rarely do chinkao or lukchin regard their gender relationships as less equal than those of their Thai counterparts. As we have seen,
Chinese nei/wai and Thai na/lang cultural principles intertwine with other
forms of social inequality to produce complex, culturally inflected gender
relationships.

A recent study suggests that Vietnamese American women gain more
power and enjoy more gender equality in the United States because of the
impact of American culture, increased job opportunities for working-class
women, and a shift in the scope and significance of women's homemaking
activities (Kibria 1993:109, 111). However, expressions of power and forms
of gender inequality can vary from culture to culture and from time to time.
No simple criterion of high versus low status can measure the social status
of women cross-culturally (Atkinson and Errington 1990:7). We should not
assume that gender relations in the United States are necessarily more egal-
itarian than they are in Southeast Asia, or that gender relations in Southeast
Asia are less hierarchical than in East Asia. Instead of measuring current
cultural principles and practices against those of an earlier time, we should
examine how they are reorganized and given new meanings, and how men
and women renegotiate their gender relationships in new contexts. In this
way we can better understand the process through which identities are
reproduced and transformed over time. Otherwise, we could easily misread

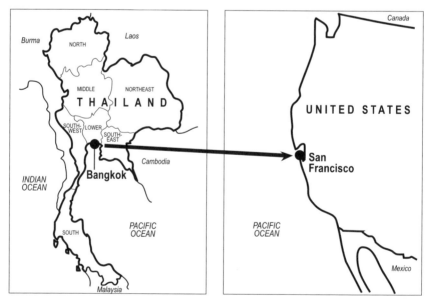

Migration from Thailand to the United States

changes in gender relations as linear and progressive—just as assimilation theorists have misread the issue of identity.

There is, of course, more than one perspective with regard to gender relations among Asian Americans. As the literary critic Sau-Ling Wong notes, the image of emasculated Asian men versus ultrafeminized Asian women prevails in Asian American literature (1992:111–129). The emasculated Asian man is contrasted with an overmasculinized African American man and an undefined "ideal" white masculinity. In the same way, the notion of an ultrafeminized Asian woman is added to the discourse about "white" and "black" femininity. In this context, notions about sexuality are associated with gender differences, for it is ethnic or racial groups, and not just individuals, who are being characterized.

The prevailing racial discourse that Sau-Ling Wong has sorted out for us reveals how categories of ethnicity and race are filtered through particular conceptions of sexuality and gender. In the United States, as in Thailand, sexuality is deployed to draw boundaries and marginalize others by speaking from a superior position. Racial hierarchies and discourses within class and race-stratified settings, therefore, shape Asian masculinity, femininity, and sexuality. Indeed, we cannot think about ethnic and racial identities without thinking about sex and gender, since subjects are made into men and women.

However, my focus here is not just on the racialized discourse in American society, but also on everyday gender relations within the Chinese Thai American community. Having examined marital practices among Chinese Thai Americans, I am convinced that Chinese Thai American men are not really emasculated because patriarchy has not disappeared. Despite being displaced, much of their gender privilege remains; they express their power and authority in different configurations as their masculinity is being reconstructed in new power settings. In the same vein, Chinese Thai American women have not become ultrafeminized because they do not stop negotiating with the patriarchal system when they move to the United States. Some women in Thailand may appear submissive but are actually very determined—like Phi Salapi in chapter 9, a decision maker who acted as her husband's indispensable assistant.

Like identity, sexuality and gender relations are unstable; they are influenced by ethnic and racial relationships, and vice versa. The masculinity and femininity of chinkao and Chinese Thai Americans has been constructed twice, first in the society in which they were born, and then again in the society to which they have immigrated. The transformation from money-oriented masculinity to what I call "economically responsible womanizing masculinity" directly shaped the cultural identity of chinkao and lukchin men, and it helped set up the boundaries they perceive between themselves and others. Although socioeconomic upward mobility has provided chinkao and lukchin women with a certain degree of power and autonomy, they are constrained by gender-specific regulations of sexuality embedded in the political and economic power structures of Thai society.

In contrast, Chinese Thai American men are constrained by American middle-class sexual morality. Monogamy, or at least the appearance of it, has become the ideal. Polygyny, visiting brothels, or seeking sexual conquests, are much less frequently seen as key indicators of masculinity in the United States, and they may sometimes even work against middle-class respectability. However, some men continue to patronize brothels when they go back to Thailand—especially if their male friends or business associates invite them out to have "fun" (*sanuk*). As one woman put it: "When the plane lands [in Bangkok] he stops being my man." Transnational mobility renders Chinese Thai American masculinity even more complicated, fluid, and temporal.

Remaining faithful to one's husband continues to be an important aspect of a Chinese Thai American woman's middle-class feminine identity. However, in the San Francisco Bay Area at least, a single woman need not be sexually detached in order to be respectable. In response to the new cultural environment, some unmarried women have begun to seek sexual pleasure, a fact that recalls how the early male Chinese migrant laborers responded to the relaxed sexual regulations in Siam. Nonetheless, these women are not entirely free, for if they were to have a child out of wedlock or if they were to have a relationship with a married man, their respectability would be instantly called into question—which shows how gender-specific constraints can take different cultural forms. More important, they are simultaneously engaging with and are being judged by competing American, Thai, and Chinese cultural criteria.

In Thai society, being Thai confers more cultural privileges than being Chinese Thai, but collectively the Chinese Thai occupy a more privileged class position than many Thai and any other ethnic group in Thailand. It would be simplistic to think, however, of the Chinese Thai as economically powerful but culturally inferior. Chinese Thai economic capital has been transferred into the political arena. Wealthy Chinese entrepreneurs or their male descendants have become members of parliament, cabinet officers, and even prime minister; but no matter how powerful they become, their ethnic Chinese background leaves them vulnerable—as Prime Minister Banharn's case revealed in chapter 6. Although Chinese migration and the immigrants' cultural practices have profoundly influenced Thailand's economy, language, and cuisine, the politics of assimilation minimize or dismiss such an impact. Without a careful consideration of that impact, our understanding of the history of Thai nation-building and Thai nationalism will remain incomplete.

Most Chinese Thai who immigrated to the United States before the 1970s were from elite or middle-class families. However, since it requires more capital and a more extensive socioeconomic network to start up a business in the United States, some of them experienced downward mobility. In addition, few can afford to maintain the privileges of middle-class life in Thailand, such as having a live-in maid to cook and clean. As a group they have found it difficult to transplant into American society the political and economic power that they enjoyed in Thailand, for the political, economic, cultural, ethnic, and racial landscapes of Thailand and the United States are different. And while the Chinese Thai are virtually invisible politically and economically in the United States, the color of their skin makes them socially visible—and vulnerable to discrimination. In Thailand they may pass as a "real" Thai by adopting a Thai name, speaking central Thai, and acting Thai, but it is much harder to pass as a "real" American. Even if they are American-born and able to speak perfect English, they are often asked "Where do you come from?" or "What's your nationality?" This makes them wonder: who counts as an American? Why do those who claim to respect diversity so often demand conformity rather than appreciating differences?

Identity is never static but continually changing, like a river. Currents flow at different speeds depending on the condition of the riverbed, and of course the river itself can widen or narrow as the flow of water changes. It may curve gracefully or zigzag drunkenly; it may meander peacefully, then abruptly sing or roar. No snapshot can capture its energy or do justice to its shining surface or craggy depths. And since a river is also part of a larger system, one must also try to understand the geography of its surroundings.

We need to break down the boundaries between Asian Studies and Asian American Studies so that we can connect identity formation among Chinese Thai in the United States with chinkao and lukchin identity formation in Thailand. If we study Asian Americans in only one setting, such as American society, we will fail to understand their history, how they have been transformed, and how they make different connections with various nation-states and cultures. No immigration or economic history is possible without a cultural history: a history of displacement, class, sexuality, gender, the division of labor, names, and acts. We also run the risk of ascribing to them a certain homogeneity of experience and end up examining a snapshot of the river instead of seeing the river itself in motion. But by studying Asian Americans as a cluster of flowing currents, we may be able to understand how previous cultural practices have been disrupted, or reproduced, or reconfigured in the new setting.

From "Married-Out Daughters" to Transnational "Bridge Builders"

While dining in a Bangkok restaurant one evening, I talked with Thaokae Zi, the cosmopolitan polygynist who appeared in chapters 4 and 5, about what it meant to be Chinese in Thailand. Thaokae Zi, who often identified himself as Teochiu, turned philosophical: "I am a Thai. Since China is my natal family (*niangjia* [M]), I am like a married-out daughter (*chujia de nüer* [M]). I have my own family (*ziji de jia* [M]). I visit my parents' home [China], but it is not my home." By evoking the asymmetrical gender and kinship systems, Thaokae Zi, though biologically male, described himself as a socially disadvantaged female, a married-out daughter. This metaphor captures the experience of the Chinese Thai throughout the twentieth century: marginalized in Thailand because of their ethnicity and marginalized in China for living abroad as overseas Chinese. They have been caught between China/niangjia, their natal family, and Thailand/*pojia*, or the family of their in-laws—tolerated but not fully accepted in either place.

A married-out daughter occupies the most marginal and peripheral position in the kinship structure in China. Only when she has a son and hence her "own family"—or to use Margery Wolf's phrase, a "uterine family" (1972)—does she become a significant member of her pojia, the family of her in-laws. Her status and identity remain in flux throughout her life. A married-out daughter is caught in a web of relationships between those in her own home, those in the home of her in-laws/Thailand, and those in the home of her natal family/China. She must act according to several conflicting and unstable identities imposed upon her by the hierarchical kinship structure.

Since implementing its open-door policy in late 1978, China has encouraged the overseas Chinese to "bridge" the gap between post-Mao China (in Mandarin, the word for bridge puns with "*qiao*," the word for overseas Chinese) and "the four modernizations" that China has been attempting to achieve (Zhao 1993; *People's Daily* 20 July 1994).[2] For the first time in its history China has provided overseas Chinese with investment opportunities more advantageous than those offered to any other group of foreigners.

Some of the wealthiest married-out daughters have established close social and economic ties with China, especially in the emigrant regions. For example, Bangkok Bank opened its first branch office in mainland China in 1993 in Shantou, the cradle of Chinese migration to Thailand (Simons and Zielenziger 1994; Wang 1993). Choosing Shantou was more than simply a business decision: it was a way for the bank to honor its ancestors and pay respect to their birthplace. Only after opening the Shantou branch did Bangkok Bank then establish its headquarters on the Bund in Shanghai's financial district. In 1993 Thai Prime Minister Chuan Leekpai, whose Chinese name is Lu Jiwen, acknowledged that "Thailand has more foreign investments in China than in any other foreign country in the world" (*People's Daily*, 27 August 1993). By 1997 the largest foreign investor in China was the CP Group—Charoen Pokphand, a multinational Chinese Thai family enterprise (Vatikiotis 1997:38–44). An increasing number of Chinese Thai are becoming major economic players in Thailand, China, and the global economy.

When China suffered severe flooding in 1991, hundreds of delegations in Thailand spontaneously formed to gather donations for flood relief. In less than a month, money, medicine, and rice worth US $5.2 million was collected, a large percentage of which came from married-out daughters in Thailand.[3] One male volunteer who helped distribute these donations in China excitedly told me, "Now, because of us, people in Anhui province know where Thailand is." He was very proud of being a "bridge builder" between Thailand and China.

Although the Chinese Thai have established political, economic, and financial networks in China, very few have gone back to settle there permanently. The Chinese Thai were among the first to send their children to study and live in Hong Kong, Singapore, Europe, and the United States, but China is not currently considered a "safe haven."

Internet access and modern transportation have enabled more and more Chinese Thai to reach out to countries all over the world through business and professional networks. The most visible change is that dialect association gatherings or conferences are no longer organized at the township or national level but internationally. This engenders a new collective

The Second International Federation of Hainanese Association was held in Bangkok in 1991. Such gatherings have helped engender a new collective sense of Hainanese-ness and Chinese-ness. (Photograph by the author.)

sense of Teochiu-ness or Hainanese-ness among individuals, no matter where they now live, and the transnational connections of these associations make them see the world and themselves from a global perspective. Rather than treating displacement as a disadvantage, they use it as an opportunity to mobilize their capital, human resources, and skills. They have been gradually transforming themselves from married-out daughters into transnational bridge builders, forging links between China and Thailand to be sure, but also connecting China with other countries, communities, and families throughout the world.

Chinese Thai Americans in the San Francisco Bay Area

In the early 1970s there were no Thai restaurants in the Bay Area; by 1997 there were more than 200. One restaurant owner, Mr. Zhang, said that "90 percent of my customers are white Americans—Thais usually do not eat in Thai restaurants." These restaurant owners often use their knowledge of Thai culture to promote business. Some dress their waitresses in Thai sarongs and waiters in formal Thai outfits; others invite musicians and dancers trained at Thai temples to perform. This marriage between cultural diversity and marketing has made Thai restaurants important sites for displaying and celebrating Thai American identity and culture.

Both Thai and Chinese Thai participate in a Kathin ceremony, the annual robe presentation ritual, at a Buddhist temple in the San Francisco Bay Area (1997). American dollar bills are attached to a Buddhist "money tree." (Photograph by the author.)

At the same time Bay Area Thai restaurants are fashioned to satisfy the taste of American customers. Typically, Bay Area Thai food is much less spicy than in Thailand, and the presentation of Thai food culture has adjusted to local cultural expectations. When Mr. Zhang first opened his restaurant, no chopsticks were provided. For him, offering only forks and spoons—the utensils commonly used in Thailand—symbolized Thai culture differentiating itself from Chinese food culture. His customers kept requesting chopsticks, however, so Chinese chopsticks are now laid out with the forks and spoons at each table in his restaurant. A popular Thai saying captures this sentiment: "When you move to a city of cross-eyed people, you also have to become cross-eyed" (*khaomuang tariu, tong riuta tam*).

Between 1951 and 1960 only 458 people were registered as immigrants from Thailand to the United States.[4] But after passage of the Immigration Act of 1965, the number of immigrants from Thailand increased more than tenfold, to 5,256 for the period 1961 to 1970 (U.S. Immigration and Naturalization Service 1984:4, 7). Many were the descendants of wealthy Chinese Thai who had originally come to the United States to earn college degrees. Jacqueline Desbarats (1979:308) found that half of her survey participants in Los Angeles had "at least one Chinese parent" and that the majority came from "the Phra Nakhon province, which includes the twin cities of Bangkok and Thon Buri," where the Chinese Thai are concentrated. Many Chinese Thai students were supported by their families, and unlike students supported by Thai or U.S. government scholarships, they were not obligated to return to Thailand after graduating or required to finish their degrees within a specified period of time. As a result, some remained in the United States and became permanent residents or American citizens.

These pioneering Chinese Thai immigrants, who were classified legally as Thai, entered the United States from the 1950s through 1970. Like the Chinese labor migrants who first came to Thailand, they were overwhelmingly male. But the two groups differed dramatically in class status and educational and occupational backgrounds: the Chinese Thai who came to the United States were mostly cosmopolitan professionals from middle- and upper-class families; the Chinese laborers who migrated to Thailand were mostly illiterate and penniless peasants. In the past, pioneering Chinese women went overseas to join their husbands and unify the family. Nowadays some women immigrate to the United States in an effort to preserve their marriages. For example, Anan's grandfathers had immigrated from China to Thailand to escape poverty decades ago. Now, almost fifty years later, in an attempt to work out family and marital conflicts, Anan and his family have immigrated from Thailand to the United States. Anan gave me this account:

> As you know, in Thailand there are a lot of men who have extramarital affairs. It's very, very common—almost a norm. If you ask any men, most of them are playing around. And my dad was the *king* [laughed a bit nervously]. Problems started even before my older brother was born, which was about a year after they got married. He worked for his [widowed] mother, my grandmother, a very strong Asian figure. He would leave work early, go off to a brothel or a bar, play poker with his friends, come home late. Whatever. So my mother suffered a lot of emotional hardship, and there were always conflicts between my mother and her mother-in-law. Always. I think that was partly why my parents moved to America: to get my father out of that environment and to take care of the problem between my grandma and my mother.
>
> The first year we were here, I could tell that my dad was very unhappy. It was hard for him to stay home at night and watch TV. And my mom also worked at reminding us of how he was in Thailand, and how everybody should prevent that from ever happening [in the United States]. I think she went to an extreme. She ended up almost creating paranoia. She was strictly against him finding other Thai friends because she was afraid "they would

bring him down again." And this affected me and my brothers too. If my dad went out to see a Thai friend, to other people that sounded like a very normal situation. But when I heard about it, I said: "Oh, my God. Uh oh. It's going to start all over again." We were living in tension and fear. *I was baby-sitting my father, you know?* In a way, we look at our father, not as a model, but almost as an "anti-example."

Drawing upon the American cultural principle that marital fidelity matters, Anan's mother, Supang, attempted to control her husband's behavior by isolating him from his friends in the Bay Area. In Bangkok a father may take his adolescent son to visit a sex worker as a rite of passage, so the idea of having a son "babysit" his father would be virtually unimaginable. Relocation and cultural disruption provided Supang with new space in which to monitor and curtail her husband's chaochu masculinity. Thus transnational movement reshaped marital practices.

Anan's rich grandmother provided enough capital for her son's family to immigrate to the United States and purchase a Burger King franchise to operate as a family business. By doing so, she hoped to prevent the break-up of her son's family and perhaps also find a way to make her own life in Thailand more peaceful. Interestingly, Anan did not refer to his grandmother as a strong Thai figure but rather a "strong Asian figure"; he spoke from his position in the United States, lumping Thai into the larger category "Asian."

Although he rejected his father as a role model, Anan resented his mother for "creating paranoia" in the family. He expressed a mixture of sympathy and resentment toward his parents. Supang had to negotiate with her husband, who had been shaped mainly by Thai culture, and with her sons, who were more influenced by American culture. With the family still traveling back and forth between Bangkok and the Bay Area, this gender battle is far from over.

While entire families are sometimes uprooted, some families may send just one individual abroad. Lum, an only son, was sent to a boarding school in the Bay Area when he was eight years old, having spent the previous six years in boarding schools in Bangkok. His parents, preoccupied with business and marital conflicts, rarely spent time with him. The telephone became his lifeline to his family.

Today the largest Thai community outside of Thailand is in Los Angeles. According to the 2000 U.S. Census, the Thai population in the United States had reached 150,283, a growth rate of 64.6 percent for the decade;

and it is now more broadly diversified by age and class than it was in the 1970s and earlier. Unlike the Chinese, Japanese, Indian, Korean, and Filipino immigrants from the mid-nineteenth to the mid-twentieth century, as well as the more recent war refugees from Vietnam, Laos, and Cambodia, the Chinese Thai Americans have been predominately urban, educated, middle-class professionals.

"White Skin" and the New Politics of Names

Skin shades in Thailand, like skin color in the United States, have political, religious, racial, and ethnic meanings. The Thai term *phiukhao* literally means "white skin." A lighter skin shade is considered desirable and—especially for women—beautiful. In addition, it is said that "the Buddha classified human beings into six different categories according to the color of their minds": black-minded people are bad, white-minded people are good, and in between there lies a wide range of people with "other colored minds" (Wiyada 1979:118). Some temple murals vividly depict the link between the color of minds and skin shades. The higher the status, the lighter the skin; the lower the status, the darker the skin: the hierarchical order descending from the Buddha, down through angels, monks, lay people, and those in hell is unmistakably expressed visually through skin shade. Skin shade is used to legitimize hierarchical relationships.

Not surprisingly, chinkao and lukchin often emphasized that "white skin" (*bai pifu* [M]) was a feature of the Chinese. Of course, it is easily shown that some ethnic Chinese are actually darker than some ethnic Thai, and that there is no biological basis for the supposed superiority of lighter skin shades. However, the social impact of such beliefs is very real: "When my mother was pregnant with me, she prayed to Buddha every day asking for my skin to be light like hers, not dark like my father's," said Candy, a college student who had a lukchin mother and a Thai father.[5]

Ruth Frankenberg points out that in the United States not talking about color consciousness is a white privilege; seemingly neutral "color blindness" actually supports white racism by refusing to acknowledge the links between racial ideologies and socioeconomic structures (1993). The United States constructs a racial continuum with whites at one end and blacks at the other. Asians (lumped together as "yellow") and other racial minorities fall at various places in between (Espiritu 1997:109).

Chinese Thai Americans quickly discovered that being Thai or having a Thai name in the United States no longer carries the privilege it had in

Thailand. Indeed, in the United States, Chinese are better known than Thai. Mary's experience was typical: "When I say, 'I am Thai,' they say, 'Oh, Taiwanese.' I say 'Thailand' and they say 'Oh, Taiwan.'" Sometimes it is simply easier to identify oneself as Chinese or Chinese American, a category often considered a "model minority."[6]

Sae, a symbol of Chinese-ness in Thailand, creates confusion in the United States that would never arise in Thailand. For example, Susan said, "In the past [in the United States], when I separated Sae and Jiang [Susan Sae Jiang], people thought Sae was my middle name. Now I put them together, but I capitalize them," as in Susan SaeJiang.

Chinese Thai Americans, especially the younger generation, tended to change their first names rather than their family names. "In my primary school there were only two Asians," Mary said. "The other kids made fun of my name and my eyes [she used her hands to slant her eyes]. They thought my name was strange, but it was a combination of my parents' names. They always teased me. I couldn't stand it, so I changed my name to Mary." Mary's predicament reminds us of how chinkao and lukchin, nearly fifty years earlier, changed their names and downplayed their Chinese identity in an effort to pass as Thai.

Chinese Thai Americans are usually not committed to any particular name. They change their names in response to both national and transnational regulations. Restoring a Chinese family name, for example, does not necessarily reveal a desire to disassociate oneself from being Thai and to become more Chinese. Changing a Chinese name into a Thai-ified Chinese name, then changing it back to a Chinese or an American name reveals a heterogeneous process of identity formation. And Chinese Thai Americans are not alone in manipulating names and identities. An increasing number of Chinese Southeast Asian war refugees identify themselves as Chinese Americans, "a phenomenon that contributed to a significantly higher count of the Chinese population in the 1990 census" (L. Wang 1994:197). In order to avoid being identified as refugees, they sought to locate themselves in a better position within the class- and race-stratified society of the United States. Clearly, the politics of naming plays an important role in identity formation and transnational migration.

"Chinese-Slash-Thai"

Bill, a young computer scientist, had immigrated twice by the time I interviewed him in 1994. Not long after the fall of Saigon in April 1975, his parents, who feared that communists would take over Thailand, moved the family to Hong Kong. Later, after his father bought a hotel in California, the family immigrated again, this time to the United States.

"When I first came to California," Bill said. "I lived in a small middle-class town where we were the only nonwhite family. I was called 'oriental.' But now, in Berkeley, I have had to rethink who I am. I am *Chinese-slash-Thai.*" While he rejected the colonialist category "oriental," Bill embraced two other categories and integrated them into one of his own: "Chinese-slash-Thai." The "slash" reflects a sense of newness, hybridity, and ambiguity; the "slash" not only connects two divided identity categories, but joins the past and the present by delineating what Homi Bhabha calls "contingent 'in-between' space" (1994:7). This hybrid category "creates a sense of the new as an insurgent action of cultural translation" (ibid., 7). "In Thailand, the mentality is different," Bill said. "If you are Chinese, you have a lot of difficulties. You play down being Chinese. But it is very easy to get mixed up because there is not much difference between the religions or physically [as there is in the United States]." From Bill's perspective, despite the physical and cultural similarities shared by Thai and Chinese people in Thailand, he found it easier to be Chinese in the United States.

When the conversation shifted to the job market, he switched his previous position: "My parents told me I had to be better than a white [person]. If I am only just as good as him, I will not be hired." Aware that he lacked the "appropriate" racial and cultural "origin," Bill apparently believed that higher education and better skills might compensate for racial inequality. He also talked extensively about his family in relation to his own sense of identity:

> I would not say I am Thai because my parents said I am Chinese. I would say I am Chinese, but born in Thailand. I can speak Teochiu with my grandma who does not speak Thai. Many of my friends do not even know their family names. I am Sae Dang. . . . Chinese-ness means you respect your parents. You will support them when they get old; you will not dump them in an old folks' home. At sixteen, I was at a rebellious stage. I yelled at my father, "Fuck you." He said: "Fine," then he left. If he had yelled at me, I would have felt better. He did not. He made me feel very guilty. I never did that again.

His sense of Chinese-ness, at this moment, was rooted in his Teochiu language skills, his Thai-ified Chinese family name, and the cultural principles that he learned from his family: respect hierarchies, take care of the elderly, and show filial piety. His statement "I would not say I am Thai because my parents said I am Chinese" contradicts his earlier Chinese-slash-Thai identity, however. His self-identification seems to be characterized by inconsistency and ambiguity. Living somewhere between Chinese and Thai, he has embraced parts of each category in a U.S. setting.

Bill's multiple cultural belongings and hybrid identities are inseparable from his struggle to exist between different social categories and between different cultures and nation-states. Many Chinese Thai Americans I knew shared his strategy of taking the middle path, or assuming, as he put it, a Chinese-slash-Thai identity. While regarding themselves as Chinese, they are also proud of being Thai.

The Naturalization of Ethnicity/Race

In Bangkok, in 1991, Thailand's former finance minister, Huang Wenbo, delivered the keynote address entitled "The Second Generation Hainanese" at the Second International Federation of the Hainanese Association Conference. He began as follows: "I apologize that I use Thai because I cannot speak fluent Hainanese. In my body my Hainanese blood is as thick as yours. . . . I will remain Hainanese forever (*cha raksa khuamphenhairam talotchiwit*)." He was warmly applauded, especially when he emphasized his Hainanese blood and Hainanese-ness. Although what he meant by Hainanese blood was never explained, the audience seemed to understand what he meant: Hainanese identity—a regional as well as a dialect identity—as articulated through blood heritage. He seemed to share the view of Achan Paisan in chapter 6, that authenticity is somehow connected with percentages of inherited blood.

This blood metaphor is used to draw boundaries within Chinese communities, distinguishing Hainanese from Teochiu, or Teochiu from Hakka, and so on. It is also used to mark the boundaries between Chinese and Thai. "My parents said I 'put family honor and social status into a drawer' (*kiat-diyot chusiang khaonai linchak*), which means that I was disgracing the family," is how thirty-nine-year-old Phi Rattana recalled her chinkao parents' opposition to her marriage to her Thai schoolmate. "Among my eleven siblings no one married a Thai. I was told that no one who married a Thai ever had a happy life. My neighbor married a Thai man and she ended up divorced; she alone supported her children." I asked her husband, Phi Ae, who sat quietly next to her, for his opinion. He replied: "Our marriage was an economic issue. I was poor. Her parents thought their daughter would suffer if she married me. Now things are reversed. I am richer than they are." Ethnic and cultural differences can disguise underlying class differences. However, Phi Rattana believed that ethnicity also played a role in her parents' initial opposition to the marriage. "Phi Ae is very handy. He is able to do many things and does them well. He is so much like a Chinese, I even wonder if he might have some Chinese blood in him." She attributed her Thai husband's diligence and economic success to possibly possessing Chinese blood. On the one hand, Rattana conformed to Chinese logic by attributing cultural identity and entrepreneurship to "Chinese blood." On the other hand, suggesting that her husband might have inherited some Chinese blood could imply a wish to regain the Chinese cultural membership she had lost by marrying a Thai.

The naturalization of ethnicity and race has deep historical and cultural roots. China's regime has used the Chinese blood metaphor to reach out to overseas Chinese. In Thailand, kings are believed to have inherited a large store of positive karma through their blood from previous incarnations, so they "have merit" (*mibun*), which gives them the right to rule (Keyes 1987a:417). This blood discourse has continued in the Bay Area. Chonan, a former employee of a U.S. intelligence agency during the Vietnam War and now a finance officer in Oakland, talked about the pain he experienced from racial discrimination in the United States—which reminded him of the discrimination ethnic Chinese faced in Thailand. He said:

> I will tell you the truth: every time I feel that I am being discriminated against, I have sympathy for the Chinese people in Thailand. Remember, I am 25 percent Chinese. My grandfather came from China and married a Thai. He sent my father back to China for more than ten years because he wanted him to be a Chinese merchant. My father returned as a Chinese immigrant, then he married my mother, who was Thai. Chinese people in Thailand have been seriously discriminated against for a long, long time. But I never felt it so strongly until I lived in the United States.

Chonan resented the ethnicized regulations that the Chinese Thai had to endure in Thailand. And yet he conformed to Chinese and Thai cultural logics by identifying himself as only "25 percent Chinese," based upon his blood heritage; he regarded the loss of his Chinese blood heritage as equivalent to the loss of his Chinese cultural identity. A half century earlier his grandfather had tried to turn his "mixed blood" father into a "Chinese merchant." In contrast, Chonan conceived of his father's identity as based solely on blood descent and not on cultural aspects, such as having lived in China or manipulated Thailand's immigration laws. I often heard an individual say "I am half X and half Y," but never "I am doubled"; this is the power of naturalization and evidence of how notions of race and ethnicity are ingrained in the language. Chonan took identity politics so much for granted that he failed to recognize that things which seem natural—such as the significance of blood or skin shade—are actually culturally constructed.

Chonan also claimed that he had to perform better than his white counterparts in order to get hired or earn a promotion:

> I went through all the pain, all the sweat, and all the tears in order to get my job. But they [his supervisors at work] would not let me attend the management training program. Another person who didn't have a degree got to go. He is a white American. I don't want to use that term [racism], but I don't know why I didn't get it. I worked very hard for three and a half years to learn the job. I started as a part-timer and became the manager. I had surpassed everybody in terms of knowledge and skill. Khun Latsami [my Thai name], *you have to outclass them by a lot. You cannot be just a little better than they are. If you are only a little ahead of them, you will lose everything* [he raised his voice and became emotional].
>
> They look at me as Thai because of the way I talk, the way I look. If it talks like a dog and walks like a dog, it is a dog. As a Buddhist, I ignore them, but I still feel the pain. Buddhism helps me to eradicate these pains. I am richer than many Americans who have been here for more than 200 years.

Chonan appears to have been unevenly shaped by Thai and Chinese culture. Thai Buddhism deeply affected how he lived his life. He discovered that his bachelor's degree in economics from a university in Thailand and his Thai cultural capital had little value in the United States (although they were valued by the U.S. intelligence services during the Vietnam War). In addition, his physical appearance and his foreign accent singled him out as nonwhite. However, like many Chinese Thai Americans, Chonan was very class conscious and his middle-class income made him feel superior to working-class white Americans. He sometimes brought up his economic success as a way of compensating for the discrimination he has endured.

Mary brought up the issue of gender in relation to blood when she once stated that her brother is "more Chinese" than she is. When I asked her what she meant by "more Chinese," she said: "My brother can do whatever he wants. It's because he's a boy, because he's got a penis. Right now, he's thirteen years old. Once I went home to visit my family in San Francisco over spring break. He went out and he didn't come home for three days. . . . If I had done that, there would have been police at the door looking for me. But with him it's okay because he's a boy." Blood heritage—which conflates gender—made Mary feel that her brother had more rights than she did, despite each having inherited "100 percent" Chinese blood. What Mary felt recalls what the Chinese Thai women encountered in Thai society: chinkao and lukchin women automatically forfeited their Chinese cultural membership when they married out of the Chinese community; lukchin women sometimes were not even considered to be "Chinese children" (lukchin) because of their gender; many were deprived of inheritance rights just because they were daughters; and until very recently, lukchin women, but not lukchin men, would lose their Thai citizenship if they married individuals who were not Thai citizens. Thus the logic of patriarchal kinship plays a significant role in regulating Chinese cultural membership and Thai citizenship.

Nevertheless, for Mary, being a Chinese daughter in the United States did not reduce her educational opportunities, as was the case for her mother in Thailand and her grandmother in China. Her family moved from a small town in California to San Francisco so that Mary could attend one of the best public high schools in the country. Her mother, a laboratory technician, and her father, a doctor of microbiology, expected her to become a physician. To some degree, their middle-class respectability depended upon their daughter's success: "They want me to be a doctor. I do want to be a doctor, but not just a doctor: I want to be a cardiothoracic surgeon. But they think that is too much. They want me to be a physician, STOP, and then start a family, just like that. But I don't think that way." Mary's career options were constrained not because she lacks intelligence or ability but because of family expectations related to her gender. Being a heart surgeon is considered a man's job, and marriage is secondary in importance to a man's career. Mary, on the other hand, is expected to marry and bear children before she grows too old. These aspects of gender, racial, and ethnic inequality are sometimes so deeply naturalized that they are completely taken for granted.

Transforming Middle-Class Respectability, Masculinity, and Femininity

While womanizing as proof of masculinity is marginalized in the United States, being a successful breadwinner continues to be a key indicator of middle-class masculinity for Chinese Thai American men. Material goods have become increasingly important for showing off class status. Driving a prestigious car, having a home in a desirable community, having the children attend elite schools, having a privileged job—all have become strong status-evoking indicators of masculinity. For those who have experienced downward mobility in the United States—and especially when they encounter former acquaintances—material goods have become even more important symbols of power, status, and identity. This transformed masculinity typified by materialism is deeply rooted in the American culture of capitalism. This does not mean that materialized masculinity is not meaningful in a Thai context. It is. But in Thailand individuals tend to show off their class status by owning a shop or a business, by the number of maids they can afford to hire, and by the ability to speak fluent English.

Although premarital sex is still a sensitive issue, many Chinese Thai American women in the Bay Area gain space from the loosened sexual restrictions. Having premarital sex, for example, no longer automatically labels a woman as "bad"—as long as she conforms to other rules, such as doing well in school, avoiding pregnancies, and not changing boyfriends too often. American-born Candy feared that her mother "would kill her" if she found out that she and her Thai American boyfriend, Visut, were living together. But when she finally told her mother the truth, it was Candy who was shocked:

> My mother was so relieved. She said she felt better that I had somebody to protect me. When my auntie came from Thailand to visit me, Visut moved out. My mother told me to clean out the closet and to take away all of Visut's clothing. She said: "I do not want her to think that I raised my children wrong." The first thing my aunt did was to go through everything, all my clothing, everything. I thought, "My God, how did my Mom know this?"

Cultural disruptions produce unpredictable results. Candy was surprised to discover that her mother, Watdi, had also been changed. Watdi, who had previously taught Candy to protect her virginity until her wedding night, now conspired with her daughter to hide the fact that she lived with her boyfriend. She subtly connected premarital sex with her daughter's safety rather than with immorality, while still maintaining gendered expectations: Candy needed a man to protect her from other men.

By saying that she did not want her sister "to think that I raised my children wrong," Watdi expressed the anxiety created by consciously crossing boundaries. Although she did not see her daughter's premarital sex as threatening her middle-class respectability in the Bay Area, Watdi wanted her sister to think that she still obeyed Bangkok's rules about middle-class respectability, which dictate chastity and a daughter's virginity before marriage. She remained concerned about what those left behind in Bangkok think about her and her daughter. Thus the diasporic Chinese Thai are regulated not only by the nation-state in which they currently reside; they are also unevenly influenced by the nation-state they have left behind. So while appearing to be monogamous has become meaningful for Chinese Thai American men, the appearance of not having become "morally loose" remains meaningful for Chinese Thai American women. Watdi's prediction of her sister's conduct springs from the Thai stereotype regarding *farang* girls: Euro-American girls are regarded as sexually "easy" or "loose" compared with Thai women. Since immigrant women and their daughters live in a "cross-eyed" country, they are consequently suspected of having become "cross-eyed" themselves.

Racializing or ethnicizing the girls of another culture is a way to assert that we and "our girls" are better. Cultural imaginations and stereotypes can cut both ways. In Japan, Germany, and the United States, young Thai women have often been imagined to be sex workers (Borthwick 1999:216; Cook 1998:256). As Mary said: "Here [in Berkeley] people, including my TA [teaching assistant], think every Thai girl is a prostitute." Pikul, a graduate student, told me that when she first immigrated to Berlin, she was shocked to discover that in Germany being a Thai woman was synonymous with being a sex worker. Her anger and shame summoned up memories of similar emotions she had experienced in Thailand, where she had denied her Chinese identity and prohibited her parents from calling her by her Chinese nickname in front of her friends. Like Chonan, Pikul's diasporic encounter forced her to rethink her own identity. In an effort to reclaim a Chinese identity she had long rejected, she enrolled in a Chinese language class.

In contrast to Candy and Watdi's nervous performance, Visut was guilt free. No one, in Thailand or the United States, questioned his privilege to have premarital sex. For a man in the Bay Area, it is extramarital, not premarital sex that might call his middle-class respectability and masculinity into question. The emotional lives of Chinese Thai American women and men, like those of their family members in Thailand and China, are deeply gendered with regard to the politics of sexuality and marriage.

Chinese Thai Americans feel the tension between where they came from and where they live now in virtually every aspect of their lives. American individualism had a profound impact on Watdi. She divorced her husband less than two weeks after discovering his affair, for she now regarded her divorce as an individual matter. For many chinkao and lukchin, men and women alike, a wife who endures her husband's sexual privilege and sacrifices herself for her children is respected and regarded as a strong woman. But in the United States, Watdi was transformed into a new type of "strong Asian woman": she worked full time and went to school at night to earn a degree in order to get a better job, and raised her daughter by herself.

While it was easy for Watdi to divorce her husband, collecting alimony payments from him proved very difficult. She and her daughter suffered a sharp drop in their standard of living. Only after many years of supporting her daughter on her own did she finally sue her ex-husband for nonpayment of child support. The meanings of middle-class respectability and of being a "good" man or woman in Chinese, Thai, and American society are not the same; individuals experience constraints that are specific to each culture and gender-specific expectations that shape how they feel about themselves as well as how they believe they should act.

Flexible Acts within Persistent Constraints

Chinkao, lukchin, and Chinese Thai Americans live at different distances from the so-called original Chinese, Thai, and American cultures. Their identities are far from being bounded, coherent, and easily apprehended; instead they are ambiguous, inconsistent, and sometimes apparently contradictory. In responding to ever-changing identity politics, shifting political and economic structures, and different cultural milieus, they have developed hybrid identities, sensibilities, and lifestyles. In their Chinese-ness there is Thai-ness, and in their Thai-ness there is Chinese-ness. For Chinese Thai Americans, various aspects of Thai-ness and Chinese-ness are integrated into their American-ness. New hybrid practices and meanings emerge from the diasporic in-between space—between where they came from and where they are now, between ideologies and practice, and in the spaces between different categories, nation-states, and cultures. Authenticity is constantly being challenged and refined. And yet, hybridization and partial belonging do not represent a free oscillation between chosen identities; rather they represent the effects of transnational migration, cultural displacement, and the penetration of different kinds of ideologies into different social spaces.

As cultural actors and reactors, chinkao, lukchin, and Chinese Thai Americans move in and out of various social categories, including Teochiu,

Chinese, chinkao, lukchin, Thai, overseas Chinese, chek, married-out daughter, Chinese-slash-Thai, Chinese Thai American, American, and Asian American. Individually and collectively they are in a perpetual dialogue with one another by virtue of the continuous cultural struggle in which they are involved. Their generational differences cannot be explained as the result of a single "progressive" linear transformation. Nor can these transnational individuals be understood if we conceive of them as belonging to a single social category, such as Thai, Chinese, or American. Because of their particular attachments to each of these categories at different times in their lives, chinkao and lukchin would like, at the very least, to be seen as Chinese Thai, instead of either Thai or Chinese. Many Chinese Thai Americans want to encompass aspects of all three categories—to be simultaneously Thai, Chinese, and American. Clearly, the meanings of identity are not circumscribed by national boundaries. And for many, the struggle to articulate their cultural differences in various national settings has been a source of strength. Thus we are challenged to grasp identities in motion at the points where many competing constructions collide.

Marriage fosters and reproduces fundamental ideas of identity, masculinity, and femininity. Among the diasporic Chinese Thai, the constructions of masculinity and femininity embody asymmetrical gender relationships, with masculinity occupying a superior position. In addition, masculinity is not meaningful only for men, or femininity only for women; the two categories are in dialogue with each other while also interacting with categories of class, ethnicity, race, and citizenship. Among these people, feminine and masculine identity, at least in part, is defined and mediated by marriage and the family, first in China, then in Thailand, and now in the United States. Diasporic Chinese Thai masculinity and femininity must be understood as being many-faceted rather than singular.

The institution of marriage constrains men and women structurally, politically, economically, emotionally, and physically. But perhaps its most profound effect is with regard to sexuality. The individuals I interviewed practice marriage but do not wholeheartedly believe in it. Among their greatest accomplishments are the strategies they have created to maintain the institution of marriage and to reap the benefits that the nation-state provides them for doing so.

Only by studying both men and women will we become conscious of how gender-specific practices contribute to the boundaries between masculinity and femininity. It is impossible to overemphasize the significance of including women and heterosexuality in a study of the diasporic Chinese

Thai. It is also important to remember that the people described in this project are not only citizens of different nation-states but also actual *men and women* with individual dreams, desires, and responses to different political and economic systems.

Class greatly affects gender and heterosexual practices, and sexual conduct expresses class just as education, occupation, money, and material goods do. The Chinese Thai have developed what I call "gender-specific middle-class sexuality." Economic capital and the breadwinner role are crucial for chinkao and lukchin men, both in terms of social status and in terms of having an exclusive right to cross nei/wai sex boundaries. In contrast, chinkao and lukchin women emphasize their middle-class morality and sexuality by marginalizing the Other—working-class Thai women who cross sexual boundaries. These gender-specific acts contrast with another kind of marital practice in the United States, serial monogamy: that is, marriage, divorce, and remarriage. Chinese Thai Americans must rearticulate their masculinity and their femininity, just as they rearticulate their Chinese Thai cultural identity in the United States.

Diasporic Chinese Thai men and women articulate their classed sexuality differently because of different experiences of personal and institutional power. But what remains consistent across all three generations is that conjugal sex serves many purposes besides reproduction. Sex, like class, ethnicity and race, also plays an important role in the process of identity formation. Furthermore, class inequality is interlocked with inequalities of sex, gender, ethnicity, and race. No one kind of inequality is independent of the others, just as no single aspect of identity—sexuality, gender, ethnicity, race, or class—can be accorded *a priori* primacy.

In this book we have encountered not only transformation and differences but also persistence and sameness in the formation of diasporic Chinese Thai identity. Monogamy and heterosexuality are two of the most prevalent and the most taken-for-granted cultural elements passed along from generation to generation. Three different nation-states—China, Thailand, and the United States—fashion marriage to make it appear as a natural institution. But heterosexuality, production, and reproduction are not automatically yoked together; they are consciously organized around the institution of marriage in culturally specific ways by the different nation-states. Regardless of where they live, most chinkao, lukchin, and Chinese Thai Americans continue to wrestle with identity politics and marriage, fully aware of the political, economic, and judicial privileges each confers.

NOTES

Chapter 1: Introduction

1. In Thailand, two hill tribes, the Mien and the Hmong, also use *sae* before their surname, based on the logic that they share Chinese culture.

2. Suryadinata estimated the number of Chinese descendants to be about 13 percent of Thailand's total population or approximately six million in 1985 (1989:1).

3. The Thai Buddhist notion of karma is, roughly speaking, a system of merits and demerits accumulated from past lives.

4. Someone might argue that the chinkao had not bought houses in Thailand because Chinese citizens did not have the right to buy property. But I would argue that legal access was not the major reason. If they really had wanted to buy a house, they could have done so—by purchasing one in the name of a Thailand-born child, for example. They found ways around many other regulations and could have circumvented this one as well.

5. In discussing transnational migration, I use the terms "migration" and "immigration." Prior to the twentieth century, many Chinese men went abroad for long periods but then returned to China. No passport was required. A son born in China might go abroad and replace his father at work so that his father could return to China and live out his remaining years. This practice continued through several generations. I call these people "migrants" and their movement between countries "migration." Immigration came into being when the modern nation-state emerged, and people could no longer legally cross borders without documentation.

6. As Ien Ang points out, diasporic space is often seen as "in-between," the space between "where you're from" and "where you're at" (1993:9, 13 quoting Gilroy 1991). This space, she notes, is not empty; it is filled up by new forms of culture that are the result of the collision between the old and the new.

7. The notion that "all Chinese are rich" is a false stereotype. Class differences among Chinese Thai in Bangkok are readily apparent. Some elderly Chinese Thai men and women I met no longer had the strength to do heavy labor but still did casual work. One chinkao man in his seventies told me that he earned 17 baht for every kilogram of bean sprout roots he could pinch. Working dawn to dusk, he could pinch about 10 kilograms and earn 170 baht (a little less than US $7 based on the 1996 exchange rate of 25 baht = US $1). A wide gap between rich and poor was visible. While the middle class live in homes with air conditioners, many from the working class are crowded together in rundown shacks in slums. In one building I surveyed, residents were crammed together in tiny windowless rooms, almost suffocating in Bangkok's debilitating heat. On each floor there were two water faucets shared by several families. These faucets were kept locked and the water turned on only twice a week. Each family had to rush and compete for water, saving it in big basins so they would have enough for the next several days.

Chapter 2: The Ongoing Process of Identity Formation

1. How gender relates to Southeast Asian Chinese cultural identity formation is rarely discussed (e.g., Cushman 1991; Cushman and Wang 1988; Suryadinata 1997; Wang 1997, 1992, 1991). For instance, Judith Nagata focuses on situational identities (1974); Leo Suryadinata points out that Chinese in China and Southeast Asia are deeply heterogeneous (1985); and Wang Gungwu argues for multiple identities (1988).

2. In writing about marriage in Southeast Asia, anthropologists tend to analyze kinship systems, marital structure, marriage rules, and rituals (e.g., Aphichat 1984; Freedman 1979; Spiro 1977). These aspects are exemplified in Maurice Freedman's classic, *Chinese Family and Marriage in Singapore* (1957). Except for Melford Spiro's work (1977), these studies tell us surprisingly little about heterosexual practices. A notable exception to the tendency to dismiss the links between sexuality and class has been the work of Aihwa Ong and Ann Stoler.

3. I wish to thank Hubert L. Dreyfus for sharing this insight with me.

4. During my fieldwork in 1992, male seniors at Chulalongkorn University still took male freshmen to visit a brothel as a social outing.

5. The terms *neiren* and *waizi* are still used by chinkao in Thailand but rarely used in mainland China today.

6. A small number of women who chose not to marry did migrate abroad to work as maids (Topley 1959:213).

Chapter 3: The Gendered Politics of Migration and Marriage

1. Among the eight chinkao men that I interviewed in depth, seven were child laborers when they immigrated to Thailand. All eight had family members who had migrated to Thailand, or another Southeast Asian country, for at least two successive generations.

2. I learned these two folk songs during my fieldwork in Shantou.

3. According to the 1909 records there were 1,441 Chinese women, 950 Siamese women, 56 Annamese women, and 50 Lao women registered that year (Dararat 2000:30).

4. Even though the amount of money remitted by individual migrants might be relatively small, over the years the collective total was substantial. Today scholars disagree as to how much money was sent back. James Ingram speculated that if remittances averaged approximately US $10 million from 1890 to 1941, based on the exchange rate of the time: US $1 = 2.5 baht, the total remitted would have been about 1.25 billion baht or a little over US $500,000,000. But Landon reckoned, as Ingram noted, that total remittances likely totalled "not more than 2 percent of the 'wealth' created by the Chinese, and not more than 10 percent of their net profits," a much lower figure (Ingram 1971:204; Landon 1941:165–167; see also Skinner 1957:125, 226, 364–365).

5. In Malaysia the Baba Chinese, who incorporated aspects of Chinese, Malaysian, and occasionally European culture into their own, usually preferred that their daughters marry Chinese immigrants instead of local Malays (Tan 1983:56–78; Freedman 1979:84). In the Philippines some *mestiza* (individuals with Chinese fathers and Filipino mothers) also married back into the Chinese community (Omohundro 1981:130).

6.　　*Chinese Immigration to Thailand by Year and Gender*

Year	Total	Male	Female
1919	260,194	205,470	54,724
1929	445,274	313,764	131,510

Year	Total	Male	Female
1937	524,062	335,524	188,538
1947	476,582	319,196	157,386

Source: Coughlin, *Double Identity* (1960:23), citing *Statistical Yearbook of Thailand, 1939–44 (1952).*

7. Of the nine chinkao women I interviewed in depth, six came to Thailand as wives, two as daughters, and one was sold as a maid. All nine were the first generation of women in their families to immigrate.

8. An amendment to the 1941 Land Act, signed into law in March 1999, now permits Thai spouses of foreigners to own land (Temsak 1999).

9. Any offspring of an unregistered married couple is considered only the mother's legal child.

10. A horoscope or "eight characters" (*bazi* [M]) consists of four pairs, indicating the year, month, day, and hour of a person's birth; each pair is made up of one Heavenly Stem and one Earthly Branch. Compatible horoscopes were considered essential for a good marriage.

11. Grandma Jinzhi's face was scarred from smallpox, so a go-between had arranged a marriage for her with a bald-headed migrant man in Thailand. The logic was simple: both had physical drawbacks so neither could complain about the other on their wedding day; each impediment was seen as canceling the other out and thereby making it a "fair" match.

12. Although it was considered a good match to share the same dialect and regional identity, sharing the same name was taboo. People with identical surnames were thought to share the same ancestors.

13. The chinkao I interviewed used a "remittance office" (*piju* [M]) to send money to China.

14. Chen reported that some migrants wrote to their wives in China as few as three times in thirteen years, or twice in twenty-one years (1940:142).

15. According to Skinner, "in 1955, the government revealed that its annual income from the opium monopoly approximated 117,000,000 baht, including 67,200,000 from the sale of opium to licensed dens and 47,300,000 in tender bids for den licenses" (1957:364–365).

Chapter 4: Middle-Class Chinese-ness, Nei/Wai Politics

1. In the 1940s, 25 sadang = 1 salung; 4 salung = 1 baht; 20 baht = US $1.

2. For a more detailed discussion, see Hewison (1981:395–412); Ingram (1971:231); Riggs (1966:251–310).

3. The well-known Asia Trust group was chiefly made up of Teochiu speakers who came from Caoyang and Chenghai counties (Suehiro 1992:46).

4. According to Mackie, in the 1990s "Thailand's commercial and industrial activity is dominated by about thirty large conglomerates of which all but two (the Crown Property Bureau and the military-owned Krung Thai Bank) are owned by Sino-Thai" (1992a:174).

5. By the 1950s it was easy to find live-in Chinese domestic workers because of the large number of female immigrants.

6. In the 1990s most domestic workers in Bangkok were ethnic Thai from northern Thailand or ethnic Lao from northeastern Thailand.

Chapter 5: Changes in Sexual Practice: "Same Bed, Different Dreams"

1. Emily Ahern remarks that ideas about sexual intercourse that have been widespread in China since ancient times perhaps still influence the attitudes of country people today. Ahern writes: "According to these ideas, during intercourse a man absorbs the female yin essence, which strengthens his vital powers. Ejaculation, however, results in the debilitating loss of vital yang essence. Too frequent intercourse so drains a man's vital essence that he is vulnerable to several serious diseases" (1975:209).

2. Brown and Xenos report that having extramarital affairs or visiting sex workers is more prevalent in Thailand than in some other Asian countries (1994:5).

3. For various reasons—e.g., fear of disease, reluctance to spend the money—some men would accompany their friends on brothel visits but then wait outside or in the bar (Van Landingham et al.,1995:xii, 21).

4. For a detailed discussion of "Chinese-traditional" as opposed to "cosmopolitan-modern," see Skinner (1958:54–60).

5. Registration does not provide people working in private businesses with health insurance or maternity leave, as it does for government service employees.

6. *Khun Chang Khun Phan* (Mr. Chang and Mr. Phan), a work by Sunthon Phu, one of Thailand's greatest poets, explicitly plays upon this theme in recounting a complicated love story (Anuman 1988:69–70). Khun Phan, a legendary hero, is represented as both a great warrior and a prodigious philanderer.

7. The number of Sarit's mistresses has been variously reported; Susanne Thorbek reported he that had more than 200 (1987:113). Penny Van Esterik writes: "Prime Minister Sarit was a particular connoisseur of beauty contest winners and used to take his mistresses (numbering over fifty) (Wyatt 1982, 285), to his 'pink heaven,' his bedroom" (1996:212). Thak Chaloemtiarana notes that "while the public in general did condemn him for using government funds for his own personal enjoyment, he was widely admired for having the effrontery to acquire mistresses on such a grand scale. Practically no one was immune to his overture—beauty queens, movie stars, night club hostesses, university and secondary school students, young and not so young. His elaborate network of procurers was the envy of many" (1979:338–339). A few years after Prime Minister Sarit's death (in December 1963), it was revealed that his estate amounted to approximately $145 million and that he had used government funds to invest in businesses and to maintain his mistresses (Keyes 1987b:79).

8. The Service Establishments Act of 1966 legitimized the entertainment industry and sought to control its operation and effects on the public order and morals. In practice, "special services" are left open to the customers' request and customers are exempt from penalty (Truong 1990:156).

9. Thai officials made it explicit that sex workers were to be regarded as an economic asset (Truong 1990:128, 179). General Prapas Charusathiarana, minister of the interior and one of Thailand's most influential men in the 1960s, declared that the sex industry "attracted tourists and was good for the economy" (Bamber, Hewison, and Underwood 1997:49).

10. The World Tourism Organization reported that international tourist arrivals in the developing countries increased from 6 million in 1962 to 40.2 million in 1978 (Truong 1990:101).

11. The first case of AIDS in Thailand was reported in 1984, but it was not until the beginning of 1994 that the epidemic "moved from a rare and obscure condition to one having a significant impact on every Thai family" (Bamber, Hewison, and,

Underwood 1997:51). In 1992 most chinkao of my acquaintance did not know how one acquired HIV.

A Johns Hopkins research team found that the HIV rate among 1991 draftees studied during 1991 to 1993 was five times higher than the rate among 1993 draftees studied during 1993 to 1995 (Smith 1998; Beyrer 1998:33). According to the World Health Organization, as of the year 2000, the estimated prevalence of HIV in Thailand, a country of 61 million people, is a little over 2 percent among those fifteen to forty years old (Prangtip 1997). More recently, a Thai state policy requiring "100 percent condom use" in brothels has reduced new HIV infections. But some men still refuse to use condoms. For example, "one sex worker recalled asking a client to use a condom. He replied that since he had spent money to 'buy' her services, he would not be getting his money's worth if he used a condom" (ibid.).

12. Vasectomies among chinkao men were not that common. Many were afraid it would decrease virility and make them less capable of performing hard work.

13. Fighting against the imposed social stigma, sex workers have created new terms such as "working with guests" (*thamngang kap khaek*) to dignify themselves.

Chapter 6: Hybrid Identities

1. While Bangkok's Chinese New Year celebration overtly exploited women's bodies, the Chinese New Year's parade in Nakhon Sawan was much more subtle. For example, four young girls marched in the parade dressed in ethnic Thai and ethnic Chinese outfits carrying a banner that read: "The Chinese and the Thai are as close as family members" (*Zhong Tai yijia qin* [M]).

2. Although masculinity is hidden and mute within the beauty contest, chaochu masculinity never stops communicating with the ongoing construction of femininity. A wealthy womanizer can convert a beauty queen's attractiveness into social capital by marrying her or taking her as his mistress. A beauty queen can also transform her beauty into economic capital.

3. Female beauty has played a crucial part in both the negotiation of Thai customs and the process of establishing Thai civilization. Thongchai Winichakul points out that ancient Siam saw itself as one, not the only, overlord in the region. India and China were recognized as the world's two great powers, cultural and otherwise, until Europe emerged as the new center of global power (2000:533). Siam's pursuit of civilization in the late nineteenth and early twentieth centuries was "an attempt originated by various groups . . . to attain and confirm the relative superiority of Siam; as the traditional imperial power in the region, Siam was anxious about its position among modern nations" (ibid., 529). Changes that leaders thought would make Siam civilized included revised etiquette and dress codes and white teeth (ibid., 529).Women's appearance was tied into the image of the nation and its relationship with other states. Siamese women were asked to stop chewing betel nut, which stained their teeth black, to let their hair grow long instead of maintaining their short crewcut style, and to give up their "comfortable draped pants," which were also worn by men (Van Esterik 1996:213) because the old practices would make the outside world think that Siam customs were those of "jungle people" (Vella 1978:153). Thus, Thai femininity was refashioned to respond to the needs of building a modern nation. This official reconstruction of beauty apparently accompanied the national struggle for civilized imagery.

4. Because of his "stubbornesss," as Lu Laoshi called it, they continued living in a rented apartment. Only after Geng Xiansheng died in 1986 did Lu Laoshi finally buy a house. But she enjoyed her house for only a few years before dying of colon cancer in 1993.

5. Banharn was also accused of plagiarizing part of his MA thesis, and his daughter Kanchana was accused of illegally profiting from land she sold to the Bank of Thailand (Mintier 1996).

6. The documents Banharn presented were later verified by the Suphan Buri police chief and the leaders of five coalition parties, who pronounced themselves satisfied with the findings (*Bangkok Post* 21 September 1996).

7. Originally chek was a Teochiu term for uncle, but it came to be used as a derogatory epithet directed at the ethnic Chinese in Thailand.

Chapter 7: *What's in a Wedding?*

1. As Sandra Cate has noted, Bangkok residents in the 1990s "have rated traffic as their foremost concern—dramatically ahead of wages, poverty, government effectiveness, or inflation" (1999:28). To make it on time for school or work, thousands of students and workers had to leave home at 5 a.m. or even earlier. Some middle-class parents carried sleeping children from bedroom to car, drove them to school, then fed and dressed them in the parking lot. Some elite-class men and women hire chauffeurs. In November 2000, golfer Tiger Woods, whose mother, Kultida, was born in Thailand, came to Bangkok to play in a tournament. The *Bangkok Post* reported "Confirming his star status, Tiger will travel each day to the Alpine Golf and Sports Club by helicopter to escape the city's notorious traffic snarls" (Thangarajah 2000).

2. Even though this is regarded as a Thai tradition, the Hong Kong Chinese have this custom too (Watson 1985:121). In Hong Kong the entryway is blocked by a group of unmarried girls; no jewelry is involved. Here both married and unmarried men and women block the groom.

3. There are six pairs of clashing birth years: rat and horse, cow and goat, tiger and monkey, rabbit and chicken, dragon and dog, and snake and pig.

4. For homage to ancestors and Buddha worship, three incense sticks were lit and three dishes—pork, chicken, and fish—were served as offerings. However, when paying homage to the Chinese house deity, five of each item was required: five sticks of incense, five cups of tea, five vegetarian dishes, five meat dishes, and five bowls of yi. This notion of five, I was told, was related to the idea that there are five primary materials of life: wood, fire, soil, metal, and water. Bananas and oranges are considered ideal fruit for rituals. Bananas symbolize continuity of the family line—generation after generation—and oranges connote prosperity and good luck.

5. Thai weddings are usually held in even-numbered months based on the lunar calendar. August and September are exceptions to this rule. August, an even month, is considered unlucky because it is the first month of Buddhist Lent. September, an odd month and the ninth month of the year, is considered lucky because the number nine is associated with good fortune. Each year, it is believed that there is a special lucky month to hold weddings; for 2000 the most auspicious month was November (*Bangkok Post*, 4 November 2000).

6. Funerals are the exception; four monks are usually invited to conduct funeral services.

7. A groom is required by law to furnish *sinsot khongman* to the bride and her parents. *Khongman*, often in the form of jewelry, serves as an engagement gift for the bride; *sinsot*, often in the form of cash, is given to the bride's parents. In Thai society it is quite common for parents to receive "compensation" for their daughter when she marries. A bride from a wealthy family, or who is considered exceptionally beautiful or highly edu-

cated, commands more "milk money." Born in the 1950s, Mani was the only lukchin in this project who refused milk money, believing that accepting it meant "selling herself." When Mani's widowed mother found out, she was outraged. She said, "If I had known you would turn out like this, I would have put ashes (*khithao*) into your mouth [to smother her] when you were born." She believed that the amount of milk money reflected her daughter's worth. Not receiving any milk money indicates that something is "wrong" with the bride, threatens middle-class respectability, and violates family gender politics. An "appropriate" marriage payment is related to the family's public face. Privately some middle- and upper-class parents voluntarily give back the milk money as a gift to their daughter or to the newlywed couple. And yet, milk money serves as an index of the daughter's "worth" and the family's status within the community. Middle-class respectability and status are articulated at several levels: ideological discourse, economic power, sexual practices, and cultural symbols.

8. I want to thank Kanokwan Tharawan and Siranush Archavanitkul for confirming the meanings of the pomegranate leaf.

9. Some lukchin were too poor to afford a wedding ceremony. Chuchu Jie said, "I got married without a wedding. It felt like eloping." When I interviewed her, she was already in her fifties, the mother of two adult children. After all these years, she still felt stigmatized for not having had a wedding ceremony. For her the wedding was public acknowledgment of a couple's marriage and carried more social significance than legal registration.

10. Although they held the wedding in a Catholic church, a friend of the family told me that the newlyweds also conducted Chinese rites at home (also see *Bangkok Post*, 6 February 1997).

11. See Bangkok Bank's official website at http://www.bangkokbank.com.

12. Some elite-class couples are known to have paid a large sum of money to Thailand's most famous "national fortune teller" to read their horoscopes and schedule their wedding ceremony for the most propitious time for this "once in a lifetime" event.

13. It was quite common for chinkao to give their children and grandchildren both Chinese and Thai names to be used as needed in different cultural contexts.

14. The price for a full-page announcement or advertisement in the *World News Daily* was 10,000 baht; a half page cost 5,000 baht, and a quarter page went for 2,500 baht.

Chapter 8: Naturalized Sexuality and Middle-Class Respectability

1. Fletcher and Gearing have observed that polygyny "affects all layers of society. Even men who are not well-off end up taking a minor wife" (1997). One-fifth of the women who sought help from the Friends of Women Foundation in 1997 did so because of issues related to their husbands having minor wives (ibid.). While polygyny is common in Thai society, there has been no comprehensive study of it, and there are no official statistics to measure its scale.

2. In his study of Chinese families in Taiwan, Myron Cohen also recognized this: "Women are accused of harboring a mutual antipathy which threatens the relationship between the men when actually it is the men who by keeping the [polygynous] family together set the women against each other" (1976:201).

3. A belief in *yuan*, a kind of supernatural force related to a person's past lives that predetermines relationships in future lives, is often used to explain why two unlikely people happened to become a couple.

4. I only met Lan Jizhe's wife once. She was a divorcée with a son from her previous marriage. However, Lan Jizhe would not allow her son to live with them, so her only child had to live with her sister.

Chapter 9: Shang Jia: *"Family Business"*

1. In the late 1970s, discouraged by her circumstances in Thailand, Guihua had bribed an immigration officer and immigrated to Australia disguised as a Laotian refugee. However, she could only find employment as a factory worker and felt terribly lonely. She returned to Bangkok to attend her mother's funeral in 1993, and Lili Jie offered her a job. Although Chen Laoban could have married Guihua without divorcing Lili Jie, the divorce was a legal stratagem primarily designed to accomplish two goals: to meet Lili Jie's demand that she be the sole legal owner of most family property and to avoid paying a large fee to restore Guihua's Thai citizenship, which was necessary so that she could work legally in Thailand.

2. Their four daughters were opposed to the marriage and had refused to attend the wedding.

Chapter 10: Multiple Belongings

1. In her study of family life in northern Thailand, Sulamith Potter observes that within matrilocal families formal decision-making authority is vested in men (1979:21). So even though Thai men may not directly control money, they enjoy the privilege of being considered the head of the family, for "authority is passed from man to man" (ibid., 20).

2. The "four modernizations" refer to industry, agriculture, science and technology, and national defense.

3. Personal communication from a reporter at the Xinhua News Agency in Bangkok (10 August 1991).

4. *Thai Immigrants Admitted to the United States from 1951 to 1984.*

Year	Number admitted
1951–1960	458
1961–1970	5,256
1971	2,915
1972	4,102
1973	4,941
1974	4,956
1975	4,217
1976	8,100
1977	3,945
1978	3,574
1979	3,194
1980	4,115
1981	4,799
1982	5,568
1983	5,857
1984	4,885

Source: U.S Department of Justice. *1984 Statistical Yearbook of the Immigration and Naturalization Service,* pp. 4, 7.

5. The difference in skin color between whiteness/*khao* and darkness/*dam* is very meaningful to the Chinese Thai and the Thai, but it may be imperceptible to many Americans.

6. Lisa Lowe points out that the model minority myth constructs "Asians" as aggressive overachievers: "it is a homogenizing fiction that relies upon two strategies common in the subordinating construction of racial or ethnic otherness—the racial other as knowable, familiar ('like us') and as incomprehensible, threatening ('unlike us')" (1991:40). The model minority myth renders Asian immigrants as "almost white but not white" and serves to homogenize all Asian groups by erasing the variety of class and cultural differences among these groups. It also further marginalizes those who are not "successful."

GLOSSARY

This glossary contains both Thai and Chinese terms. The symbol [M] is used to distinguish Mandarin from Thai.

achan	teacher; professor
ayi [M]	aunt
biaomei [M]	maternal-side female cousin
bobo [M]	older uncle
chaochu	a womanizer or being flirtatious
chek	a derogatory term used to refer to the Chinese Thai
chinkao	Chinese immigrants who came to Thailand before 1949, or elderly Chinese immigrants
i nan	"that woman" (a derogatory reference to the other woman)
jie [M]	older sister
jizhe [M]	journalist
khonchin	Chinese citizen; ethnic Chinese
khuam pen chin	Chinese-ness
khun	a term of address which conveys respect; it can be used in front of either a first name or a family name for both men and women
laoban [M]	entrepreneur; business owner
laoshi [M]	teacher
liangtoujia [M]	transnational polygyny, or a polygynist who has a family "on both ends"
lukchin	"Chinese children"; Chinese descendants who were born in Thailand
maeban	mother of the house; housewife
mama [M]	mother
mianoi	a mistress or a minor wife
na/lang	front/behind
nainai [M]	grandma
nei/wai [M]	inside/outside
neizhu [M]	inside assistant
pa	aunt
phi	a man or a woman who is older than the speaker
phuchuai	assistant
sae	a prefix attached to the surname of the ethnic Chinese and some hill tribes (the Mien and the Hmong) in Thailand, to single out their "Chinese" cultural background. Sae literally means "family name" in Teochiu Chinese
thansamai	modernity
thaokae	head of the business

tongyangxi [M]	little daughter-in-law
wai	showing respect through a gesture of putting one's palms together at chest level and bowing one's head to the palms
xiansheng [M]	Mr.
xiaozhang [M]	school principal

BIBLIOGRAPHY

Abu-Lughod, Lila. 1993. *Writing Women's Worlds.* Berkeley: University of California Press.

Ahern, Emily. 1975. The power and pollution of Chinese women. In *Women in Chinese Society,* edited by Margery Wolf and Roxane Witke, 193–214. Stanford, CA: Stanford University Press.

Anderson, Benedict. 1991. *Imagined Communities: Reflections on the Origin and Spread of Nationalism.* Revised edition. New York: Verso.

Ang, Ien. 1993. To be or not to be Chinese: Diaspora, culture, and postmodern ethnicity. *Southeast Asian Journal of Social Sciences* 21, 1:1–19.

Anjira Assavanonda. 1 January 2000. Love moves mass marriage. *Bangkok Post,* http://scoop.bangkokpost.co.th/bkkpost/2000/_jan/bp20000101/010100_news08.html (accessed 10 October 2001).

Anuman Rajadhon. 1988. *Essays on Thai Folklore.* Third edition. Bangkok: Thai Inter-Religious Commission for Development & Sathirakoses Nagapradipa Foundation. Distributed by Kled Thai Co. and Suksit Siam.

———. 1973. The story of Thai marriage custom. *Asian Culture Quarterly* 1, 2:56–62.

Aphichat Chamratrithirong, ed. 1984. *Perspectives on the Thai Marriage.* Institute for Population and Social Research, No. 81. Mahidol University. Bangkok: Sri Ananta Press.

Atkinson, Jane M., and Shelly Errington, eds. 1990. *Power and Difference: Gender in Island Southeast Asia.* Stanford, CA: Stanford University Press.

Bamber, Scott, Kevin Hewison, and Peter Underwood. 1997. Dangerous liaisons: A history of sexually transmitted diseases in Thailand. In *Sex, Disease, and Society: A Comparative History of Sexually Transmitted Diseases and HIV/AIDS in Asia and the Pacific,* edited by Milton Lewis, Scott Bamber, and Michael Waugh, 37–65. Westport, CT: Greenwood Press.

Bamrung Amnatcharoenrit. 21 December 1999. Wedding bells chime big bucks. *Bangkok Post,* http://scoop.bangkokpost.co.th/bangkokpostnews/bp20001104/041100_business10.html (accessed 11 February 2001).

Bangkok Post. 4 November 2000. Wedding business booming. http://scoop.bangkokpost.co.th/bkkpost/2000/bp2000_nov/bp20001.../041100_business10.htm (accessed 17 October 2001).

Bangkok Post. 18 March 1997. Wife on the run as penis takes off. Home section: 3.

Bangkok Post. 6 February 1997. Chinese New Year. Tradition strong, but business is business: Top families observe customs, but long holidays are rare. Business section: 1, 12.

Bangkok Post. 1 October 1996. Broken vow lends weight to Banharn's lowly image. Opinion and Analysis: 13. [Editorial reprinted from *Matichon Daily*].

Bangkok Post. 21 September 1996. Nationality document is verified: Police Gen produces original registration. First section: 1.

Bangkok Post. 20 September 1996. PM shows proof of nationality: Disputed paper says father came in 1907. First section: 1, 3.

Barlow, Tani E. 1994. Theorizing woman: Funu, guojia, jiating. In *Body, Subject and Power in China,* edited by Angela Zito and Tani E. Barlow, 253–289. Chicago: The University of Chicago Press.

Basch, Linda, Nina Glick Schiller, and Cristina Szanton Blanc. 1994. *Nations Unbound: Transnational Projects, Postcolonial Predicaments, and Deterritorialized Nation-states.* Langhorne, PA: Gordon and Breach.

Bei, Wenxi. 1988. Gen guiqiao zuojia du ai chang 'Guofan' shange. [Singing folk songs about 'migrating to barbarian lands' with emigrant writer Du Ai.] In *Shantou Qiaoshi Luncong. Shantou Huaqiao Lishi Xiuehui,* Vol. 1, 295–297.

Berman, Marshall. 1988. *All That Is Solid Melts into Air.* New York: Verso.

Beyrer, Chris. 1998. *War in the Blood: Sex, Politics and AIDS in Southeast Asia.* New York: Zed Books.

Bhabha, Homi K. 1994. *The Location of Culture.* London and New York: Routledge.

Boonsanong Punyadyana. 1971. *Chinese-Thai Differential Assimilation in Bangkok: An Exploratory Study.* New York: Cornell Thailand Project, Interim Reports Series No. 13.

Borthwick, Prudence. 1999. Developing culturally appropriate HIV/AIDS education programs in northern Thailand. In *Genders and Sexualities in Modern Thailand,* edited by Peter Jackson and Nerida Cook, 206–225. Chiang Mai, Thailand: Silkworm Books.

Bourdieu, Pierre. 1977. *Outline of a Theory of Practice.* Cambridge: Cambridge University Press.

Brown, Tim, and Peter Xenos. 1994. AIDS in Asia: The gathering storm. *Asian Pacific Issues* 16:1–14.

Cabrera, Jaime. 8 December 1996. Evolution of sexual perspectives. *Bangkok Post,* http://scoop.bangkokpost.co.th/bangkokpostnews/bp961208/0812_pers05.html (accessed 2 February 2001).

Cate, Sandra. 1999. Cars-stuck-together. In *Converging Interests: Traders, travelers and tourists in Southeast Asia,* edited by Jill Forshee with Christina Fink and Sandra Cate, 23–43. International and Area Studies Monograph No. 36. Berkeley: University of California Press.

Celentano, David. 1996. Risk factors for HIV-1 seroconversion among young men in northern Thailand. *The Journal of the American Medical Association* 275, 2:122–127.

Chang Noi. 6 February 1997. Political styles: Gangster, monk, or Chinese. *The Nation,* http://www.geocities.com/changnoi2/main97.htm (accessed 3 March 1997).

———. 29 August 1996. Cultural revolution in Thailand. *The Nation,* http://www.geocities.com/changnoi2/main96.htm (accessed 3 March 1997).

Chen, Ta. 1940. *Emigrant Communities in South China.* New York: Institute of Pacific Relations Press.

Cohen, Abner. 1974. *Two-dimensional Man: An essay on the Anthropology of Power and Symbolism in Complex Society.* London: Routledge & Kegan Paul.

Cohen, Myron L. 1976. *House United, House Divided: The Chinese Family in Taiwan.* New York: Columbia University Press.

Cook, Nerida. 1998. "Dutiful Daughters," Estranged Sisters: Women in Thailand. In *Gender and Power in Affluent Asia,* edited by Krishna Sen and Maila Stivens, 250–290. London and New York: Routledge.

Coughlin, Richard J. 1960. *Double Identity: Chinese in Modern Thailand.* Hong Kong: Hong Kong University Press.

Cushman, Jennifer. 1991. *Family and State: The Formation of a Sino-Thai Tin-mining Dynasty 1797–1932.* Edited by Craig J. Reynolds. Oxford: Oxford University Press.

Cushman, Jennifer, and Gungwu Wang, eds. 1988. *Changing Identities of the Southeast Asian Chinese Since World War II.* Hong Kong: Hong Kong University Press.

Dararat Mettariganon. 2000. Kha yingchin khamchat nai prawatsat sangkhumthai. [A history of trafficking in Chinese women in Thailand]. In *Silapawatthanatham [Art and Culture]*, 20 February:26–39.

Desbarats, Jacqueline. 1979. Thai migration to Los Angeles. *Geographical Review*, 69, 3: 302–318.

Duan, Lisheng. 1983. Teochiu pioneer immigrants in Thailand [Chaochin Teochiu thi opphayop mayang Thai nai raya raek]. In *Two Hundred Years of Ethnic Chinese Under the Bounties Bestowed by Kings*, edited by Vitaya Vitamnuikhun, Vol. 2, 27–29. Privately printed.

Embree, John F. 1950. Thailand—A loosely structured social system. *American Anthropologist* 52:181–193.

Errington, Shelly. 1998. *The Death of Authentic Primitive Art and Other Tales of Progress.* Berkeley: University of California Press.

Espiritu, Yen Le. 1997. *Asian American Women and Men.* Thousand Oaks, CA: Sage Publications.

Fei, Hsiao-Tung. 1939. *Peasant Life in China.* London: George Routledge and Sons, Ltd.

Fletcher, Matthew, and Julian Gearing. 6 June 1997. A wife in the shadows: Many Thai men have concubines, but they are meant to keep them well-hidden. *Asiaweek*, http://www.asiaweek.com/asiaweek/97/0606/feat2.html (accessed 1 April 2002).

Foucault, Michel. 1983. The subject and power. In *Michel Foucault: Beyond Structuralism and Hermeneutics*, edited by Hubert L. Dreyfus and Paul Rabinow, 208–226. Chicago: The University of Chicago Press.

Frankenburg, Ruth. 1993. *White Women, Race Matters: The Social Construction of Whiteness.* Minneapolis: University of Minnesota Press.

Freedman, Maurice. 1979. Chinese kinship and marriage in early Singapore. In *The Study of Chinese Society, Essays by Maurice Freedman*, edited by G. William Skinner, 84–92. Stanford, CA: Stanford University Press.

———. 1957. *Chinese Family and Marriage in Singapore.* Colonial Research Studies No. 20. London: Her Majesty's Stationery Office.

Gilroy, Paul. 1992. *The Black Atlantic: Modernity and Double Consciousness.* Cambridge, MA: Harvard University Press.

———. 1991. It ain't where you're from, it's where you're at. *Third Text* 13:3–16.

Greenhalgh, Susan. 1994. De-orientalizing the Chinese family firm. *American Ethnologist* 21, 4:746–775.

Hall, Stuart. 1991. The local and the global: Globalization and ethnicity. In *Culture, Globalization, and the World System*, edited by Anthony King, 19–39. London: Macmillan.

———. 1990. Cultural identity and diaspora. In *Identity: Community, Culture, Difference*, edited by Jonathan Rutherford, 222–237. London: Lawrence & Wishart.

Hamilton, Annette. 1997. Primal dream: Masculinism, sin and salvation in Thailand's sex trade. In *Sites of Desire, Economies of Pleasure: Sexuality in Asia and the Pacific*, edited by Lenore Manderson and Margaret Jolly, 145–165. Chicago: University of Chicago Press.

Hamilton, Gary, ed. 1991. *Business Networks and Economic Development in East and Southeast Asia.* Hong Kong: Centre of Asian Studies, University of Hong Kong.

Harris, Olivia, and Kate Young. 1981. Engendered structures: Some problems in the analysis of reproduction. In *The Anthropology of Pre-Capitalist Societies,* edited by Joel Kahn and Josep Llobera, 109–147. London: Macmillan.

Harrison, Rachel. 1999. The Madonna and the whore: Self/"Other" tensions in the characterization of the prostitute by Thai female authors. In *Genders and Sexualities in Modern Thailand,* edited by Peter Jackson and Nerida Cook, 168–190. Chiang Mai, Thailand: Silkworm Books.

Heidhues, Mary F. Somers. 1974. *Southeast Asia's Chinese Minorities.* Hawthorn, Victoria, Australia: Longman.

Hewison, Kevin. 1989. *Bankers and Bureaucrats: Capital and the Role of the State in Thailand.* New Haven, CT: Yale Center for International and Area Studies.

———. 1981. The financial bourgeoisie in Thailand. *Journal of Contemporary Asia* 11: 395–412.

Hochschild, Arlie. 1989. *The Second Shift: Working Parents and Revolution at Home.* New York: Viking.

Hsiung, Ping-chun. 1996. *Living Rooms as Factories.* Philadelphia: Temple University.

Huang, Zhongyan. 1985. Shilun woguo qiaoxiang shehui de xingcheng tedian he fazhan qushi. [On the formation, characteristics, and future of China's emigrant communities]. In *Huaqiao Huaren Lishi Luncong,* 6–36. Guangdong: Zhongshan Daxue Dongnanya Lishi Yanjiushuo.

Ingram, James C. 1971. *Economic Change in Thailand 1850–1970.* Palo Alto, CA: Stanford University Press.

———. 1955. *Economic Change in Thailand Since 1850.* Palo Alto, CA: Stanford University Press.

Johns Hopkins Gazette. 11 March 1996. Marriage biggest risk for HIV Thai women. http://www.jhu.edu/~gazette/janmar96/mar1196/11briefs.html (accessed 5 June 2003).

Kasian Tejapira. 1992. Pigtail: A pre-history of Chineseness in Siam. *Sojourn* 7, 1:95–122.

Kendall, Laurel. 1996. *Getting Married in Korea.* Berkeley: University of California Press.

Keyes, Charles F. 1989. Buddhist politics and their revolutionary origins in Thailand. *International Political Science Review* 10, 2:121–142.

———. 1987a. Thai religion. In *The Encyclopedia of Religion,* edited by Mircea Eliade, vol. 14, 416–421. New York: Macmillan.

———. 1987b. *Thailand: Buddhist Kingdom as Modern Nation-State.* Boulder: Westview Press, 1987.

Khukrit Promote. 1983. Fang . . . Khukrit Phut Ruang Chin [Listening to . . . Mr. Khukrit talk about the Chinese]. In *Two Hundred Years of Ethnic Chinese under the Bounties Bestowed by Kings,* edited by Vitaya Vitamnuikhun, vol. 2: 11–13. Privately printed.

Kibria, Nazli. 1993. *Family Tightrope.* Princeton, NJ: Princeton University Press.

Kulp, Daniel H. 1925. *Country Life in South China: The Sociology of Familism.* Volume I. New York City, Bureau of Publications, Teachers College, Columbia University.

Landon, Kenneth Perry. 1941. *The Chinese in Thailand.* London: Oxford University Press.

Li, Shuji, Jikun Cai, et al. 1815. Lie nu [The exemplary wife]. In *Denghai Xianzhi,* vol. 19.

Lim, Linda. 1983. Chinese economic activity in Southeast Asia: An introductory review. In *The Chinese in Southeast Asia: Ethnicity and Economic Activity*, edited by Linda Lim and L. A. Peter Gosling, vol. 1, no. 6:1–29. Singapore: Maruzen Asia.

Lim, Linda and L. A. Peter Gosling, eds. 1983. *The Chinese in Southeast Asia*. Vols. 1 and 2. Singapore: Maruzen Asia.

Lim, Mah Hui. 1981. *Ownership and Control of the One Hundred Largest Corporations in Malaysia*. Kuala Lumpur: Oxford University Press.

Lock, Margaret, and Patricia A. Kaufert. 1998. Introduction. In *Pragmatic Women and Body Politics*, edited by Margaret Lock and Patricia A. Kaufert, 1–27. Cambridge: Cambridge University Press.

Lowe, Lisa. 1991. Heterogeneity, hybridity, multiplicity: Making Asian American differences. *Diaspora* 1, 1:24–44.

Mackie, Jamie. 1992a. Changing patterns of Chinese big business in Southeast Asia. In *Southeast Asian Capitalists, Cornell Southeast Asian Program*, edited by Ruth McVey, 161–190. Ithaca, NY: Southeast Asia Program, Cornell University.

———. 1992b. Overseas Chinese entrepreneurship. *Asian Pacific Economic Literature* 6, 1:41–64.

Mallory, Walter H. 1956. Chinese minority in Southeast Asia. *Foreign Affairs* 34, 2: 258–270.

Manderson, Lenore. 1995. The pursuit of pleasure and the sale of sex. In *Sexual Nature, Sexual Culture*, edited by Paul R. Abramson and Steven D. Pinkerton, 305–329. Chicago and London: The University of Chicago Press.

———. 1992. Public sex performances in Patpong and explorations of the edges of imagination. *The Journal of Sex Research* 29, 4:451–475.

Matsui, Yayori. 1989. *Women's Asia*. London: Zed Books.

McDonald, N. A. 1884. The Chinese in Siam. In *Siam and Laos as Seen by Our American Missionaries*, edited by Mary Backus, 145–161. Philadelphia: Presbyterian Board of Publications.

McMahon, Keith. 1995. *Misers, Shrews, and Polygamists*. Durham, NC: Duke University Press.

Mills, Mary Beth. 1999. *Thai Women in the Global Labor Force: Consuming Desires, Contested Selves*. New Brunswick, NJ: Rutgers University Press.

Mintier, Tom. 18 September 1996. Thai PM faces no-confidence motion: Allegations against Banharn follow dive in economy. *CNN Interactive*, http://www.cnn.com/WORLD/9609/18/thailand/ (accessed 18 July 2003).

Mongkol Bangprapa. 12 June 2003. Draft gives women 3 options. MP's proposal to go to parliament. *Bangkok Post*, http://search.bangkokpost.co.th/bkkkpost/2003/june2003/bp20030612/news/12jun2003_news2.html (accessed 8 August 2003).

Mosse, George L. 1985. *Nationalism and Sexuality: Middle-Class Morality and Sexual Norms in Modern Europe*. Madison: The University of Wisconsin Press.

Muecke, Marjorie. 1992. Mother sold food, daughter sells her body: The cultural continuity of prostitution. *Social Science and Medicine* 35, 7:891–901.

———. 1984. Make money not babies: Changing status markers of Northern Thai women. *Asian Survey* 24, 4:459–470.

Mydans, Seth. 20 June 2003. A famed resort where tourists fear to tread. *The New York Times*, http://www.nytimes.com/2003/06/20/international/asia/20THAI.html?8hpib=&pagewanted= . . . (accessed 20 June 2003).

Nagata, Judith. 1974. What is a Malay? Situational selection of ethnic identity in a plural society. *American Ethnologist* 1, 2:331–350.

Napaporn Chayovan. 1989. Marriage registration among Thai women. In *Health and Population Studies Based on the 1987 Thailand Demographic and Health Survey*, 205–221. Chulalongkorn University, Institute of Population Studies, Serial No. 1.

Nian, Lamei. 1991. Sile zhangfu haokaixin [I'm happy my husband died]. In *Longfu Ji*, 11–12. Thailand: Dazhong Sheyin Guanggao Youxian Gongsi.

Nonini, Donald M., and Aihwa Ong. 1997. Chinese transnationalism as an alternative modernity. In *Ungrounded Empire: The Cultural Politics of Modern Chinese Transnationalism*, edited by Aihwa Ong and Donald Nonini, 3–33. New York: Routledge.

Omohundro, John T. 1981. *Chinese Merchant Families in Iloilo: Commerce and Kin in a Central Philippine City.* Athens, OH: Ohio University Press.

Ong, Aihwa. 1999. *Flexible Citizenship.* Durham, NC, & London: Duke University Press.

———. 1993. On the edge of empires: Flexible citizenship among Chinese in diaspora. *positions* 1, 3:745–778.

———. 1987. *Spirits of Resistance and Capitalist Discipline: Factory Women in Malaysia.* Albany: State University of New York Press.

Ortner, Sherry. 1998. Identities: The hidden life of class. *Journal of Anthropological Research* 54, 1:1–17.

———. 1996. *Making Gender: The Politics and Erotics of Culture.* Boston: Beacon Press.

———. 1974. Is female to male as nature is to culture? In *Woman, Culture and Society*, edited by Michelle Rosaldo and Louise Lamphere, 76–88. Stanford, CA: Stanford University Press.

People's Daily (Overseas edition). 20 July 1994. Zuohao 'qiao' zi da wenzhang [Do a good job on the overseas Chinese/bridge], 1.

People's Daily (Overseas edition). 27 August 1993. Li Peng zhuchi yishi relie huanying Chuan Li Pai [Li Peng holds ceremony to welcome Chuan Leekpai], 1.

Potter, Sulamith. 1979. *Family Life in a Northern Thai Village.* Berkeley: University of California Press.

Prangtip Daoreung. 4 September 1997. Thailand-health: Women's unequal status undercuts AIDS campaign. *Inter Press Service*, http://www.aegis.com/news/ips/1997/IP970903.html (accessed 28 May 2001).

Redding, Gordon. 1990. *The Spirit of Chinese Capitalism.* Berlin and New York: Walter de Gruyter.

Reid, Anthony. 1988. Female roles in pre-colonial Southeast Asia. *Modern Asian Studies* 22:629–645.

Reynolds, Craig J. 1991. Introduction: National identity and its defenders. In *National Identity and Its Defenders, Thailand, 1939–1989*, edited by Craig J. Reynolds, 1–40. Melbourne: Monash University, Center of Southeast Asian Studies, Monash Papers on Southeast Asia.

Riggs, Fred W. 1966. *Thailand: The Modernization of a Bureaucratic Polity.* Honolulu: East-West Center Press.

Rofel, Lisa. 1999. *Other Modernities.* Berkeley: University of California Press.

Rosaldo, Michelle. 1974. Woman, culture, and society: A theoretical overview. In *Woman, Culture and Society*, edited by Michelle Rosaldo and Louise Lamphere, 17–42. Stanford, CA: Stanford University Press.

Rubin, Gayle. 1984. Thinking sex: Notes for a radical theory of the politics of sexuality. In *Pleasure and Danger*, edited by Carole S. Vance, 267–319. Boston: Routledge & Kegan Paul.

Sacks, Karen Brodkin. 1994. How did Jews become white folks? In *Race*, edited by Steven Gregory and Roger Sanjeck, 78–102. New Brunswick, NJ: Rutgers University Press.

Said, Edward W. 1999. *Out of place: A memoir.* New York: Knopf.

San Francisco Chronicle. 9 October 1993. Angry wives in Thailand got their revenge in the '70s. A8.

Sanitsuda Ekachai. 10 July 2003. Breaking the rules governing polygamy. *Bangkok Post*, http://search.bangkokpost.co.th/bkkkpost/2003/july2003/bp20030710/news/10jul2 003_news3.html (accessed 16 July 2003).

———. 19 March 1997. Adultery is for women only. *Bangkok Post*, http://scoop. bangkokpost.co.th/bangkokpostnews/bp9703119/1903_news31.html (accessed 10 February 2001).

———. 8 July 1991. Choices in a modern marriage. *Bangkok Post.* Section 3. Outlook.

Simons, Lewis M., and Michael Zielenziger. 26 June 1994. Enter the dragon. Building the Chinese powerhouse. *San Jose Mercury News*, http://acc6.its.brooklyn.cuny.edu/ ~phalsall/texts/chinpress.html (accessed 5 January 2004).

Skinner, G. William. 1973a. Chinese assimilation and Thai politics. In *Southeast Asia: The Politics of National Integration*, edited by John T. McAlister, 383–398. New York: Random House.

———. 1973b. Change and persistence in Chinese culture overseas: A comparison of Thailand and Java. In *Southeast Asia: The Politics of National Integration*, edited by John T. McAlister, 399–415. New York: Random House.

———. 1964. The Thailand Chinese: Assimilation in a changing society. *Asia* 2:80–92.

———. 1958. *Leadership and Power in the Chinese Community of Thailand.* Ithaca: Cornell University Press.

———. 1957. *Chinese Society in Thailand.* London: Oxford University Press.

Smith, Michael. 3 March 1998. Condom use in Thailand dramatically cut HIV infection. *United Press International* (Internet edition), http://www.aegis.com/news/upi/1998/ UP980301.html (accessed 28 May 2001).

Somchai Meesane. 18 September 1996. Banharn needs to answer each and every allegation. *Bangkok Post*, Analysis/Censure debate, 1.

Somchai Meesane and Wut Nontarit. 16 September 1996. Banharn insists he won't quit: Activists may launch anti-PM campaign. *Bangkok Post*, International Edition, Politics, 1.

Spiro, Melford E. 1977. *Kinship and Marriage in Burma.* Berkeley: University of California Press.

Stoler, Ann. 1997. Carnal knowledge and imperial power. In *The Gender Sexuality Reader*, edited by Roger Lancaster and Micaela di Leonardo, 13–36. New York and London: Routledge.

Streckfuss, David. 1993. The mixed colonial legacy in Siam: Origins of Thai racialist thought, 1890–1910. In *Autonomous Histories, Particular Truths*, edited by Laurie J. Sears, 123–153. Madison: University of Wisconsin Press, Center for Southeast Asian Studies. Monograph Number 11.

Suehiro, Akira. 1992. Capitalist development in postwar Thailand: Commercial bankers, industrial elite, and agribusiness groups. In *Southeast Asian Capitalists*, edited by Ruth McVey, 35–63. Ithaca, NY: Southeast Asia Program, Cornell University.

Sumalee Bumroongsook. 1995. *Love and Marriage: Mate Selection in Twentieth-Century Central Thailand.* Bangkok: Chulalongkorn University Press.

Suryadinata, Leo. 1997. *Ethnic Chinese as Southeast Asians.* Singapore: Institute of Southeast Asian Studies.

———, ed. 1989. *The Ethnic Chinese in the ASEAN States: Bibliographical Essays.* Singapore: Institute of Southeast Asian Studies.

———. 1985. *China and the ASEAN States: The Ethnic Chinese Dimension.* Singapore: Singapore University Press.

Szanton Blanc, Cristina. 1989. Gender and inter-generational resource allocation among Thai and Sino-Thai households. In *Structures and Strategies: Women, Work and Family,* edited by Leela Dube and Rajni Palriwala, 79–102. New Delhi: Sage Publications.

———. 1983. Thai and Sino-Thai in small town Thailand: Changing patterns of interethnic relations. In *The Chinese in Southeast Asia, Identity, Culture and Politics,* edited by Linda Lim and Peter Gosling, vol. 2, 99–125. Singapore: Maruzen Asia.

Tambiah, Stanley J. 1976. *World Conqueror and World Renouncer: A Study of Buddhism and Polity in Thailand against a Historical Background.* Cambridge: Cambridge University Press.

Tan, Chee-Beng. 1983. Acculturation and the Chinese in Melaka: The expression of Baba identity today. In *The Chinese in Southeast Asia: Identity, Culture and Politics,* edited by Linda Lim and Peter Gosling, vol. 2, 56–78. Singapore: Maruzen Asia.

Temsak Traisophon. 24 March 1999. Land controls on spouses of foreigners relaxed. *Bangkok Post,* http://search.bangkokpost.co.th/bkkpost/1999/march1999/bp19990324/240399_news04.html (accessed 16 July 2003).

Thailand. Office of the Prime Minister. 1990. Royal Thai Government and National Statistical Office. *Statistical Yearbook of Thailand 1990.* No. 37.

Thailand. Royal Institute. 1968. *Romanization Guide for Thai Script.* Bangkok: Royal Institute.

Thak Chaloemtiarana. 1979. *Thailand: The Politics of Despotic Paternalism.* Social Science Association of Thailand. Bangkok: Thammasat University.

Thangarajah, Edward. 15 November 2000. Tired Tiger feted on his arrival. *Bangkok Post,* http://search.bangkokpost.co.th/bkkpost/2000/bp2000_nov/bp20001115/151100_news01.html (accessed 5 June 2003).

Thongchai Winichakul. 2000. The quest for "Siwilai": A geographical discourse of civilizational thinking in the late nineteenth and early twentieth-century Siam. *The Journal of Asian Studies* 59, 3:528–549.

———. 1994. *Siam Mapped: A History of the Geo-Body of a Nation.* Honolulu: University of Hawai'i Press.

Thorbek, Susanne. 1987. *Voices from the City: Women of Bangkok.* London: Zed Books.

Topley, Marjorie. 1959. Immigrant Chinese female servants and their hostels in Singapore. *Man,* December: 213–215.

Truong, Thanh-Dam. 1990. *Sex, Money and Morality: Prostitution and Tourism in Southeast Asia.* London: Zed Books.

U.S. Census Bureau. 2002. *Census 2000.* Data derived from analysis by the Asian American Federation Census Information Center (Federation CIC), http://www.aafny.org/cic/table/ust.asp (accessed 7 February 2002).

U.S. Department of Justice. 1984. *1984 Statistical Yearbook of the Immigration and Naturalization Service,* 4–7. Washington, DC: U.S. Government Printing Office.

Vance, Carole. 1991. Anthropology rediscovers sexuality: A theoretical comment. In *Social Science and Medicine* 33, 8:875–884.

Van Esterik, Penny. 1996. The politics of beauty in Thailand. In *Beauty Queens on the Global Stage*, edited by Colleen Ballerino Cohen, Richard Wilk, and Beverly Stoeltje, 203–216. London: Routledge.

———. 1982a. Introduction. In *Women of Southeast Asia*, edited by Penny Van Esterik, 1–15. Monograph Series on Southeast Asia, Occasional Paper No. 9. Dekalb: Northern Illinois University, Center for Southeast Asian Studies.

———, ed. 1982b. *Women of Southeast Asia.* Monograph Series on Southeast Asia, Occasional Paper No. 9. Dekalb: Northern Illinois University, Center for Southeast Asian Studies.

VanLandingham, Mark, John Knodel, Chanpen Saengtienchai, Anthony Pramualratana, eds. 1995. *Friends, Wives and Extramarital Sex in Thailand.* Bangkok: Chulalongkorn University.

VanLandingham, Mark, Somboon Suprasert, Werasit Sittitrai, Chayan Vaddhanaphuti, Nancy Grandjean. 1993. Sexual activity among never-married men in northern Thailand. *Demography* 30, 3:297–313.

Vatikiotis, Michael. 23 January 1997. From chickens to microchips. *Far Eastern Economic Review* 160, 4:38–44.

Vella, Walter F. 1978. *Chaiyo! King Vajiravudh and the Development of Thai Nationalism.* Honolulu: University of Hawai'i Press.

Voravudhi Chirasombutti and Anthony Diller. 1999. Who am 'I' in Thai?—The Thai first person: Self-reference or gendered self? In *Genders and Sexualities in Modern Thailand*, edited by Peter A. Jackson and Nerida M. Cook, 114–133. Chiang Mai, Thailand: Silkworm Books.

Wang, Chuanzhen. 19 February 1993. Tai pangu yihang jiang zai hua she fenhang [Bangkok Bank of Thailand will open its branch office in China]. *People's Daily* (Overseas edition), 5.

Wang, Gungwu. 1997. *Global History and Migrations.* Boulder, CO: Westview Press.

———. 1996. Sojourning: The Chinese experience in Southeast Asia. In *Sojourners and Settlers: Histories of Southeast Asia and the Chinese*, edited by Anthony Reid, 1–14. St. Leonards, Australia: Allen & Unwin.

———. 1992. *Community and Nation.* Kensington, Australia: Asian Studies Association of Australia in association with Allen & Unwin.

———. 1991. *China and the Chinese Overseas.* Singapore: Times Academic Press.

———. 1988. The study of Chinese identities in Southeast Asia. In *Changing Identities of the Southeast Asian Chinese Since World War II*, edited by Jennifer Cushman and Gungwu Wang, 1–21. Hong Kong: Hong Kong University Press.

Wang, Ling-chi. 1994. Roots and the changing identity of the Chinese in the United States. In *The Living Tree: The Changing Meaning of Being Chinese Today*, edited by Tu Wei-ming, 185–212. Stanford, CA: Stanford University Press.

Ward, Barbara, ed. 1963. *Women in the New Asia: The Changing Social Roles of Men and Women in South and Southeast Asia.* Paris: UNESCO.

Wasant Techawongtham. 17 September 1991. Aiming to loosen the gangster's grip on prostitution. *Bangkok Post.* Section Three, Outlook, 1.

Wathinee Boonchalaksi and Philip Guest. 1994. *Prostitution in Thailand.* Nakhorn Pathom: Institute for Population and Social Research. Bangkok: Mahidol University.

Watson, Rubie S. 1985. *Inequality Among Brothers: Class and Kinship in South China.* Cambridge: Cambridge University Press.

Wertheim, W. F. 1965. The trading minorities in Southeast Asia. In *East West Parallels: Sociological Approaches to Modern Asia*, edited by W. F. Wertheim, 39–82. Chicago: Quadrangle Books.

Whittaker, Andrea. 1999. Women and capitalist transformation in a northeastern Thai village. In *Genders and Sexualities in Modern Thailand*, edited by Peter Jackson and Nerida Cook, 43–62. Chiang Mai, Thailand: Silkworm Books.

Williams, Brackette. 1995. Classification systems revisited: Kinship, caste, race, and nationality as the flow of blood and the spread of rights. In *Naturalizing Power: Essays in Feminist Cultural Analysis*, edited by Sylvia Yanagisako and Carol Delaney, 201–236. New York: Routledge.

Willmott, William E. 1967. *The Chinese in Cambodia.* Vancouver: University of British Columbia Press.

Wiyada Thongmitr. 1979. *Khrua in Khong's Westernized School of Thai Painting.* Bangkok: Akson Samphan Press.

Wolf, Arthur P. 1975. The women of Hai-shan: A demographic portrait. In *Women in Chinese Society*, edited by Margery Wolf and Roxane Witke, 89–110. Stanford, CA: Stanford University Press.

Wolf, Arthur P., and Chieh-shan Huang. 1980. *Marriage and Adoption in China, 1845–1945.* Stanford, CA: Stanford University Press.

Wolf, Margery. 1972. *Women and the Family in Rural Taiwan.* Stanford, CA: Stanford University Press.

———. 1968. *The House of Lim: A Study of a Chinese Farm Family.* New York: Appleton Century Crofts.

Wong, Sau-Ling C. 1992. Ethnicizing gender: An exploration of sexuality as sign in Chinese immigrant literature. In *Reading the Literatures of Asian America*, edited by Shirley Geok-lin Lim and Amy Ling, 111–129. Philadelphia: Temple University Press.

Wong, Siu-lun. 1980. The Chinese family firm: A model. *British Journal of Sociology* 36, 1:58–72.

World Factbook 2002. Thailand. http://www.odci.gov/cia/publications/factbook/geos/th.html#Geo (accessed 31 May 2003).

World News Daily. 24 June 1991. Zhengzhi Yigao, Nuren Nanwan [It is easy for the general to play politics, but it is difficult for him to play with his women].

Yanagisako, Sylvia, and Jane Collier. 1987. Toward a unified analysis of gender and kinship. In *Gender and Kinship: Essays Toward a Unified Analysis of Gender and Kinship*, edited by Jane Collier and Sylvia Yanagisako, 15–50. Stanford, CA: Stanford University Press.

Yanagisako, Sylvia, and Carol Delaney. 1995. Naturalizing power. In *Naturalizing Power: Essays in Feminist Cultural Analysis*, edited by Sylvia Yanagisako and Carol Delaney, 1–22. New York: Routledge.

Zhao, Jian. 5 May 1993. Qiaowu bumen jiji wei difang zhaoshang yinzi [Overseas Chinese bureau actively helps the locals to attract overseas investment]. *People's Daily* (Overseas edition), 5.

Zhao, Xiaojian. 2002. *Remaking Chinese America: Immigration, Family, and Community, 1940–1965.* New Brunswick, NJ: Rutgers University Press.

INDEX

adoption, 45, 46–47
agency: Chinese entrepreneur's, 98. *See also* alliances; boundary crossings; family business; games; performance; women's agency
AIDS, 22, 82, 133, 194n.11
alliances: Chinese entrepreneurs with Thai state elites, 17, 38–39, 54, 56, 72, 97, 98, 170–171; class, 54, 57; ethnic, 54, 57; social, 69. *See also* global networks; kinship position; marriage; politics
Americans, 171, 188; African Americans, 55, 169, 178; business ties with Thailand, 34, 58; gendered housework, 67; Jews, 17, 55; married women's nationality, 27; nationalisms, 17; racism, 14, 17, 55, 169, 171, 178, 182–183; sex tourism in Thailand, 81; sexual hierarchies, 169
ancestor worship, 107–108, 115, 146
Asian Americans, 14, 168–169, 188. *See also* Chinese Thai Americans
assimilation, 19–20, 52, 169, 171
assistants: husbands not as, 158; wives as, 49, 59–60, 71, 145, 148–149, 154, 155, 163

Bangkok: Chinese Thai population, 28, 102; ethnic occupations of *chinkao*, 57; Miss Chinatown beauty pageant, 95–98; publishing in Chinese, 141; sex industry, 21, 58, 81–84; strike against tax increase, 41; traffic, 105, 106, 107, 118, 122; wedding rituals, 105–124
beauty, women's: beauty pageants, 94, 95–98, 195n.3; hidden by family, 140–141; women's ethnicized bodies, 13, 38–39, 42, 52, 83, 85–86, 97–98, 113, 178, 195n.3. *See also* dress; skin color
blood: Chinese, 181–184; gender and, 183–184; interethnic marriage, 38; kinship, 17; race, 17, 181–184; Thai and Chinese fusion, 100. *See also* ethnicizing

bodies: women's ethnicized, 13, 38–39, 42, 52, 83, 85–86, 97–98, 113, 178, 195n.3; yin/yang, 25. *See also* beauty; dress; skin color
boundary crossings: *nei/wai*, 189; wedding ritual, 109–110; women's, 27, 94, 99–100, 127, 129, 146, 147, 185–186, 189. *See also* hybridity
breadwinner role: Chinese Thai American men, 184–185; *chinkao* men, 32, 48–52, 54, 59, 65–66, 72, 75, 85, 189; husband's responsibility, 26–27, 48–52, 59, 69–71, 126, 134, 139; masculinity, 9, 11, 23, 32, 69–71, 73, 85, 134, 146, 184–185, 189; naturalization of, 48, 73, 79, 146; women's downplayed, 63–65, 71, 73, 145, 156, 158, 162–163. *See also* economic production; entrepreneurs; remittances
Buddhism, Thai Theravada, 24, 40, 74–75, 150; karma, 7, 24, 112; making merit, 130; mandala, 110; middle way, 143, 150, 151, 181; political identity, 102–103; San Francisco Bay Area, 175; sexual detachment, 143; and skin color, 178; wedding rituals, 106, 107, 108, 109, 111–112, 115, 116, 117, 119. *See also* monasticism
business: Chinese-ness of, 41, 53, 55–58, 71, 72, 182; global, 13, 16, 18, 34, 81, 120, 173–174; learning new skills and technologies, 63, 65–67, 154, 157; merit vs. origin as basis for, 58–59; state regulations, 53–59, 72, 98; Teochiu as language of, 40; Thai restaurants, 174–175. *See also* capitalism; economic production; entrepreneurs; family business; sex industry

Cantonese: language, 10–11; occupations, 57
capitalism, 16, 18, 20, 57–58, 118–122, 124
Catholicism, wedding rituals, 106, 109, 111, 112, 118, 119, 122
chaochu masculinity, 13, 81, 84–87, 125–143, 176–177. *See also* men's extramarital sex

213

69–71, 72, 189; political power of,
170–171; and responsible extramarital
sex, 9, 69, 85, 87, 126, 134, 139, 170;
sports, 126; Thai-ness, 101; transnational migration motive, 32; and wedding rituals, 113, 120. *See also* business;
economic production; entrepreneurs;
money; upward mobility
economic production: class and, 20. *See
also* breadwinner role; business; capitalism; economic capital; entrepreneurs; labor; occupations; women's
income-producing work; working
class
economy: global, 13, 16, 18, 34, 81, 120,
173–174; Siam, 34, 38, 41; Thai,
57–58, 81. *See also* economic production; labor; money
education: Chinese Thai overseas, 173,
175–176, 177, 184; names reflecting,
6; teaching, 61–62, 65, 66–67;
women's, 46, 127–128, 138, 145–146,
153–154, 157, 161, 184
elite class: capitalist wedding ritual,
118–122, 124; China, 61; Chinese
business alliances with, 17, 38–39, 54,
56, 72, 97, 98, 170–171; Chinese Thai
American immigrants, 171, 175;
donations honored by, 69–70; male
sexual privilege, 9; modern identity,
120–121, 122, 124; royal interethnic
marriage, 38–39; Siamese royal, 3, 4,
38–39, 56
emotion: Chinese Thai American
women's sexual politics, 186; extramarital sex and, 130, 135, 141,
155–156, 158, 176; family business
and, 13, 49, 145, 149–153, 155–156,
158; widows of living ones, 36–37; in
writing, 141–142. *See also* desire;
pleasure
endurance, 74–76; men's, 75; women's,
75–76, 78–79, 89, 130, 134–135, 136,
151, 187
entrepreneurs: alliances with state elite,
17, 38–39, 54, 56, 72, 97, 98,170–171;
chinkao, 13, 31, 38–40, 53, 56–72, 82;
lukchin, 13, 141, 144–163; women, 13,
63–64, 141, 144–149, 155–163, 169
ethnic Chinese, 11, 12, 103; economic
image, 53, 71; New Year, 50, 95–98;
population in Thailand, 5; sex services
for, 82–83; upward mobility in Southeast Asia, 11, 12–13, 49, 53–73. *See
also* Chinese; Chinese Thai; diasporic
Chinese
ethnicity: classed, 9, 17, 19, 20; natural-

ization of, 72, 181–184; sexuality and
gender and, 169; state-defined, 4, 5,
12, 27–28, 103, 176, 182. *See also*
Americans; blood; Chinese; ethnic
capital; ethnicizing; ethnic politics
ethnicizing, 87; Chinese image, 53, 71;
on class lines, 9, 17, 19, 20; domestic
work, 68; friendship, 69; gender-
specific, 87–88, 186; Lao, 68, 124;
marriage, 87; occupational, 34, 54–59,
68, 72, 82; political, 19, 94, 97–98;
sexual, 22–23, 82–88, 97, 133,
134–135, 169, 186; women's bodies/
beauty, 13, 38–39, 42, 52, 83, 85–86,
97–98, 113, 178, 195n.3. *See also*
Chinese-ness; ethnicity; racism;
Siamese-ness; Thai-ness
ethnic politics, 19, 94, 97–98, 101–104,
170–171. *See also* ethnicizing; name
politics; racism
extramarital sex. *See* men's extramarital
sex; prostitution; women's extramarital sex

family business, 13, 144–163; assistants,
49, 59–60, 71, 145, 148–149, 154,
155, 163; children's labor, 64, 153,
160; cofounded by husband and wife,
146–153; divorce's effect on, 74,
149–150; donations promoting, 70;
established by wives, 147, 157–162;
female inheritance, 65, 161; gender-
specific practices, 9, 13, 26–28, 48,
49–50, 59–73, 140–141, 144–163;
inherited by husband, 147, 153–157;
male inheritance, 59, 64, 147,
153–157, 161; masculinity of, 70, 145,
148, 149; polygyny and, 49, 59,
128–130, 150–162; wife's compensation, 71, 162–163; wives' work in,
28, 49, 59–61, 71, 140–141, 144–163;
women as primary providers, 63–65,
73, 147, 159–162; women's economic
ability, 13, 63–65, 73, 141, 144–146,
147–149, 155–163; women's strengths
downplayed, 13, 54, 63–65, 73,
144–145, 148–149, 161, 162–163. *See
also* family relationships; gendered
division of labor
family gender politics, 9, 11, 31–52, 167,
188; Chinese Thai American,
176–177; daughters' status, 45, 46–48,
80, 109, 146, 157, 161; husband's
responsibilities, 9, 26–28, 48–52,
59–72, 79, 85, 86, 126, 134, 139, 153;
interethnic marriage and, 117–118;
modern, 105, 117–118; *na/lang*, 28,

patrilineal system; polygyny; sexuality; sex workers; women's agency
generations: *chinkao*, 14, 153; differences/similarities, 14, 147, 188; generation gap, 137–138; family business, 147, 153, 154; *lukchin*, 14, 105, 147, 153, 154; wedding rituals, 105. *See also* children; modernity
gifts: to compensate for extramarital sex, 86; major to minor wife, 151; for sex, 133, 134, 135; wedding ritual, 108, 111, 112, 114–115, 117, 196n.7
global networks: business, 13, 16, 18, 34, 81, 120, 173–174; dialect groups, 173–174, 181; political, 103. *See also* colonialism; immigration; tourism; transnational migration
governmentality, 10, 18, 25–26. *See also* discipline; regulations; state

Hainanese: cross-dialect marriage, 157; global networks, 173–174, 181; language, 10–11; occupations, 57
hierarchical systems: American sexual, 169; children's seniority, 46, 47–48; Chinese Thai community, 48; East Asia/Southeast Asia, 168; extramarital sex and, 7–8, 9, 21; family business, 59–60, 145, 154; father and daughter, 125; gestures related to, 12; major and minor wives', 7–9, 42, 59, 81, 88, 99–100, 126–127, 129–131, 150–152, 158–159, 161; marriage interconnected with, 31; married-out daughters, 172; religious, 111–112; titles and terms of address and, 7–8; wedding rituals revealing, 111–112, 121; wives over maids, 21, 68, 74. *See also* class; inequalities; patriarchy; racism; social stigma; upward mobility
housekeeping: men choosing tasks, 67–68; mother of the house (*maeban*), 7–8, 28, 145–147, 163; wife's responsibility, 11, 28, 54, 60, 67–68, 145–147, 163. *See also* domestic work; maids
husbands: domestic work, 54, 65–68, 72–73; family business cofounded by wives with, 146–153; family business inherited by, 147, 153–157; responsibilities, 9, 26–28, 48–52, 59–72, 79, 85, 86, 126, 134, 139, 153; of woman entrepreneurs, 156–157, 158. *See also* breadwinner role; family gender politics; men's extramarital sex; polygyny

hybridity, 12, 18–19, 93–124, 180, 187

identity: ambiguous, 5, 18–19, 43, 72, 101, 180–181, 187; categories, 5, 16–17; cosmopolitan-modern, 80–81; double, 19–20; ethnicizing others as articulation of, 87; flexibility, 6; formation, 3, 10–28, 52, 93, 127, 171–174, 189; games, 15–16, 101–103, 130, 179; in-between-ness, 18–19, 180, 187; marriage as site of constructions of, 8, 10, 24, 27, 42–43, 51, 60, 188; multiple geographies, 17–18, 167–189; socially constructed and malleable, 12, 101. *See also* Americans; blood; Chinese; class; ethnicizing; family relationships; gender; hybridity; identity politics; immigration; language; marriage; social categories; Thai
identity politics, 14–19, 101–103, 167, 182–183, 189. *See also* ethnic politics; gender politics; interethnic marriage; name politics
imagined community, nation as, 17
immigration, 11; family ethnic politics and, 101–102; family gender politics and, 89; illegal aliens, 101; laws, 5, 99, 175; after Qing dynasty fall, 41; undocumented, 13, 84, 101, 133. *See also* diasporas; migration; transnational migration
in-between-ness, 18–19, 180, 187
inequalities, 189; class, 72, 126, 189; gender, 14, 80, 89, 126, 131, 133–134, 137, 140, 143, 167–168, 184, 188, 189; naturalized, 126, 131, 133–134, 137, 140, 143; sexual, 89, 133–134, 143, 189. *See also* discrimination; hierarchical systems; power relations
inheritance, 88; family business, 59, 64, 65, 147, 153–157, 161; female, 65, 161; male, 13, 45, 46, 59, 64, 147, 153–157, 161; men's extramarital sex and, 23, 161–162; registration of marriage and, 81. *See also* blood; patrilineal system
interethnic marriage, 5, 27; Chinese women's appeal to Siamese/Thai men 38–39, 42, 113; *chinkao* with Thai, 15–16, 39–43, 52; cross-dialect, 44, 157; *lukchin* with Thai, 93–94, 99, 100, 113–118, 123, 128–130, 181–182; Thai women marrying non-Thais, 39–41, 42, 43, 52, 99, 184; wedding rituals, 113–118, 123. *See also* polygyny

ABOUT THE AUTHOR

Educated in Beijing and Vientiane, Bao received her Ph.D. from the University of California at Berkeley. She is associate professor of anthropology at the University of Nevada, Las Vegas.

Production Notes for Bao/MARITAL ARTS

Cover and interior design by Trina Stahl in Janson Text Hawn, with display type in Cicero

Composition by Trina Stahl

Printing and binding by The Maple-Vail Book Manufacturing Group

Printed on 60 lb. Text High Opaque, 426 ppi